PARIS

IN AMERICA.

BY

DR. RENÉ LEFEBVRE,

PARISIAN

de la Société des Contribuables de France et des Administrés de Paris;

DES SOCIÉTÉS PHILADELPHIQUE ET PHILHARMONIQUE D'ALISE ET D'ALAISE, ETC.;

DE LA REAL ACADEMIA DE LOS TONTOS DE GUISANDO;

Pastore nell' Arcadia in Brenta (detto Melibeo l'Intronato)

Mitglied des Groß- und Klein-Deutschen Narren-Landtags;

Mitglied der K. K. Hanswurst-Akademie zu Gänsedorf;

MEMBER OF THE TARLETON CLUB, OF COVENTRY, F. R. F. S. M. A. D. D., ETC.

COMMANDEUR DE L'ORDRE GRAND DUCAL DELLA CIVETTA;

CHEVALIER DU MERLE BLANC (LXXXIXe CLASSE) AVEC PLAQUE

ETC., ETC.

ÆGRI SOMNIA.

(ÉDOUARD LABOULAYE.)

TRANSLATED BY

MARY L. BOOTH,

TRANSLATOR OF MM. DE GASPARIN AND COCHIN'S WORKS ON AMERICA, ETC.

NEW YORK:

CHARLES SCRIBNER, 124 GRAND STREET.

1863.

W. H. Tinson, Stereotyper.

John F. Trow, Printer.

TRANSLATOR'S PREFACE.

At a time when it is the fashion of a faction among us to carp at American institutions and greatness; to declare that democracy is a failure; that the masses are incompetent to govern themselves; that the titled inequality of Europe is better than the glorious equality which proclaims us all sovereigns, and predestines no one to the humiliation of being obliged to bow his head at home or abroad, and acknowledge another his superior; and to ape this inequality by striving to raise up factitious social distinctions—at such a time, the appearance of a work like the present cannot fail to be of marked utility. A profound, sagacious and acute student of the United States, bringing to the research an appreciation and love of liberty and democracy, as embodied in the ideal of our Republic, M. Laboulaye, well styled in Paris *le plus américain de tous les Français*, and whose knowledge of America is perhaps greater than that of any other man in Europe, was admirably calculated to draw a parallel between the practical workings of these principles in America, and the effects of monarchism in Europe, which may lead us as a nation to set a higher value on the blessings within our grasp, and more fully to realize the picture which our friend has drawn of us. Nor is this picture wholly eulogistic. On looking closely the reader will discover many a pungent satire on our absurdities, follies and shortcomings, which we would do well not to pass by unheeded. Perhaps some brief note of the author himself may not be an ill-timed introduction to the work.

Édouard René Lefebvre Laboulaye was born in Paris in 1811, where he studied law, and first became known through a "History of the Law of Real Estate, from Constantine to the Present Times," published in 1839, and crowned by the Academy of Inscriptions and Belles Lettres. This was followed, in 1842, by a life of the celebrated German jurist Frederick Charles de Savigny. In the same year, he became advocate in the Royal Court of Paris. In 1843 he published "Researches on the Civil and Political Condition of Woman from the Romans to the Present Times"—a work crowned by the Academy of Moral and Political Sciences, and in 1845 an "Essay on the Criminal Law of the Romans, respecting the Responsibility of Magistrates," which was also crowned by the Academy of Inscriptions and Belles Lettres. In 1849 he was chosen a member of the latter academy, and in the same year Professor of Comparative Legislation in the Collége de France. Among his other writings may be quoted, "The Political History of the United States, A.D. 1620–1783," the first volume only of which has yet appeared (1855); "Contemporary Studies on Germany and the Slavic Nations," (1855), and on "Religious Liberty," (1856); "Souvenirs of a Traveller," (1857); "Studies on Literary Property in France and England," (1858); an Arabic novel, "Abdallah," (1859), and "Moral and Political Studies," (1861). He has also made numerous translations: "Walter's History of Civil Proceedings among the Romans," (1845); "The Social Works of Channing," preceded by an "Essay on His Life and Doctrines," (1854); "Channing's Slavery," preceded by a "Preface," and "Study on Slavery in the United States," (1855), etc. He has also edited various legal works, and contributed largely to to the *Revue de législation et jurisprudence*; is one of the directors of the *Revue historique de droit français et étranger*, and collaborateur of the *Journal des Débats*, *Revue germanique*, *Revue nationale*, etc. His lectures this season in the Collége de France on the American Revolution have attracted especial attention and applause.

In a recent lecture, after commenting on the intense sympathy which existed twenty or thirty years ago between Americans and Frenchmen, when all seemed inspired with the friendship of Lafayette and Washington, M. Laboulaye asked: "Why is it that this friendship has cooled? Why is it that the name of American is not so dear to us as it was in those days? It is due to slavery. We had always hoped that something would be done to put an end to an institution which was regarded by the founders of the Constitution as fraught with peril to the country; but, instead of this, the partisans of slavery having obtained the ascendant, have continually been engaged in efforts to perpetuate it and extend its limits, so that we have ceased to feel the same interest in Americans." He concluded the same lecture with the words: "America is the future of civilization; America is the future of liberty. When her territory shall become as populous as that of France, 200,000,000 freemen will occupy it, with a system of government which will, with irresistible force, draw all the world to follow the example. It is for this that I am so interested in American progress; it is for this that I wish to direct your attention toward it. You, young men, particularly; for it is to you that the world looks for advancement."

The appearance of *Paris en Amérique* has excited marked attention in France, where, although it is somewhat wounding to the self-love of the French nation, it passed in two weeks to a third edition. While it exhibits so intimate a knowledge of American peculiarities, that Americans in Paris refuse to believe that the author has never visited this country, which however is the case.

That our nation may justify the wishes and faith of its enthusiastic champion; that it may achieve the great work which it has undertaken; that it may continue the standard-bearer of liberty and, the blessings of peace once regained, resume its onward course as a truly free nation, glorying in its republican institutions, and esteeming the sovereign title of American citizen above that of all nobility, as the lord is above his follower, let him rank as high as he may—with these earnest wishes, I submit this volume to the perusal of my countrymen.

MARY L. BOOTH.

NEW YORK, *May* 1, 1863.

TO THE READER.

FRIENDLY reader, I offer thee this little book, written for thy pleasure and mine. I dedicate it neither to fortune nor glory; fortune is a damsel that, for six thousand years, has pursued after the young; glory is a vivandière that takes delight only in soldiers. I am old, I have killed no one, therefore I have no longer any wish but to seek the truth in my own guise, and to tell it in my own fashion. If I have not all the gravity of an ox, a goose, or a—(choose whatever name you like), forgive me; the first acts of life make us weep enough to justify us in laughing before the curtain falls. When one has lost his illusions of twenty, he takes neither the comedy nor the comedians in earnest.

If this little book please thee, it is well; if it scandalize thee, it is better; if thou castest it aside, thou art wrong; if thou comprehendest it, thou hast known it longer than Machiavel. Make it the breviary of thy wasted hours; thou wilt not regret it: *Non est hic piscis omnium.* The paradoxes of the eve are the truths of the morrow. A word to the wise is sufficient.

One day, perhaps, by the light of my lamp, thou wilt see all the deformity of the idols which thou adorest to-day; perhaps, too, beyond the decreasing shadows, thou wilt perceive, in all the charm of her immortal smile, Liberty, the daughter of the Gospel, the sister of justice and pity, the mother of equality, abundance and peace. On that day, friendly reader, do not suffer the flame which I confide to thee to die out; enlighten, enlighten that youth which already presses on our footsteps and urges us forward, while asking us the path of the future. That it may be madder than its fathers, but in a different way, is my prayer and hope.

Upon which, I pray God to preserve thee from ignorant men and fools. As to the wicked, it is thy own affair; life is a mêlée: thou art born a soldier, defend thyself; or still better, take back from the Americans the old motto of France, *Forward! always and everywhere, forward!*

Adieu, friend,

RENÉ LEFEBVRE.

NEW LIBERTY (VIRGINIA), *July* 4, 1862.

PARIS IN AMERICA.

ÆGRI SOMNIA.

CHAPTER I.

AN AMERICAN MEDIUM.

"You are respectfully invited to attend the psychical and medianimic soirée of Mr. Jonathan Dream, spiritual and transcendental medium of Salem (Mass.), to be given next Tuesday, April 1st, at his residence, No. 33 rue de la Lune.

"Somnambulism, trance, vision, prevision, prophecy, second sight, distant sight, divination, penetration, abstraction of thought, evocations; preternatural conversation, poetry and chirography; thoughts from beyond the tomb, arcana of the future life unveiled, etc. etc.

"*Doors closed at eight o'clock precisely!*"

"*Pardieu!*" thought I, again reading the letter, "I shall not be sorry to make acquaintance with an American medium, a brother in *experimental and positive pneumatology;* for I too am a medium. I am not only a simple citizen of Paris; I have already, as well as others, evoked Cæsar, Napoleon, Voltaire, Madame de Pompadour, Ninon, etc; and even, if it must be told, whatever it may cost my modesty, these illustrious personages have not eclipsed me by their genius; all have answered me as if I had whispered them. Let us see whether Mr. Jonathan Dream, with his American pretensions, has more spirit or more spirits than your servant, Daniel Lefebvre, D.M.P., the pupil in spiritism of M. Hornung of Berlin, M. de Reichenbach, and Baron de. Guldenstubbe. The medium will find more than his match."

In a fine suit of rooms, at the bottom of a drawing-room, hermetically closed, but blazing with light (which is not usually the case in our spiritual meetings), I found Mr. Jonathan Dream seated before a round table. He had the melancholy gaze and inspired countenance of sibyls. Opposite him sat half-a-dozen adepts, with a meditative air—nervous people, women not understood, majors or widows on the retired list—the audience is always the same. Each one was writing on a slip of paper the names of the dead whom he wished to interrogate; I did like the rest.

The names were jumbled together in a hat, and the first that was drawn was that of Joseph de Maistre. Jonathan meditated a moment, put his hand to his ear to listen to the voice which whispered to him, and wrote rapidly as follows:

"There is no sterile knowledge; all knowledge is like that spoken of in the Bible—Adam knew Eve, and she brought forth.

"No creed, no credit."

"Ah, ah!" thought I, "these paradoxes sound well, they have all the swaggering of their father; only it seems to me that I have seen them somewhere else—in Baader, if I am not mistaken. After all, perhaps there is no literary property on high, and, for the sake of distraction, it is possible that one amuses himself there by pilfering ideas."

Hippocrates came next; he had the kindness to speak French, and his shadow wrote as follows:

"The man who thinks most is the one who digests least; other things being equal, he who thinks least is he who digests best."

"Alas!" said a little woman, with a thin face buried beneath waves of grey hair, "this is a doctor's answer, a coarse answer, made by men and for men. It is not the thought which preys upon the heart, it is"——
And she sighed.

Nostradamus was summoned, and his opinion asked on the future of Poland, France and Italy. This is the answer of the great diviner, a sublime genius who always left to others the care of understanding what he said:

"En France, Italie et Pologne,
Beaucoup d'esprit, peu de vergogne;
En France, Pologne, Italie,
On est sage après la folie;
En Italia, Pologne et France,
Moins de bonheur que d'espérance." *

We were forced to content ourselves with this oracle, too profound to be clear. It was Kosciusko's turn. This evening, the Polish Washington was in a bad

* In France, Italy and Poland,
Much wit, little shame;
In France, Poland and Italy,
One is wise according to folly;
In Italy, Poland and France,
Less happiness than hope.

humor; nothing could be obtained from him but the Latin motto, "*In servitute dolor, in libertate labor;*" In servitude suffering, in liberty labor. Three times he was questioned, three times he made this sullen reply, and flung it in our face as a reproach that we had even ceased to feel.

The last slip of paper demanded that Don Quixote, Tom Jones, Robinson Crusoe or Werther should be questioned; which made the cœnaculum laugh, although, to tell the truth, it had little wish to do so. The author of this piece of impertinence, I am ashamed to confess, was myself. I had been so long wearied both of the dead and the living, that I should have been delighted to know what entered the brain of men who had never existed.

Jonathan Dream flung the unlucky billet into the fire, announced that the sitting was over, and accompanied us to the door with many bows. As I was about to go, he laid his hand on my shoulder, and entreated me to remain.

Once alone—"It was you, brother," said he with a peculiar smile, "that addressed to me a demand which these profane beings deem indiscreet; perhaps even you are of their opinion. Blind man, who hast never fathomed the arcana of eternal truth! Do you fancy that Don Quixote and Sancho Panza, Robinson Crusoe and Friday, Tom Jones and Sophie never lived? What! man cannot create an atom of matter, yet you suppose that he can create entire souls who will never perish. Do you not believe in Don Quixote more than in all the Artaxerxes? Is not Robinson Crusoe more living to you than the Drakes and Magellans?"

"What! the ingenious Don Quixote has lived? And

I can talk with the wise governor of the island of Barataria?"

"Doubtless. Know then, what is a poet. He is a seer, a prophet, who mounts to the invisible world; there, among the millions of beings who once lived and whose remembrance is lost here below, he chooses those whom he wishes to revive in the memory of mankind. He evokes them, he listens to them, he writes under their dictation. What foolish humanity takes for an invention of the artist is only a confession of the unknown dead; but you, a medium, or pretending to be such, how is it that you do not yourself recognize a preternatural voice? How is it that you suffer yourself to be deceived like the crowd? Are you so little advanced then in the ways of mediumship?"

While speaking thus, Jonathan Dream threw his head backwards, and waving his arms and opening and shutting his hands, advanced towards me as if to drown me with his fluid.

"Brother," said I, "you are, I see, a man of wit, although a medium; I have no doubt that you could write us a little speech in the style of Don Quixote, or some new proverbs worthy of Sancho Panza. But we are alone, and both of us are augurs; we have the right to look each other in the face, and even to laugh while looking. Stop where you are, and believe that I wish you a happy success. In France, the thing is easy; the people who believes itself the most *spirituel* in the world, is naturally the easiest to lead by the nose. Ask the women of Paris."

"Stop!" cried my magician in a furious tone. "Am I mistaken? Are you a false brother? Do you take me for a charlatan, a mystifier, a mountebank? Know that Jonathan Dream never spoke a word that was not true. Ah! you doubt my power, my little gentleman. What proof of it do you wish? Shall I take away all your ideas, which would not be difficult; shall I put you to sleep, make you pass through cold, heat, wind and rain; shall I?"——

"No magnetism," said I, "I know that there is in it a natural phenomenon, as yet imperfectly known, of which you take advantage. If you wish to convince me, do not begin by putting me to sleep. We are not at the Academy."

"Well!" said he, fixing his glittering eyes upon me. "What would you say if I transported you to America?"

"I? I must see it to believe it."

"Yes, you," he exclaimed, "and not only you, but your wife, your children, your neighbors, your house, your street, and, if you say the word, all Paris. Yes," added he, with feverish agitation, "yes, if I will it, to-morrow morning, Paris will be in Massachusetts; there will be no longer on the shores of the Seine but an inhabited plain."

"My dear sir, you should sell your secret to the prefect of the Seine; it would perhaps save us many millions. In the absence of the Parisians, there might be made for them a wholly new, regular and monotonous Paris like New York; a Paris without past, without monuments, without memories; all our architects and administrators would be ready to die with joy."

"You jest," said Jonathan, "you are afraid. I repeat it to you, to-morrow, if I wish, Paris will be in Massachusetts and Versailles with it. Do you accept the challenge?"

"Yes, certainly, I accept it," answered I, laughing.

Nevertheless, the assurance of this devil of a fellow troubled me. I was no stranger to gasconade; I read twenty journals a day, and I have heard more than one minister on the rostrum; but this voice of one of the illuminati awed me despite myself.

"Take this box," said the magician in an imperious tone; "open it; there are two pills, one for you and the other for me; take which you like and ask me no questions."

I had gone too far to draw back. I swallowed one of the globules, Jonathan Dream took the other, and bade me adieu, saying in a sepulchral voice, "till to-morrow, on the other side of the ocean."

Once in the street, I found myself in a singular state. I felt brisker, lighter and more elastic than ever was human being; it seemed as if with a bound I could touch the horns of the moon, just rising above the horizon. All my senses were of incredible acuteness. From the Place de la Concorde, I saw the carriages turning the corner of the Arc de l'Étoile, I heard the ticking of the hand that marked the hour on the clock of the Tuileries. The blood coursed through my veins with unheard-of warmth and velocity. I asked myself whether some invisible hand had not already borne me beyond the Atlantic. To reassure myself, I looked at the pale crescent slowly mounting in the sky; sure of not having changed latitude, I returned to my house, ashamed of my credulity, and fell asleep, laughing at Jonathan Dream and his absurd threats.

CHAPTER II.

IS IT A DREAM?

During the night, I had a dream. Was it a dream? Jonathan, seated at my pillow, was looking at me with a mocking air.

"Well!" said he, "Mr. Incredulous, how do you find yourself after your journey? The voyage has not fatigued you over much?"

"The voyage!" murmured I, "I have not stirred from my bed."

"No, but you are in America. Do not spring out of bed like a madman. Wait till I give you some instructions, that the shock may not kill you. In the first place, I have turned your house topsy-turvy. In a free country, men do not live in barracks, pell-mell, without repose and dignity. Of each of those drawers, which you call *étages*, I have made an American dwelling; which I have disposed and furnished in my own manner, and have joined to it a little garden. To arrange thus the forty thousand houses of Paris has taken me two hours, I do not regret it; here you are independent at home, it is the first of all liberties. Henceforth you will not have to suffer from your neighbors, and you will no longer make them suffer. The odor of the kitchen and stables, the cries of women, children and nurses, the mewing of cats and pianos, all is at an end. You are no longer a member of a convict prison or hospital, a packed herring; you are a man; you have a family and a fireside."

"My house turned topsy-turvy! I am ruined; what have you done with my lodgers?"

"Be easy; they are here, each in a commodious little house. They are now tenants who will pay you their rent for half a century, without your needing every three years to surprise each other, and to vie with each other in artifice. I have put at your right, M. Leverd, the grocer, now Mr. Green. M. Petit, the banker on the first floor, has become Mr. Little, and is no less a personage with his millions. M. Reynard, the attorney, is called Lawyer Fox, and has not on this account lost a single one of his tricks. On your left, you will find the brave Colonel Saint-Jean, become the gallant Colonel St. John, with all his rheumatism; and lastly, M. Rose, the druggist, who is neither less majestic nor less important since he has been called Mr. Rose. As to you, my dear Lefebvre, here you are, become by right of immigration, Dr. Smith, and a member of the most numerous family that has sprung from the Anglo-Saxon stock. Make a fortune by killing or curing your patients of the New World; you will find no lack of cousins."

I attempted to cry out—the eyes of my terrible visitor nailed me to my bed. "By the way," said he, laughing, "you will be somewhat astonished to hear your wife, children, and neighbors speak English through their nose. They have left their memory in the Old World, and are no longer but pure-blooded Yankees. An admirable effect of climate, already remarked by the prince of mediums, the great Hippocrates! Dogs no longer bark on approaching the pole; wheat, under the equator, is nothing but sterile couch grass; a Yankee in Paris believes himself born a gentleman; a Frenchman in the United States loses the abhorrence of liberty. As to you, Mr. Incredulous, I have left you both your prejudices and your memories. I wish you to judge of my power with full knowledge of the case. You shall know whether Jonathan Dream is a medium; here you are sewed in an American skin, and you will not leave it except at my good pleasure."

"But I cannot speak English," I exclaimed; I stopped suddenly, frightened at whistling like a bird.

"That's not bad," said the insupportable mocker, "before two days are over, you will confound *shall* and *will, these* and *those*, with all the ease and grace of a Scotchman. Adieu," added he, rising; "adieu, I am expected at midnight by the Sultan, at his harem in Constantinople; at two o'clock, I must be in London, and I shall see the sun rise at Pekin. A last counsel—remember that a wise man is astonished at nothing. If you should chance to see a strange figure about you, don't shout the devil; you will be shut up with our lunatics, which would impede your observations."

I started up; three handfuls of fluid, flung in my face, rendered me mute and motionless. My betrayer saluted me with a sardonic laugh; then, seizing a moonbeam which trailed into the room, he wound it about his waist, darted through the window and vanished in air. Fright, magnetism or sleep, I felt myself overpowered:

"I' venni men, così com' io morisse,
E caddi, come corpo morto cade."

CHAPTER III.

SAMBO.

When I again came to myself, it was daylight. My son was singing the *Miserere* from *Trovatore* at the top of his voice; my daughter, a pupil of Thalberg, was playing with incomparable *brio* the variations of Sturm on a varied air of Donner. In the distance, my wife was quarreling with the nurse, who answered her in a shrill tone. Nothing was changed in my peaceful abode; the pangs of the night were only an idle dream; freed from these chimerical terrors, I might, according to my tranquil habit, dream with open eyes while awaiting the hour of breakfast.

At seven o'clock, according to custom, the servant entered my room and brought me the journal. He opened the window and put aside the blinds; the brightness of the sun and sharpness of the air affected me most agreeably. I turned my head towards the light;—horror! My hair stood on end, I had not even strength to cry out.

In front of me, smiling and dancing, was a negro, with teeth like piano keys, and two enormous red lips overshadowing his nose and chin. Dressed wholly in white, as if afraid of not appearing black enough, the animal approached me, shaking his woolly head and rolling his great eyes.

"Massa slept well," sung he, "Sambo very glad."

I closed my eyes to drive away this nightmare; my

heart beat almost to bursting; when I ventured to look up, I was alone. To spring from the bed, run to the window, and feel my hands and head was the work of an instant. Opposite me was a row of small houses, ranged like pasteboard monks, three printing establishments, six newspaper offices, placards everywhere, wasted water overflowing the gutters. In the street were busy, silent men, hastening along, with their hands in their pockets, doubtless to hide revolvers there—no noise, no cries, no loungers, no cigars, no coffee-houses, and, as far as my eye could reach, not a *sergent de ville*, not a *gendarme*. It was all over with me; I was in America, unknown, alone, in a country without government, without armies, without police, in the midst of a savage, violent and cupiditous people. I was lost!

More forsaken, more desolate than Crusoe after his shipwreck, I let myself fall into an easy chair, which immediately began to dance beneath me. I sprang up, trembling. I looked in the glass. Alas! I no longer recognized myself. In front of me was a lank man, with a bald forehead, sprinkled with a few red hairs, and a freckled face, framed with flaming whiskers, which fluttered upon the shoulders. See what the malice of fate had made a Parisian of the Chaussée-d'Antin! I was pale; my teeth chattered; the cold chilled the very marrow of my bones. "Be a man!" exclaimed I to myself. "I have a family, and the French name to maintain. I must regain over my senses the empire that is escaping me. Adversity makes heroes!"

I wished to call; there was no bell. I perceived a brass knob, which I pressed by chance. Suddenly, Sambo appeared, like one of those devils which spring from a box, bowing and thrusting out their tongue.

"Fire!" I exclaimed, "bring me fire. I want a large fire in the fire-place."

"Hasn't Massa any matches?" said Sambo, pointing to a box on the mantel. "Can't Massa stoop down?" added he, in an ironical tone. Then, turning a screw at the bottom of the fire-place, and putting a match to the brass log, a thousand tongues of fire spouted forth. "Oh dear!" exclaimed, he, on going out, "must a poor negro be disturbed in this way when he is sunning himself?"

"A savage people," thought I, approaching the fire and reanimating myself by its soft and equal heat—"a savage people, that has neither shovel, nor tongs, nor bellows, nor charcoal, nor smoke; a barbarous people, that does not even know the pleasure of stirring the fire! To turn a screw to kindle, extinguish, or regulate one's fire is truly the work of a race without poetry, that leaves nothing to the unforeseen, and that is afraid of losing a moment, because time is money."

Once warmed, I thought of my toilette. I had before me a mahogany table, overloaded with copper swans' heads, and other ornaments in bad taste, but furnished with that English china which delights the eye by its richness of color and design. There were upon this table, and in profusion, brushes, sponges, soaps, vinegars, pomatums, etc., but not a drop of water. I again pressed the knob, and Sambo reëntered, more sulky than at his departure.

"Hot and cold water for my toilette; quick, I am in haste!"

"This is too much!" cried Sambo. "Massa can't turn the hot and cold water faucets there in the corner? Upon my word, it is enough to make one give warning. I can't stay with a master that doesn't know how to see." And he went out, slamming the door in my face.

"Hot and cold water at any moment, and everywhere! This is convenient," thought I; "but it is the invention of a people that thinks only of its comfort. Thank God, we have not come to this! Centuries will pass before glorious France will stoop to this search for luxury, this effeminate cleanliness."

Nothing refreshes the ideas so much as shaving. Having trimmed my beard, I found myself quite another man. I even began to be reconciled with my long visage and front teeth. "If I were to take a bath," thought I, "I would be perfectly composed. I could brave with more courage the sight of my wife and children. Perhaps, alas! they are no less changed than I!" I rang. Sambo appeared, with cast down looks.

"My good fellow, where is there a bathing establishment in the city? Show me the way."

"A bathing establishment, Massa! For what?"

I shrugged my shoulders. "Blockhead, to bathe in, it would seem."

"Massa wants to take a bath," said Sambo, gazing at me with mingled surprise and affright. "And it was for this that Massa disturbed me?"

"Of course."

"This is too much!" cried the negro, tearing out a handful of hair. "What! There is a bath-room by the side of every bedchamber, and Massa makes Sambo come up-stairs to ask him, 'Where shall I bathe?' An American isn't to be made a fool of in this way." And pushing open a little door concealed beneath the hangings, the negro made me enter an elegant closet, in which was a marble bath-tub.

"Come, Sambo," sung he, in a furious but comical tone, "turn the faucet for Massa; the cold-water faucet, the hot-water faucet; get the bath ready; put the linen to warm by the register; play the nurse, Sambo; Massa does not know how to use his hands!"

I had nothing to do but to be silent. I let Sambo exhaust his rage, and endeavored not to see that he thrust out his tongue at me. But I execrated to myself these horrible American houses; unsocial abodes; true prisons, from which one cannot go out, since he finds ready at hand all that at Paris we have the pleasure of going in quest of outside our houses, at a dear rate, it is true, but at a great distance.

CHAPTER IV.

AT HOME.

Quitting the bath without having found composure there, I pensively descended the little staircase which led to the ground floor. What had been done with my house? Under what mask was I about to find my family? I entered the dining-room, no one was there; I went into the parlor, there was no one. Meanwhile, I looked about the two apartments, to accustom myself to the appearance of my new dwelling.

In the dining-room, which was furnished with a carpet, the only ornament was a heavy old mahogany chest, loaded with china cups, and britannia tea-urns brighter than silver. In front of the buffet, were three indifferent engravings; in the middle, Penn treating with the Indians under the Shakamaxon elm; on the right, the portrait of Washington, standing, with his horse and negro; on the left, the image of the sovereign, *pro tempore*, Honest Old Abe—in other words, the honorable Abraham Lincoln, once rail-splitter, now president of the United States.

"These, then," I cried, "are the protecting genii of my new fireside—mine, a Frenchman, reared in the worship of strength and success. A pacific Quaker; a general who, having it in his power to be emperor of the New World, humbled himself so far as to remain the first magistrate of a free people; a workingman, become lawyer by dint of labor, and president of his country by chance—such are the heroes of America! In this half savage land, the code of morals of the great men is also that of the citizens. What can be expected from a nation with such prejudices? It will never give a Cæsar to the world!"

In the parlor was a rosewood piano, a desk loaded with papers, and a book-case filled with books. Three or four Bibles figured therein, among the works of Francis Quarles, Bunyan, Jeremy Taylor, Law, Jonathan Edwards and Channing; great men, doubtless, but whose names I read for the first time. I stopped there, having little taste for theology, even on the nights when I cannot sleep. Next came a few historians or moralists—Franklin, Emerson, Marshall, Washington Irving, Lothrop Motley, and Ticknor; then a few didactic novels, and a host of English, American, German, and even Spanish poets. And France—where was she? Alas! to represent my country, I found nothing but a *Télémaque*, with the pronunciation figured, or rather disfigured, in English. And to think that perhaps some time, to celebrate her father's birthday, my daughter, my dear Susan, would recite to me, with her rosy lips, *Calepso ne povait se counsolère diou départe d'Ioulis!*

In spite I threw down the book, and went into the garden—a little corner of ground, shut in by four walls, ornamented with ivy and honeysuckle; everywhere were lilacs, roses, and new flowers; at the bottom was a little green-house and a Chinese kiosk, a convenient shelter to take tea, smoke a cigar, or gaze at the stars. No one was in the garden but Sambo, stretched on a white marble slab like a bronze statue. His face turned towards the sun and covered with flies, the negro, snoring, was resting from the cruel cares which I had caused him. The dog took advantage of being in my service to do nothing and sleep at full liberty.

This solitary promenade in the habitation of the Sleeping Beauty in the Woods began to perplex me strangely. I was about to awaken Sambo, were it only for the pleasure of quarreling with a Christian, when I heard voices issuing from the sub-soil of the house, or, as the French-Americans say in their dialect, the *basement*, a word which, I hope, will long be wanting in the dictionary of the Academy.

Having descended a few steps, I spied, at length, in a large kitchen, two women so much occupied that they did not hear the sound of my steps. The one whose back was turned towards me, but whom I immediately recognized by her voice, was my dear Jenny, the mother of my children; the other, whom I was ere long to appreciate, was an enormous blonde, five feet eight inches high, who had rather the air of a Scotch grenadier than of one of the daughters of Eve. This was Martha the cook, a Pennsylvanian by birth, a Tunker by religion —something like a Quaker—an excellent person, who scolded constantly, and who had but one fault, that of treating as a publican and sinner whoever wore a button on the dress or coat. To her exalted soul, the symbol of Christianity was not the cross, but a clasp.

Judging from the earnestness of both women, and the words which they were eagerly exchanging, a great culinary work was being accomplished, at this moment. Jenny (was this indeed Madame Lefebvre?) was tying a shapeless mass of dough in a napkin, which she carefully deposited in a pot full of water. In her turn, Martha placed this precious vessel in an iron furnace, which occupied the whole length of the kitchen. This was a monumental structure, with stories like a house, and I know not how many drawers and cupboards, from which the smoke was escaping. Ovens for baking and roasting, laundry, stove, hot water, hot air, everything was found in this monster furnace, which bore the inscription, like a triumphal arch—

G. Chilson's Cooking Range, Boston.

I doubt whether Satan himself, with all the resources at his disposal, ever invented a better heated furnace.

When all was in place, and an army of pots and pans had been moved and ranged in line, my wife turned round, and uttered a cry of joy on seeing me.

"Good morning, my love," said she; "I hope that you have slept well. You are looking at our preparations; it is a pudding, like the one you thought good the other day. I have just made it myself; I know your taste better than Martha. You will be pleased with me, I hope, and will reward me for all the trouble, or rather pleasure, which I take in serving you."

Saying this, she approached me and offered me her forehead. Strange! It was my wife, and yet it was not she. There was the same face, the same features, as in the Old World, except that the end of the nose was somewhat reddened, but at the same time an indescribable calmness and limpidity in the glance, gentleness in the speech, and affection in the gesture, which I had never remarked in our household in ancient Paris. I felt myself loved and cared for, and it delighted my heart. Without troubling myself, therefore, about Martha and our twenty years' marriage, I tenderly embraced Madame Lefebvre—I mean, Mrs. Smith. Pardon me, Parisian husbands, I was in America!

"Martha," said my wife, taking off a kitchen apron and letting down her dress, which was tucked up and fastened behind, "Martha, go to Mr. Green's. His last coffee was not good; it was Brazilian; my husband likes none but Mauritius. Get a small, round kernel; I will burn it myself. I have seen early cherries in market; buy enough to fill one of those nice pies which you make so well, and which my husband and children liked so much last summer. Tell Hoffman, the florist, that there are pinks everywhere except in our garden, and that my husband is waiting for the three new varieties he promised me. Don't forget the lily which I selected for Susan, and the geraniums which I ordered for Henry. Finally, take from the library Dr. Bellows' last speech on the state of the nation; it is an eloquent and patriotic work, and my husband, who reads so well, will read it to us this evening. My children and I will enjoy it so much."

Weak hearts that we are! I felt myself attracted and charmed by this new music, in which my name and my children's recurred at every measure. In Paris, in France, I heard quite a different strain. My wife had all the virtues, but her extreme modesty rendered life somewhat hard to me. To *do like other people* was the motto of Madame Lefebvre; God knows what it cost me not to distinguish ourselves. To be lodged *like other people*, we lived in a suit of rooms a hundred and ten steps high, in a princely hotel, it is true, and whose porter, who laughed at me, had a man servant and a floor rubber. To be waited on *like other people*, we had a great rascal of a lacquey, a drunkard and liar, a magnificent dog in plush breeches and red waistcoat, who cost me dear, served me at cross purposes, and who permitted me neither to dress, nor eat, nor drink, in my own fashion. To be attired *like other people*, my wife and daughter must have dresses at an insane price, and crinolines, each of which filled a whole carriage. Lastly, to go *where other people went*, I was forced to run after invitations, and to smile on men whom at the bottom of my heart I despised with sovereign contempt. It was the custom. The fashionable world wished that fortune should be adored and men should ruin themselves to appear in it. I had taken care not to separate myself from good society; this would have been originality, a vice in the worst possible taste, which France leaves to the English. Thanks to my wife and her wise counsels, we played a difficult part, I think, with propriety; those who saw us every day, at a fixed hour, at the *Bois*, must render us this justice. I venture to say that we maintained our position at Paris, and that we led with honor the most busy life that can be imagined; we paid twenty visits every morning, and never missed a soirée. All this was good; but, must it be confessed? in a savage country my grosser nature gained the ascendancy; I was glad to hear nothing more of *other people;* it pleased me that my wife occupied herself only with me, and saw nothing beyond her husband, children, and house. I felt myself king in my habitation, and I was so well satisfied with my subjects and their obedience, that, in ascending the staircase, I passed my arm around Jenny's waist, and embraced my wife a second time, which made her blush prodigiously. "For shame, Mr. Smith!" murmured she, in a tone which made me believe that both she and I had grown twenty years younger.

CHAPTER V.

NO DOWRY.

WHILE Sambo fatigued himself with sleeping, and my wife and Martha laid the table and served breakfast, I set about reading the Paris Telegraph, an enormous cheap journal, which bore as its motto, "The world is governed too much." The coarse tone of this sheet displeased me. Thank God! we are given a better education. We are not suffered to acquire the odious habit of calling *a cat a cat, and Rollet a rascal.* Who would believe, for instance, that the Paris Telegraph dared brand with the name of robber, and even of assassin, an honest millionaire who, by a mistake excusable without doubt, had furnished to the Northern army sixty thousand pairs of shoes with pasteboard soles, which had illy resisted the dampness of the camps? Do business in a country where so little respect is paid to great speculations!

All the journal was in this deplorable tone. Nothing escaped the invectives of this miserable gazetteer. Such a law was abominable, because it encroached on the free action of the citizens; such a magistrate was a Jeffries or Laubardemont, because he set an innocent snare for the knave who was confided to justice; such a mayor was an ignoramus or a Verres, because he granted to right-minded stockholders a monopoly advantageous to all, as monopolies always are. Must one take the trouble to govern men, daily to encounter such abuse? "Wretched pamphleteer!" I exclaimed, "if thou hadst the honor of living among the most amiable and enlightened people on earth, thou wouldst know from thy birth that to criticise the law, the judge, or the office-holder, is a crime of social treason! The first dogma of a civilized people is the infallibility of authority. Accursed be the inventor of the newspaper, and above all, of the cheap, free newspaper! The press is like gas—a light which burns your eyes and poisons you at the same time."

"Why do we not breakfast?" asked I of my wife abruptly, to shake off unpleasant thoughts. "Where are the children? Why do they not come down?"

"They have gone out, my dear, but will soon return. Henry is to make his first speech this evening before the Academy of Young Readers; he wished to try his voice in the hall before speaking in public."

"And on what subject will our Cicero of sixteen declaim?"

"Here is the rough draught of his speech," said Jenny, handing me with a mother's pride a paper full of words underlined, interjections, pauses and exclamations.

The title, written in large characters, appeared to me more respectable than clear:

"*On the Moral Education of Women, considered as the Instructresses of the Human Race.*"

"Hang thyself, Cherubim!" exclaimed I, "the world will end by dint of virtue! At sixteen, if we thought of anything, it was not certainly, like my son, of the moral"——

"My dear," said Jenny. Her tone stopped me short, and so opportunely that I bit off the word in the middle, and blushed in spite of myself.

"My dear," continued my wife, who did not perceive my confusion, "I think that a change is about to take place in Henry's condition. He repeats to me every day that he wishes to choose an occupation, that he has too long been a burden on us, that the governor must be tired of it"——

"Who is the governor?"

"You know, it is the familiar name which our children give their father; in short, Henry wishes to choose a profession."

"Patience, Mrs. Smith, we have time enough; this is my care."

"My dear," resumed Jenny, "our son is already sixteen; all his comrades have a profession; he must make his way in life. Talk with him about it; no one can guide him better than you."

I began to pace up and down the room, while my wife looked out of the window to see whether our children were coming.

"Oh, my son," thought I, "it is my business to settle thee in life. I have long since arranged everything for thy success. It was not in vain that, sixteen years ago, I chose for thy godfather my friend Regelman, then sub-chief, now Chief of Bureau in the Ministry of the Finances, Section of Customs. Yes, my son, already, without knowing it, thou art candidate in aspiration to the supernumerary force of the Ministry of the Finances. In two years thou wilt be bachelor; in three years, if thou passest successfully three or four competitions, *tu Marcellus eris*. I see thee already, at thirty-five, sub-chief, with a salary of twenty-four hundred francs, and decorated like thy godfather; I see thee, like thy model, gentle, humble, polite and complaisant towards thy superiors;

severe, rigid and majestic towards thy inferiors; and rising, step by step, to the direction of the corps, I see thee become the hope and terror of ten thousand green coats. What fortune, and what a future!"

"There is Henry," cried my wife from the window. "He is talking with Mr. Green; I am sure that he is asking him for good advice, better perhaps than this."

"What do you say, my dear? Green, the grocer! What need has my son to talk with such obscure people?"

"Obscure people!" returned my wife, with an air of surprise. "Mr. Green is an honest man, a good Christian, universally respected. He is worth three hundred thousand dollars, and makes the best use of the fortune, which he owes to labor."

"Well, well!" exclaimed I. "Happy country, where grocers are millionaires, and give counsel like lawyers, if not places like ministers! Let my son then solicit His Excellency the Lord of Prunes and Molasses. But call Susan; I presume that she expects nothing from the Honorable Mr. Green."

"Susan is at her lesson in hygiene and anatomy."

"Anatomy! Good God! My daughter at nineteen learning anatomy! She is dissecting, perhaps?"

"What is the matter with you, my dear?" returned my wife, with a calmness which brought me back to realities. "Susan will some day have children. Do you wish her to bring them up and attend to them blindly, without knowing anything of their constitution? Have you not said a hundred times in her presence that the study of the human body is a necessary part of a good education?"

"And who is the physician to whose prudence is confided the care of teaching young girls anatomy?"

"It is Mrs. Hope, one of our medical celebrities."

"Women physicians! Molière, where art thou? What! in this country, where everything is the opposite of all others, men do not have the care of our wives, mothers and daughters? Women, perhaps, attend at the accouchement of ladies of good society? This is done nowhere; it is indecent, Mrs. Smith, it is indecent!"

"I thought the contrary, my dear; but you know more about it than I. Then, if ever our daughter should have one of those indispositions, whether serious or not, which a woman in her modesty scarcely dares confess to herself, you had rather that I should call in a male physician?"

"By no means; you misunderstand me, my dear. I only meant to say to you that there are ancient usages which are respectable like all ancient errors. That is to say—no, I will explain all this to you some other day. Who accompanied Susan to this lesson in anatomy?"

"No one."

"What! no one? At nineteen, and as beautiful as an angel, my daughter is running about the streets alone, without a chaperon?"

"Why should she do differently from her companions? What danger does she run? Do you imagine that there is a man criminal enough or mad enough in America to be wanting in the respect which he owes to youth and innocence? Fathers, mothers, husbands, sons, every hand would be raised to strike down the wretch—but such an indignity has never been seen in this noble country. These infamies and vices we leave to the Old World.

"Besides," added my wife with her sweet smile, "I think that Susan is well protected. Alfred, Mr. Rose's youngest son, has returned from the East Indies, I saw him walking yesterday with his father and eight brothers. I cannot get it out of my head that Susan and he have been engaged for a long time."

"Engaged! my daughter in love with the ninth son of an apothecary! And her mother coolly announces to me a piece of news of this kind!"

"Why should she not marry the one she loves?" answered Jenny, fixing her beautiful blue eyes on me. "My dear, is it not what I did? am I sorry for it? do you regret it?"

"But what profession, what fortune has this young man?"

"Be easy, my dear; Alfred is a worthy man; he will not marry Susan until he has a position to offer her. Susan will wait ten years if need be."

"And the dowry, Mrs. Smith, have you thought of the dowry? Do you know what this young gallant wants, do you know what we can do, and what part of our little property we must sacrifice?"

"I do not understand you, Daniel. Are we selling our child? Must we bribe a young man, a lover, to decide to accept for a companion a charming girl, the sight of whom rejoices the eyes, and who is as good as she is beautiful? Where did you get these strange ideas, which I hear for the first time?"

"No dowry!" I exclaimed, "in a country where from morning to night all are kneeling before the dollar!"

"In America, my dear, people love, they marry because

they love, and they are happy all their lives in repeating to each other that they have chosen each other through love. Each one brings his heart as a dowry, and I hope that in a free, young, generous nation like ours, we shall never know any other dowry than this."

"No dowry!" thought I, "no dowry! Harpagon was in the right; this changes matters greatly. Marriage is no longer a business. Rich or poor, the bride is sure of being loved; the father who tremblingly gives away his daughter does not fear at least that he is yielding her to some unworthy speculator. No dowry! Barbarous people have sometimes, without knowing it, instincts of delicacy which would do honor to our civilization."

"Here is Susan," cried my wife, who had resumed her post of observation. "Alfred is with her; I guessed it."

I ran to the door. My daughter, my dear Susan—she was more beautiful than ever! Her luxuriant, fair hair, falling in ringlets on her shoulders, her smiling glance, her confident air, her self-possessed bearing gave her a new charm. It was the innocence of the child and the grace of the woman. She flung herself on my neck like a mad-cap, I pressed her to my heart with transport and carried her in my arms to the dining-room.

There only I perceived that Susan had not entered the house alone. He was by her side, the monster who came to snatch from me my happiness and joy; Susan took him by the hand and presented him to me in the most natural manner imaginable.

"Mr. Alfred Rose, dear papa, don't you recognize him?"

I recognized him only too well; he was charming, the wretch! I sighed, and shook hands with this future son-in-law who was pleased to do me the honor to choose me as father-in-law without taking the trouble to consult me on the subject. No dowry! this was sufficient for him to think that he had a right to marry the woman he loved. Talk of propriety to brutes who always go straight ahead!

CHAPTER VI.

IN WHICH WE MAKE ACQUAINTANCE WITH MR. ALFRED ROSE AND NEIGHBOR GREEN.

WHILE we stood face to face, Alfred and I, both silent and gazing at each other, the two women were whispering together with the utmost eagerness, the mother smiling, the daughter with supplicating eyes.

"My love," said Jenny, taking the young people by the hand, "here are two children who, with the help of God, wish to found a Christian family; they ask your blessing."

My blessing! I had seen Pius IX. bless Rome and the world, with that gentle majesty which brought unbelievers to their knees; I had seen pious bishops bless the innocence and fervor of a first communion; it was beautiful and imposing, it was the overflowing of sanctity. But I, a sinner, I did not feel the right to bless even my children. I embraced Susan, I embraced Alfred; I joined their hands in mine, and wept.

They were so happy, the ingrates, that they did not see my tears; they escaped from my arms to run to Jenny, who received them, raising her voice:

"May the God of Abraham and Sarah," said she, "may the God of Isaac and Rebecca, of Jacob and Rachael, bless you, my children, and give you a Christian life!'

"Amen!" responded a voice, whose gravity made me

start. It was Martha, who approached with the look and gesture of a prophet.

"Man," said she, "thee takes this woman before God; woman, thee takes this man before God; for better or worse, in sickness and health, in life and death; do not forget it, the Eternal will remember."

"No, indeed; I will never forget it," cried Alfred, raising his hand, "I call God to witness."

Shall I confess it, to my shame? despite the excellent education which I had received in France, and although I had been accustomed from childhood to treat nothing but jests in earnest, I felt moved to the heart by the solemnity of this engagement. It seemed to me that my hearth had become sacred like that of Abraham, and that the invisible and present God descended upon it to bless the union of my children.

The entrance of Sambo chased away these grave thoughts. He had despoiled the garden and conservatory to offer an enormous bouquet to the bride; he accompanied this present with such grotesque grimaces and compliments, that I laughed despite myself.

"When is the wedding, young massa?" asked he; "to-morrow, the next day, next week? Sambo will sing, Sambo will dance."

"Susan!" exclaimed I, looking at my daughter, "the day is not fixed?"

"Dear papa, we await your pleasure," answered my daughter, with a feigned modesty which made me sigh.

"And this is all we wait for," said Alfred. "I have hired and furnished a house near here, on the corner of Fourteenth Avenue. Everything is ready to receive her who does me the honor to share my name and fortune."

"My son," said I to Alfred, (the name of son strangled

me, by the way), "Susan has chosen you; we adopt you with our eyes shut; but forgive the legitimate curiosity and anxiety of a father. How long have you loved my daughter?—and, since you speak of fortune, what will be the condition of both of you in this household, whose happiness concerns us so closely?"

"To tell you how long I have loved Susan would be difficult," replied the young man. "It seems to me that I have loved her from her birth. Indeed, I loved her already when we went to the common school together, running all the way, she quite a child and I almost a young man. Since this time, we played, talked, and prayed so much together, I saw her so often, gay, good and amiable, we conversed with open hearts so many times, I saw so many times all the beauty of her soul, that the day came when I felt that Susan was the wife whom God, in his goodness, had chosen for me. When Susan was sixteen, I asked her to accept me for her husband; we were engaged. This is the whole story of our love."

"Then," said I, sighing, "it was esteem and friendship which led you to what you call love. Nothing overpowering, nothing sudden, no passion?"

"I am twenty-four years old," said the young man; "I love Susan; I have never loved, and shall never love, any other than she; I esteem her more than any one on earth; I cherish her more than myself. Is this wisdom? is it passion? I know not; but I hope that Susan will ask no more of me, and will permit me to love her in the same manner to my dying day."

"Very well, my son, you are a sage; you will be happy, as you deserve, and have many children. Now, let us talk of money."

"I had no fortune," said Alfred. "This retarded many of our plans. I was twenty-one years old, and I resolved to make my way in life speedily; I had no doubt of success."

"You doubtless had powerful protectors—the promise of some good place under government—or perhaps your father had obliged the cousin of a lady-cousin of a senator?"

"I had my head and hands," replied Alfred, "and the motto of every true Yankee: '*Go ahead; never mind; help yourself.*' These were worth more than the support of strangers. In a country which grows as fast as ours, every man who is not a fool, and who has the will, always ends by striking a lucky vein. Employed as a chemist by a rich indigo merchant, I often heard my patron complain that the vessels sent to the East Indies were never more than half laden. To find a new article of freight was the one fixed idea of our shipping merchants. I discovered one which nobody had thought of, and the sale of which was sure. It was ice. It is impossible ever to supply the East Indies with as much as they can consume. The difficulty was to preserve it on the way; this was a problem to be resolved. Thanks to my father, I had been brought up in a laboratory; physics and chemistry had been my earliest amusements. It was necessary to find a body which should be a bad conductor of caloric, to isolate my ice. I tried sawdust, which is worthless among us. The discovery was made. Nothing was lacking but capital.

"To find money to put a good idea in execution is easy in America. I thought of Mr. Green, who does a large business in rice, coffee, spices, and indigo. He had confidence in me, and risked a shipment. I set out for

Calcutta with my cargo, which did not melt on the way. I sold my ice in such a way as to make the outward and homeward freight, and returned after having secured advantageous markets for twenty years. On my arrival, I had eight thousand dollars for my share; and here I am at the head of the firm, Green, Rose & Co. Success is certain. I could raise money on it to-day if I liked. Ten or twelve thousand dollars a year is what I can offer Mrs. Rose while awaiting something better."

"Sixty thousand francs a year!" I cried. "What a fine thing is commerce, when it is successful!" I looked at my son-in-law more closely, and detected in him an air of genius. In the forehead and lower part of the face he had something of Napoleon.

I had wholly forgotten his father's shop, when Sambo announced Mr. Rose, who had come to share in the common joy. However estimable was this excellent man, an apothecary was by no means the father-in-law I had dreamed of for my daughter. I had aspired to a sub-prefect; but what was to be done in a back country, destitute as yet of that centralization which Europe envies us?

With Mr. Rose entered Mr. Green, followed by Henry. I recognized the apothecary by that medical air which he never lost; but the grocer, in a black coat and white cravat, was to me an unknown monster. His language and manners were no less strange than his costume. Green, the seller of oil and coffee, talked with the authority and self-possession of a man that moves millions.

"Neighbor," said he to me, with affectionate good-nature, "here I am, something like one of your family, through this young man, your son-in-law, and my partner. We will not stop here. Henry has been to see me.

He is an intelligent boy, and I like him. I have found him a position. Alfred is going to settle down. A man hardly marries to rove about the world; but we must have, notwithstanding, a reliable man at Calcutta. I have thought of Henry, in spite of his youth. One never gets a taste of business too early. Three years' stay in the East Indies will form him. We will give him a share, which, if he works, will amount to four or five thousand dollars a year. You entrust me with a child, in three years I will give you back a man! What do you say of my plan? Does it suit you as well as it does Henry?"

"Oh, my son," thought I, "I had dreamed of a different future for thee! Perhaps this suits thee better; perhaps thou hast neither the political genius nor the necessary suppleness to rise to the rank of Chief of Bureau. Fate has decreed it! Thou wilt be nothing but a millionaire."

I thanked Green, who whispered to me:

"Neighbor, we will not stop here. You know Margaret, my twelfth child, a charming little girl, ten years old, with a figure already as plump as a doll's. I have an idea that in six or seven years we will make her Mrs. Henry Smith. From this time we will have an eye on this young man and his fortunes. Depend on me."

It was too much. I, Doctor Lefebvre; I, a scholar and citizen in my own country, to become the relation and protégé of a grocer! Certainly I love equality. I am a Frenchman, and have for my gospel the principles of 1789. Let this equality be proclaimed and placarded everywhere, I demand it; let it even be put in our laws, I consent, the laws are scarcely ever applied; but that this equality be brought down into our customs, never! The man who does nothing will always be more than he who soils his hands by working.

I was about to break the charm, and refuse this perfidious fortune, when, by my wife's invitation, each of our neighbors accepted a slice of ham and cup of tea.

"Daniel," said Jenny, "we are all at the table, say the blessing."

"My dear, I am so much agitated that I no longer know what I am doing. Take my place and speak for me."

"O God," said Jenny, "bless this house, and all who are found in it! Bless, above all, those who are departing from it; and mayst thou, O Lord, find among them only pure and obedient hearts!"

Each one replied "Amen" in so sincere a tone that it overthrew the whole course of my ideas. I looked at my friends, my children, my wife; Green, who with so much simplicity made the fortune of my family; Henry, who at sixteen, with the resolution of a man and the ardor of a child, resolved, by dint of labor, to conquer for himself a rank in the world, and recoiled neither before danger nor exile; Susan and Alfred, who loved each other with so pure and tender a love; lastly, my wife, my good Jenny, who thought only of others; attentive and devoted, the life and soul of the house, the queen of this hive whence the swarm was taking flight.

And I, useless drone, who knew only how to murmur; I said to myself that I was about to be left alone by this hearth, lately animated by the joy of Susan and Henry. Rose had nine children, Green had twelve. God blesses large families, and when we wish to be wiser than he, he confounds our false prudence, and condemns us to the isolation which we have sought.

And I looked at my wife, still young and fresh, with a graceful *embonpoint*, and said to myself—I know no longer what I was saying, when Sambo, pushing open the door, entered with a frightened air, crying, "The bell! the bell! Hark! it is fire!"

CHAPTER VII.

THE FIRE.

At the first cry of Sambo, the apothecary ran to the window, then turning to Green:

"Lieutenant," said he, "it is for us, the fire is in Twelfth Avenue."

"Sergeant, I am ready," said the grocer, rising. "Doctor," added he, striking me on the shoulder, "make haste, the carriage will not wait!"

"Good!" thought I, on seeing them go out, accompanied by Alfred and Henry, "see them playing the National Guard! The National Guard is a gift sent us from America by Lafayette and by which we have profited finely! Run to this useless parade, my dear friends, and much good may it do you; for my part, I shall stay at home. What is this carriage that Green speaks of? Does he imagine that I shall run like an idler to see a conflagration in a country where fires, they say, occur every day?"

I approached the window; whirlwinds of smoke were rising in the sky and throwing out fiery sparks; the fire was gaining ground.

"Quick, sir, quick, the carriage is coming," said Martha, all at once.

I turned round; before me was Sambo, a hatchet in his hand and a helmet of varnished leather on his head; Martha was holding a jacket of black cloth and a broad gymnastic belt; it was my uniform, I was a fireman!

A fireman! I! I sought to protest against this new insult of fate; but Martha had taken possession of me. In the twinkling of an eye I was dressed, strapped, helmeted and hoisted on an immense carriage. Two magnificent black horses drew on a gallop the engine and firemen.

"Fear nothing, Daniel!" cried Martha, her hand upraised, "thee is going to serve God; the Most High will bring thee back from the midst of the flames as he rescued his servants, Shadrach, Meshach and Abednego."

This Biblical benediction made me shudder, it savored of singeing. "A singular idea," I exclaimed, "to risk one's own skin for strangers, when firemen might be hired!"

"What are you saying, doctor?" interrupted a shrill voice by which I recognized my neighbor Reynard in Attorney Fox. "Citizens," added he, reciting some old speech, "if you would be free, be yourselves your police and army. To give yourselves guardians is to give yourselves masters. My dear friend," continued he, in a natural tone, "where did you get these old world ideas, are you not a friend of liberty?"

"Liberty before everything," I hastened to reply, a little ashamed of my weakness. "To fly to the assistance of our fellow citizens is a duty and pleasure which I leave to no one; I am proud of being a fireman!"

"Not so much so as Green," replied the sharp-visaged man. "He is the one that likes so well to go to fires! He is devilish smart!" whispered he in my ear; "devilish smart," he repeated four times, winking and making signs with his nose and chin.

He opened his snuff box, sighed, and took two pinches of snuff, slowly. "Our captain, the gallant Colonel St. John, is about to resign," said he, "Green is lieutenant, and ambitious. He wishes to become captain, in order to rise higher. He is devilish smart; but he has hid his cards in vain; I read his hand."

Fox had not ended his insidious confidences when we arrived at the spot. There was no police, no precaution taken; a crowd of curious people was gathered on the sidewalks, fortunately leaving free the middle of the street. In a moment, the engine was put in place, the water was everywhere. While the lieutenant ascertained the principal seat of the fire and gave orders, I set to work to pump with my amiable neighbor.

In front of us was a house on fire. The flames had broken the windows, and were bursting out on every side. All at once, piercing shrieks were heard from the second story; a white figure passed like a shadow; a woman's voice called for help. Green quickly placed a ladder along the wall, mounted, and was lost amidst the smoke.

"Devilish smart!" said Fox, with a satanic grimace, "devilish smart! He plays well, the ambitious dog!"

"Pump, boys, pump!" cried Rose, wholly occupied with drowning the flames. I bore with all my might upon the lever, but I could not detach my eyes from the window which Green had entered. My heart beat; I was breathless with anxiety.

Suddenly Green reappeared, a woman in his arms, and descended, amid the huzzas of the crowd.

Scarcely had the woman touched the ground when she sprang to her feet. "My child!" cried she, "where is my child?"

Her limbs shook; she wept; she raised her hands towards the burning windows, and wished to fling herself into the furnace. In vain we sought to restrain her; she escaped from our hands, rushed to the house, and, driven back by the flames, recoiled, uttering heart-rending shrieks, and tearing her hair.

All looked at each other. The flames were roaring like a tempest. The burning roof was about to fall in: the child was lost! At this moment I felt an indescribable sensation. The sight of this poor mother, the words of Martha, the example of Green, the idea that I was a Frenchman—I know not what—a sort of intoxication mounted to my brain. I ran to the ladder, and was at the top before I knew what I was doing.

Rose sought to stop me. "I am a father," I exclaimed. "I will not let this child die."

Once in the room, I was filled with terror. The flame whistled round me; the wainscot crackled; the glasses snapped—the sounds were sinister. Stifled by the heat and blinded by the smoke, I called, there was no answer; I cried, no echo. I was in despair, when a tongue of the red flame, piercing the darkness, showed me opposite a closed door. To break the lock by a stroke of the hatchet, enter the chamber, rush to the cradle where an infant was crying, and possess myself of the treasure, was the work of an instant. What joy, but how short! Surrounded with smoke, almost asphyxiated, I knew no longer where I was. My heart beat, my head turned, I was lost.

"This way, doctor, this way, Daniel," cried the voice of Rose. "Come on, but step aside. Take care!"

The advice was wise. I had hardly turned when a vigorous jet of water, directed by the skillful hand of the apothecary, inundated me from head to foot, at the risk of throwing me down. Thanks to this strategic diversion, which for an instant arrested the flame and dissipated the smoke, I saw the window, ran to it, and, bestriding the ladder, glided to the ground, black and smoking like a drenched firebrand. An instant after the roof fell with a horrible crash. Martha was right: God had treated me like Abednego.

To tell the joy of the poor mother would be useless. The happiest person was myself. I had saved a child, and maintained the honor of the French name. It had cost me something. I had the whole side of my hair singed, an ear flayed, and the left arm burned from the wrist to the elbow; but what was this to what I had gained?

An hour at most after these events, we returned to our district, leaving to the last comers the care of extinguishing the smoking ruins. I clambered briskly, with head erect, upon the carriage which I had mounted in the morning with such ill grace. Fox was there, winking as if he were blind of one eye.

"Green is smart," said he, pushing his elbow against my burned arm, and making me wince; "but you are devilishly smarter than he. Hurrah for Captain Smith!" added he, rubbing his hands.

I did not answer him. I was wholly occupied by a new spectacle.

Along the sidewalks was ranged an immense crowd in incredible order. Almost all the men held a paper in their hand, which they waved as we passed.

"Hurrah for the brave lieutenant! Hurrah for Green!" cried the crowd. "Hurrah for Smith! Hurrah for the gallant fireman!"

"Here they are!" exclaimed some one, pointing us out! Hats were raised, handkerchiefs fluttered; women showed us to their children, who waved their little hands as if to bless us.

By what mystery did the whole city already know my name and deed? I was ignorant, and did not ask. We quickly become accustomed to glory; but emotion overpowered me, and I vainly endeavored to gaze at the crowd with the modesty and calmness of a hero. When I approached my dwelling, I was in tears. The people surrounded Jenny, my daughter, Martha, who was preaching, and Sambo, who was dancing like a child. I threw myself into their arms, and, despite my chimney-sweeper's face, Gôd knows how heartily I embraced them all. I grimed everybody, I believe, even to Sambo.

Before entering the house, Jenny smilingly showed me the newspaper-office opposite us, that of the *Paris Telegraph*, that seditious journal. An immense placard was hoisted above the house, and half a league off might have been read the following description:

FIFTH EDITION.

PARIS TELEGRAPH.

HORRIBLE CONFLAGRATION!

The brave Lieutenant GREEN! *The gallant Fireman* SMITH!!

SUBLIME MOTTO:

"*I am a father; I will not let this child die!*"

50,000 copies sold.

SIXTH EDITION *in press.*

This was the temple whence the glory was dispensed; there was wherewith to cure vanity.

With what pleasure I hastened to the bath-room to plunge into the water, wash my face, and refresh my burned arm! This time, I found the invention admirable which placed hot water at every moment in my dwelling. As to Sambo, he would not quit me, pretending that Massa needed his services, and could not do without him. The rascal needed to make me talk to give himself importance in the neighborhood. My glory was his; he had entered the flames, by proxy.

When I descended to the parlor, the office of the Paris Telegraph, still crowded with buyers, could not satisfy the demand; the crowd pressed beneath our windows to try to obtain a glimpse of me. With my arm in a sling, my scarred cheek and burned hair, I might well believe myself a hero.

Ere long, that nothing might be wanting to the joy of this happy day, the fireman's band came to give me a serenade, and the whole company, with Green for its spokesman, made me an address. In this well-turned speech, the grocer, with touching modesty, forgot himself to speak only of the courage which I had shown; and, in the name of the company, he entreated me to accept the post of captain.

"Comrades! friends!" exclaimed I, "I am confused by your kindness, but God forbid that I forget the example set me by Lieutenant Green, and the aid lent me by Rose, the brave sergeant! To the first, I owe the honor of a good action; to the second, my life. Permit me, therefore, not to forget the debt of gratitude, and always to regard as my superiors the excellent Green and the generous Rose. I will remain with you, comrades; like you, a simple fireman in a free country. Proud of your friendship and heroism, I would not exchange our modest uniform for the gilded dress of a captain-general. Hurrah for America and liberty!"

My reply was successful, especially the end, which meant nothing. Green threw himself into my arms, Rose did the same, and Fox, taking me aside, whispered to me: "You are devilish smart, comrade, you look high; but all the same, I read you." And he winked with both eyes at once—a mysterious language, the scope of which escaped me.

On a signal from Green, the serenade again commenced. At the same moment, I saw a canvas ascend the whole length of the newspaper office, like the mainsail of a ship. Upon this transparency, lighted by colored lanterns, was read the following inscription, in letters a foot high:

EIGHTH EDITION.

PARIS TELEGRAPH.

HORRIBLE CONFLAGRATION!

The gallant fireman SMITH, *the new Cincinnatus!!!*

How America rewards virtue.

100,000 copies sold.

NINTH EDITION *in press.*

"What does this mean?" I exclaimed. "Sambo, go bring the paper; there is some bad joke under this."

The paper brought, I read in it, to my great surprise, Green's speech and my answer. I had been stenographed, and printed forthwith. My refusal had won for me the title of Cincinnatus. Why, I never knew; but the word looked well on the placard. It is something for a man to be called the *new Cincinnatus.*

Beneath my speech, under the absurd heading, "*How*

America rewards virtue," were the two following letters:

SWAN FIRE INSURANCE COMPANY.

No. 10 *Acacia St.*

(Joint Stock capital, $10,000,000. A share in the profits secured to the parties insured.)

"Sir:

"The courage displayed by you in this morning's fire has attracted the attention of the Directors of the Company.

"The position of consulting physician, to verify the wounds and accidents resulting from fire, is at this moment vacant.

"We hope that you will do us the honor to accept it. The emoluments are $400.

"X. X——

"Director of the Company.

"Dr. Daniel Smith, Fireman of Company VII."

THE PROVIDENCE CHILD'S HOSPITAL.

Supported by private subscriptions, at $10 *per annum.*

No. 25 *Walnut St.*

"Sir:

"The physician who uttered the noble words: *I am a father, I will not let this child die,* is naturally fitted, by his devotion and talent, for the care of young children.

"The place of physician in chief in our hospital is vacant; we hope that it may suit you to accept it.

"Attendance daily, from 6 to 8, A.M. Salary, $2,000.

"R——

"T——

"Governors of the Hospital.

"Dr. Daniel Smith, Fireman of Company VII."

"Sambo," asked I, "have these letters been brought me, then?"

"No, Massa, the postman has not come yet."

"It is impossible, unless there be some mystification in this journal."

"There is a knock, Massa," said Sambo; "one, two, three—it is the postman. I am coming!"

The negro brought me forty letters—a mountain of paper. Some patients asked my office hours, others entreated me to visit them as soon as possible; four physicians called me in consultation; six druggists offered me a partnership; and lastly, strange to say, two letters, carefully sealed, announced to me confidentially what the *Paris Telegraph* had already published with an indiscretion which at heart I pardoned it.

I was celebrated! my fortune was beginning! A day, an hour of courage had given me a name, and done more for me in America than twenty years of labor had done on the old continent! "But," thought I, and this thought restored to me the humility of which I had great need, "without this garrulous journal, without this trumpet, which has flung my name to all the echoes of the New World, would I have succeeded?" My first idea, nevertheless, was to thank the journalist, be this as it might. It was too late; the office was closed, the picture extinguished, my glory vanished. I postponed my visit till the next day.

I passed the evening with my old friends, my wife and children. They made me repeat the smallest details of the terrible and glorious event. Jenny grew pale when I spoke of my dangers; her cheeks glowed when I told the joy of the mother on regaining her child. Susan clasped my hand and looked at Alfred.

The conversation, I think, would have lasted all night, if Martha had not placed on the table an enormous

Bible, bound in shagreen and fastened by large copper clasps.

"Read," said she to me, "and calm thy vanity. Do not forget the story of Haman, son of Hammedatha, of the race of Agag; and remember that there is a Mordecai here who will not bend the knee before thee."

"Be easy, Martha," answered I, laughing. "There is no gallows fifty cubits high at my gate, and I wish to hang no one."

Jenny opened the Bible, and read us the third chapter of Daniel, which delighted the Quakeress, pleased Sambo no less, and made me seriously reflect on the goodness of God in my behalf. The evening was far advanced when we separated after so well filled a day. I threw myself on my bed, weary and suffering somewhat, but content with myself, and dreamed all night of serenades, placards, huzzas and speeches.

CHAPTER VIII.

TRUTH, HUMBUG & CO.

Scarcely awakened, I ran to the window; I wished to enjoy my new-born celebrity, and once more to contemplate my name proclaimed above the house-tops. The canvas was in its place; all the passers were casting their eyes on it; but, oh vanity of human glory! behold what was read there:

ARRIVAL OF THE PERSIA.

GREAT NEWS FROM EUROPE.

London. Consols 92¾.

Liverpool. Rise in Cotton, 20 per cent.
Salt pork (Cleveland), demand for 4000 bbls. at $14.

A RARE CHANCE FOR FARMERS!!!!

Four beautiful Italian Asses, first class stallions.

Apply to Ginocchio Bros., No. 70 William Street.

"Shopkeeping people," exclaimed I, shaking my fist at the passers, "gross race which carries on pell mell, and at the same pace, business, sentiments, cotton and ideas, I thank God for not belonging to thee! Long live France, the country of the ideal, that is always carried away with a high-sounding word, France that, thank God! never thinks of her own interests except when it is too late! Our folly is better than the wisdom of these Yankees; our poverty is nobler than their riches. Four

Italian asses and the price of pork, this is the great news from Europe to these ignorant farmers! And of France, the new fashions, the Court ball, the last novel, the last vaudeville, not a word! Pale Vandals, I have for you naught but contempt!"

While giving free vent to my just anger, I wished none the less to thank the journalist who had spoken of me the night before. Whatever might be this pamphleteer, it was fitting that I should not remain his debtor; to honor him with a visit was already to acquit myself of the obligation.

I entered a house of insignificant appearance, which had no other sign than a brass plate, nailed to the wall, on which was read, PARIS TELEGRAPH, *Truth, Humbug & Co., Editors and Proprietors.* A green serge door was before me; I pushed it open and found myself in the presence of a little man, dressed in black, and buttoned to the throat—it was Mr. Truth. Seated before a mahogany desk, he held in his hand an enormous pair of scissors, with which he was cutting long strips from an English journal and throwing them into a kind of letter box which communicated with the press room. It was cheap editing.

"What do you want, sir!" asked he, without raising his head or interrupting his work.

"Sir," said I in a grave and deliberate voice, "I am Dr. Daniel Smith, fireman of Company VII., the same whom you had the kindness to praise in your last evening's paper."

"Well," said the journalist, continuing his cutting, "what do you want?"

"To thank you, sir; to pay my debt of gratitude."

He looked at me with an air of surprise.

"You owe me nothing, doctor. In publishing your noble action, I was following my trade, and you were worth to me yesterday more than two hundred dollars. You are therefore under no obligations to me."

Upon which he resumed his labor, without even inviting me to be seated.

"Mr. Truth," said I in a dry and dignified tone, "I care nothing about the motives from which you acted yesterday; you have rendered me a service, and I am and remain your debtor."

I was about to depart when he raised his head, and fixed on me a pair of large black eyes whose suffering expression struck me.

"Doctor," said he in a panting voice, "if you absolutely insist on acquitting yourself of an imaginary debt, here is the opportunity. Tell me in all sincerity from what disease I am suffering, and how much longer I have to live."

He rose, laid his hand on his heart, and suddenly stopped short. A violent asthma oppressed him. I felt his pulse, listened to his respiration, and auscultated him; there were symptoms which permitted of no mistake.

"Doctor," said he, "I ask you to tell me the truth. When a man is in the habit, like me, of telling it to everybody, he has the strength to hear it on his own account. I need to know my situation."

"You have," answered I, "a disease of the heart, which is far from being incurable. Stramonium cigarettes will relieve you. But if you wish to be cured, you must have pure air, a tranquil life and repose of soul and body; all things which are not found in a newspaper office."

"Thank you, doctor," said he, "your advice is the same

which my physician gave me this morning. I must renounce the fatigues of my profession; so be it, the sooner the better. A Yankee never looks back. Doctor, buy my journal. I will sell you my share for twenty thousand dollars; in six months you will have made it. Is it done?"

"Whew!" cried I; "how you get on! I a journalist! That is an honor I never thought of!"

"Think of it, then. To a good man, it is the first of callings. Is there anything more glorious than to guide one's brethren in the way of justice and truth?"

Journalism is a profession which is little esteemed at a distance, but which near by, I know not why, every one wishes to handle. Journalists are of the same family as comedians; they are disdained, yet envied. These Bohemians have wit; in coming in contact with them, one feels himself less plebeian. There is not a beautiful lady that is not happy to approach noted coquettes; there is not a statesman that at some moment does not flatter pamphleteers, even if he do not modestly enrol himself among the makers of journals. Despite myself, the proposition of Mr. Truth tickled my vanity; the idea of leading public opinion pleased me. A man like me has so many things to teach that ignorant and stupid mass, called the public! The sentiment of my dignity alone hindered me from yielding to this folly.

"To direct a journal," said I to my patient, "is too difficult a thing for one not born in the profession."

"No, nothing is simpler. Sit down here, by my side; remain two hours, and you will have the secret of the trade. At the bottom, everything may be reduced to a simple rule of action—to tell the truth, the whole truth and nothing but the truth."

Curiosity prevailed. I threw myself into a large easy chair of yellow leather, placed my cane between my legs, and rested my wounded arm on the elbow of the chair. Once installed, I opened a forgotten snuff-box on the table, and, looking at Mr. Truth:

"My dear Aristides," said I, "your device is a fine one, but, between ourselves, is it not too fine? In point of journalism, I thought that falsehood was the rule and truth the exception."

"Where have you seen this, Machiavellian doctor? In Old Europe, perhaps? In Spain, in Russia, in Turkey, wherever the press is a monopoly in the hands of the government, the poor journalists have permision to say nothing for six days, on condition of lying officially on the seventh; but in a country of liberty, where every one can think as he likes and print what he thinks, where would be the use of lying? Truth is our merchandise, with which we buy the public. To lie is to lose our credit, and ruin ourselves disgracefully. We may have all the vices, a single one excepted. See the *London Times*. It is inconstant, abusive, violent; but lying—never! Surprised in the very act of falsehood, its proprietors would lose an income of a hundred thousand dollars. A man is not vicious at this cost; he is veracious through calculation, and virtuous through interest."

This American virtue dazzled me little; I was seeking an answer, when I perceived a weasel's paw on the latch of the door. It was my honorable brother-in-arms and neighbor, Lawyer Fox, who approached, gliding over the floor, and took us affectionately by the hand.

"Good morning, my dear Truth," said he to the journalist, smiling. "I come in behalf of Mr. Little, the banker, to talk with you about a large job. There are two thousand dollars to make for the journal—two thousand dollars," repeated he, emphasizing each syllable.

"Very well," replied the journalist coldly. "This is my partner's business."

He rang. A small door opened, and there emerged from it, not without difficulty, a fat man, whose enormous body, bald head, large ears, and projecting teeth, gave him the air of a dressed elephant.

"Good morning, Dr. Smith," cried he, bursting into laughter, "good morning; I recognise you by your arm in a sling. What do you say to my last night's bulletin, my dear Cincinnatus? It was not worth as much as to-day's. Truth, the four asses are sold; Ginocchio writes us to withdraw the advertisement. Good morning, Fox; you are so thin, that I took you for the doctor's shadow. You lawyers have such tender consciences that you grow thin by your scruples. What have you brought us?"

"This is the point in question," answered Fox, little flattered by the graciousness of Mr. Humbug. "The firm Little is making a small Mexican loan—ten million dollars to begin with. The shares are two hundred dollars each, issued at one hundred and sixty, and redeemable at par by annual drawing. Ten per cent. interest, twenty per cent. profit on the capital—it is a fine thing."

"For Little," said Humbug, laughing; "and you want to advertise, '*Mundus vult decipi, ergo decipiatur.*' Be easy, Fox; we will give you a nice little place in the journal. Between Holloway's ointment and Morrison's pills, your Mexican loan will do wonders."

"I came to agree with you about the price," said Fox.

"Do you want to know the rate of advertising? A cent a word, a dollar a hundred words. In this common forest, all humbug at a fixed price, as you well know."

"Pardon me, my dear Humbug," returned Fox, winking, "you don't understand me. When I spoke of the price, I was not thinking of the rate of advertising. Little would like to have the plan of this useful and patriotic subscription inserted in the body of the journal, so that it may not look like an advertisement. We will pay whatever is necessary. Do you understand me?"

"I am afraid I do, Master Fox," replied the fat man, without ceasing to laugh. "But, as old Plautus says: '*Stultitia est venatum ducere invitos canes.*' You rose too late, my good Fox. On this side the water, simpletons are not caught in so gross a snare; it will do for the innocents of the Old World. Besides, if my advertisements are not in question, address yourself to my partner. Do you understand what we are asked to do, my dear Truth?"

"Perfectly," replied Truth, in an abrupt voice. "Mr. Little has need of our house to place his loan; he sends to ask at what price I will sell myself."

"Truth, my dear fellow, you take things wrongly," said Fox, in a wheedling tone. "We ask nothing of you but what other journals have promised us; the *Lynx*, the *Sun*, and the *Tribune*, will recommend our loan; I hope so, at least; we are negotiating."

"Since you have these journals," resumed Truth, "why do you come here? What need have you of me?"

"For a simple reason, my excellent friend," said Fox, in a honied voice. "There is little confidence on 'Change in anything but the *Paris Telegraph;* it is quite natural that we should endeavor to have you on our side. We will make any sacrifices for it."

"Mr. Fox," exclaimed the journalist, pale with emotion, "there is the door."

"I am your servant, Mr. Truth," said the lawyer, disappearing.

"I am not yours," replied my patient. "To-morrow, I will know what this loan is, and will publish it."

"My dear sir," said I, with the authority of my profession, "you will make yourself worse; you will disabuse no one, and will make yourself mortal enemies."

"Enemies are our glory; we are soldiers; our place is in the fire."

As he said this, he put both hands to his breast, and fell back into his easy chair.

"Doctor," cried Humbug, "help him; he is suffocating. How can a man excite himself in this way, for this human rabble? Truth, you selfish dog, you are killing yourself expressly to destroy me—me, your old friend. Come! look at me."

Truth stretched him his hand, smiling sadly. Despite myself, I felt a sort of pity for this poor Bohemian, who was sacrificing his life to the most chimerical and deplorable of pursuits.

CHAPTER IX.

IN WHICH TRUTH FINDS HIS MATCH.

When the crisis had passed and the sick man had regained his breath, Humbug leaned both elbows on the table, and said in a tone which he strove to render gay, without succeeding

"My dear Truth, no longer resist your true vocation; turn preacher. Vices are tough; they suffer themselves to be maltreated without answering back. We castigate them vigorously every Sunday over the shoulders of our neighbor, after which we breakfast in peace and dine in the same way. But these bipeds who believe themselves men only because they walk on two paws, these wolves in round hats, these foxes in spectacles, these apes in neck ties, these geese in black coats—we are only to approach them to laugh at their cruelty, their avarice, their cowardice and their stupidity. Whoever takes them in earnest dies of a broken heart."

"Here is my successor," says Truth, taking me by the hand, "my dear Humbug, the doctor will make you a good partner."

"The doctor," returned Humbug, "impossible! he looks like a deer."

"Of what kind of animal then," exclaimed I, "are journalists made?"

"To make a good journalist," said Humbug, with comical gravity, "needs the face of a dog, the scent of a dog, the impudence of a dog, the courage of a dog, and the fidelity of a dog. The face of a dog to intimidate knaves, the scent of a dog to smell them from afar, the impudence of a dog to bark at them in spite of their threats and grimaces, the courage of a dog to take them by the throat, the fidelity of a dog to start, stop and return at the first call of truth."

"Mr. Superintendent of advertisements," said I, with impatience, "I did not suspect that you had so lively and disinterested a passion for truth."

"Why so, wise Esculapius?" returned he, in a bantering tone. "Do you think that I do not know that two and two make four? What regulates the price of advertisements? The number of readers. What brings readers? Public opinion. Do we gain them by deceiving public opinion? Truth is the body of the journal; the advertisements are only its crinoline, a ridiculous costume, furnished by falsehood and vanity. *Desinet in piscem mulier formosa superne.* Whose is the fault? The spirit and good taste of the public."

"Sir," said I, turning over the snuff-box in my hands to give weight to my words, "all truths are not to be spoken. There are those which disturb and break up society."

"Yes, my dear doctor, truth is revolutionary."

"At length," I exclaimed, "you confess it."

"Doubtless. See the Reformation; at what a cost did it free the human conscience?"

"That is so! that is so!" said I, rapping with my cane.

"And the Gospel," resumed Humbug, "what subversion! A system of civilization destroyed, Jupiter dethroned, the Cæsars despised and overthrown! How happy it would have been to have stifled in its beginning this truth which slew a world and brought forth a new one! Ah, my dear Hippocrates, you are silent. And the French Revolution?"

"Sir," exclaimed I, "let us not touch sacred things! It was the resistance of the privileged classes that did all the harm. Acknowledge, at length, that there are truths which appal"——

"Yes; as the light appals thieves."

"There are truths which are odious to those who hear them."

"Yes; when they disturb drunkenness, or awaken remorse."

"There are truths which are dangerous to those who speak them."

"Yes; when they have the heart of a slave or a footman."

I turned my back on this shameless sophist, who did not fear to attack wise prejudices and to shake the pillow on which the world has been sleeping for two thousand years, and addressed myself to Truth, who had resumed his cutting, and seemed not to hear us.

"What are you thinking of, my dear patient?" said I. "Our conversation wearies you, perhaps?"

"Doctor," replied he, smiling, "forgive the impertinence of my fancy, I was thinking of Pilate. I heard this grave ruler saying to Christ, '*What is the truth?*' and going out without attending to the answer. In the time of Tiberius Cæsar, you would have made an excellent governor of Judea.

"What!" added he, becoming animated, "do you not feel that to us men, truth is life and falsehood death? Seek around you the prosperous, enlightened, upright, charitable countries; are they not those where every one has a right to tell the truth, the whole truth, without distinction of persons, without respect to prejudices, privileges and abuses? Seek the miserable, ignorant, immoral countries; are they not those where, under every form, official falsehood rules? Contemplate the greatness of England, the growth of America, the rising fortune of Australia. In eighty years, what power has raised our United States from three million to thirty-one million men? Do not deceive yourself, it is truth. Leave politicians to build up systems and combine forms of government; see what are the living institutions of free peoples. Schools, associations, the rostrum, the press—what are all these, if not so many instruments to propagate truth and to win all hearts to it? Count the journals of a people, and you will have its rank in the scale of civilization—it is a thermometer which never errs. Why? Because truth is, under another name, only the law which governs the moral world; because there are natural relations between men, as between things. To recognize and respect these relations is to recognize and respect the truth, or rather, God himself, present in the world by his almighty truth."

"Dear Mr. Truth," replied I, a little moved by this flow of words, "Humbug is right, you were born to preach. But experience has long since taught me that practice is the opposite of theory. How many truths, admirable at a distance, fail on being put to the test! Every day I hear it repeated that men are brethren, that woman is the equal of man, that governments are made for the people"——

"Do you doubt it?" said Truth.

"No, I do not doubt it *theoretically;* but try to put these fine maxims in practice, and what will come of it?"

"The kingdom of Jesus Christ," replied the journalist, with singular gravity. "If you have no more noble ideal," added he, "if you have nothing to put in its place, do not play the sad rôle of Mephistopheles. Humanity needs to hope and believe."

"Come, charming doctor, you who do not believe in theory," exclaimed Humbug, with an impertinent laugh, "when you speak, do you know what you are saying? when you give a remedy to your patients, do you know what you are doing? Do not be angry; if you know, you are only putting theory in practice; if you do not know, what right have you to be so proud of not reasoning?"

I sunk into my easy chair, crossed my arms and legs, and, looking Humbug full in the face:

"Sir," said I, "listen to me seriously, if you are capable of anything serious. In theory, once more, I love truth, and I love it as much as you can do; but the press is not truth. It is a mingling of passions, insults and falsehoods which excite the indignation of a sensitive heart. The savage liberty which rules in this country is not to my taste; I have long reflected on the subject, and I will tell you, if you will deign to listen to me, how it is possible to organize the press, wisely administer the truth, abolish the license of evil, and leave nothing but the liberty of good."

"Hinder dogs from barking!" cried Humbug, bursting into laughter; "the quadrature of the circle is found."

"I suppose," continued I, without replying to this jest, "I suppose an enlightened, moral, paternal government, thinking only of the good of its subjects."

"Doctor, this is theory!"

"No, sir, this is observation. In this government there are intelligent ministers"——

"I understand," said the insupportable mocker; "enlightened, moral, paternal ministers, thinking only of the good of those under their administration."

"Yes, sir; and these ministers have under their command thousands of agents"——

"All enlightened, moral, paternal, etc.; in a word, a legion of angels in black coats."

"In Heaven's name, Humbug, be silent," cried Truth. "Let him finish his fairy tale. I fancy I hear a Frenchman who imagines that he reasons because he strings paradoxes together and sews words one upon another."

"Mr. Truth," answered I, drily, "reason and experience are speaking through my lips; listen to me. To the hands of this wise government, which knows everything, sees everything, and listens to everything—to its hands, I say, I would confide the deposit of truth—not that I would be willing to give it the monopoly of it; I am the friend of liberty, but regulated, limited, moralized! I would therefore reduce the number of printers, in such a manner as to make a prudent and discreet censorship of typography, a conservative priesthood; then I would limit the number of journals; veritable pulpits, where naught but decency and moderation would be suffered to speak. Journalists would be like priests; that is, ministers of the truth, who would receive from the government their type and character. If, despite the wise direction of the state, some insolent gazetteer, forgetting the gravity of his duties, should be wanting in the respect which he owed to the sovereign power, the personification of justice and truth, I would not have recourse to the jury, which has a heavy hand and lets more than one doubtful innocent slip through its fingers; it is to the administration, always powerful and protective, that I would leave the holy mission of blighting falsehood and, if need were, arresting it even before it was born. The administration, always prudent, enlightened and disinterested, and knowing better than any one what suited it or fettered its plans—the administration would chastise audacity and ignorance; it would stifle opposition in the bud, as Hercules strangled serpents in his cradle. Thanks to this ingenious hygiene, the journals would be innocent food, an antidote instead of a poison; the press would be a torch in the hands of the ruling power, we would no longer stand in fear of conflagration. Useful prejudices, salutary errors would be treated with circumspection; truth would be graduated to the necessities of the state and the strength of the people; and if any new doctrine appeared in foreign countries, we would wait until it had made the fortune of the country of its birth before uselessly disturbing tranquil souls with it that sighed only for repose. This is my theory, Mr. Humbug, what do you say to it?"

"Damned rascal!" exclaimed he, letting fly a blow of the fist at my shoulder, which might have knocked down an ox. "When a man is happy enough to have wit, he always has some foolish thing to say. With his solemn air, this cunning dog mystified, for a moment, an old Yankee like me."

"Mr. Humbug," said I, rubbing my shoulder, "these brutal arguments are not to my taste. To knock down is not to answer."

"No more is to strangle," cried the journalist, laughing. "Go on, doctor; you are more amusing than you think! *Verba placent et vox.* But good-bye; the hour has come to make up the paper; time is money; you are ruining me!"

Left alone with Mr. Truth, I asked him if he had not been struck, like me, with the profundity of the system which I set forth; if he could place the turbulence and disorder of the American press in comparison with this compact mechanism, which in little time must bridle the most ardent nation on earth, and give it the habit of moderation and the taste for innocent freedom.

"Doctor," said he, mildly, "I am of Humbug's opinion. You are laughing at our simplicity. I have long known this doctrine, which you present to us as a new invention. It is the dogma of the Inquisition. Truth becomes an official instrument, *instrumentum regni*, monopolized by the church and the state. Three centuries ago, Luther annihilated these dangerous chimeras, and replaced every Christian in possession of his conscience and rights. In the earliest days of the world, truth flew out of Pandora's box, with so many other blessings, which also are evils in unskillful hands. To seek for truth is the work of all, to take exclusive possession of it belongs to no one. Do not be satisfied with words. Government, ministers, functionaries—what are all these, if not men, neither more infallible nor more learned than we? To make them the dispensers of truth is a dream. Truth belongs to all, like the air and the light; the only thing possible is to stifle it, is to hinder men not from thinking but from speaking. Who would profit by so detestable an invention? The ruling power? It would be the first victim. It would be deceived unceasingly. A handful of intriguers would suffice to lead the most honest magistrate into the maddest adventures. Do you not see, moreover, that you give your government full power to act wrongly, provided it takes care to reason wrongly? Would the citizens gain by it? On the day when public affairs are no longer their affairs, you take away from them what is noblest, most beautiful, greatest in life—the love of country and the passion of liberty. Take away the agitation of the rostrum and newspapers, and society is no longer but a stagnant pool, whence arises corruption and death. Would you secure at least material prosperity, the only bait which tempts the crowd? Quite the contrary; wealth is the fruit of liberty. There is no security either of finances, or commerce, or industry, except in the countries which swarm with those journals whose voice importunes you. Silence is the triumph of fools; darkness is not the kingdom of honest men; leave us light, noise, and life. Remember that at Rome, likewise, there was an outcry against the loquacity of the rostrums; that one day Sylla silenced them, to the great joy of the witlings, and that thenceforth commenced the decline from which Christianity even could not upraise the universe."

"I beg your pardon," replied I, astonished at the turn which the discussion was taking; "I do not pretend to have found the philosopher's stone in politics. Every system has its abuses; it is a question of proportion. Admit that the language of your journals is frightful, and that there is no more terrible evil than their unbridled license."

"Doctor, you know what the Gospel says: *By their fruits ye shall know them.* Find me a country where there is more enlightenment, more charity, more material prosperity, than in America."

"I see nothing but scandal everywhere," answered I. "The very foundations of society are giving way in that quicksand which you call democracy. What do you respect? Religion? Well, let a pastor be wanting in his duty—let his conduct be light—directly twenty journals begin to laugh at him, like the unworthy son of Noah, instead of hiding from all eyes a weakness, the shame of which is reflected upon the church."

"The shame," said Truth, "is to the church which espouses the cause of the criminal, not to the one which casts out of it a corrupt member."

"Do you spare justice? Yesterday even, your journal attacked, with cynical bitterness, a judge who had spoken roughly to some knave in a moment of ill humor. How do you expect the judge to be respected, if he is not infallible?"

"Justice," said Truth, "is made for the accused, and not the accused for justice."

"Let a subaltern exceed his powers," I continued; "let him forget the law by chance, and arrest by mistake an innocent person; directly ten journals will howl at the tyranny, like dogs barking at the moon. They will set the country in a blaze for the cause of the vilest of wretches, for a beggar or a thief, thrown in prison without the forms having been observed."

"They will do right," said Truth. "The liberty of the vilest of wretches is the concern of all. As soon as legal forms are violated, as soon as a citizen is unjustly attacked, all are menaced. Whoever does not feel this, does not know what is liberty."

"Is it not sometimes necessary to veil the statue of the law, and to save the country in spite of a false legality?"

"Doctor, you have a weakness for Pilate. He likewise was not checked by a false legality; he chose rather to condemn an innocent man than to risk his place. He was a man of ability; I know not why the world is so severe with him."

"What has come of it?" continued I, more and more irritated by the coldness of Truth. "Twelve or fifteen newspapers—these are the masters of public opinion and the republic."

"Fifteen newspapers!" said Truth, astonished; "what do you mean by that? We have three hundred, which is very little for sixteen hundred thousand souls. Boston has a hundred for less than two hundred thousand inhabitants. It is true that in Boston, a Puritan city, liberty and civilization are understood otherwise than at Paris."

"Three hundred newspapers!" exclaimed I, surprised at this formidable number. "Who, then, directs and governs public opinion? The first comer can, without a mission, set himself up as a prophet and legislator; the first dreamer can say what he will, and impose his opinions on the crowd. It is an atrocious despotism!"

"My good friend," said Truth, lowering his voice to bring me back to a less noisy pitch, "do not again begin your jests; they amuse Humbug, but hurt me. Where all the world can speak, there is neither *mission* nor *prophet*, nor *first comer*. There is a right which belongs to every citizen, and which every citizen uses for his private interest, or for the interest of the whole. Among a free people, who ever dreams of directing and governing public opinion? Certainly not a Yankee, who lays down for himself his own rule of action, and chooses his party and colors with full knowledge of the case. The press is an echo which repeats the ideas of all the world, nothing more. These innumerable newspapers have but one object—to accumulate facts, information, and ideas—to increase and diffuse enlightenment! The more of these there are, the more opportunity has each citizen to read, reflect, and judge for himself. To place the truth within the reach of all—this is our ambition. This pretended newspaper despotism exists only in your imagination. At most it would be possible only where an ill-advised government, making of journalism a monopoly against itself, would permit only ten or fifteen sheets, and would thus oblige parties to coalesce against it, which, by their nature, tend to disperse. But in America, where there are eight or nine hundred newspapers, where new ones spring up every day, the number of tyrants has killed the tyranny.

"So be it. It is a system not foreseen by Aristotle—a paper democracy. In this happy country, everything is government, except the government itself. You journalists (and everybody here is a journalist), you are more than the Church, more than the law, more than the State. What are you then?"

"The answer is too easy," said Truth. "We are society."

"But if society—if the people govern, who then are the governed?"

"Doctor," answered the journalist, smiling, "when you conduct yourself into the street, who then is conducted? Through love of a word, must you have leading strings? When you govern your passions (which you do not always do), who then is governed? There is an age of maturity for peoples as for individuals. Let China grow old in an eternal infancy, I pity her; but we Christians, we citizens of a great country, we are not a people of idiots and outlaws. We have long since escaped from tutelage, and managed our own affairs. What is this popular sovereignty which we have placarded for seventy years at the head of our constitutions, if not a declaration of majority?"

"Comparisons prove nothing," returned I, drily "What is true of an individual is not true of a nation."

"Still words, doctor. A nation is a collection of individuals. What is true of ten, twenty, a thousand persons, is also true of a million. At what number then does incapacity begin?"

"No," said I, "it is not true that a nation is a simple collection of individuals. It is quite a different thing."

"That is to say, the total of a column of figures is a different thing from the sum of all the units."

"Wrong!" I exclaimed, wearied of arguing with a narrow mind. "The difference here stares one in the face. To rid themselves of private interests, what is the magical word invoked by all statesmen? The general interest. When it is wished to annul rights and petitions which incommode the government, what is alleged? A superior interest, the social interest. Public utility is the negation of individual rights; such, at least, is the manner of reasoning and acting in all civilized countries. If it were enough to listen to the will of the majority, and to sum up interests and wishes, let me just ask you what politics would be? A grocer's trade, a rôle within the reach of the first honest comer. Picture to yourself a Cæsar, a Richelieu, a Cromwell, a Louis XIV., listening to the voice of a peasant, or taking the votes of a few thousand citizens! What would become of the combinations, the alliances, the wars, the conquests?—all those brilliant strokes, all those freaks of fortune by which heroes triumph? To drag a nation to victory and glory, to impose on the popular masses ideas which are not their own, to make them serve an ambition and projects which in no wise concern them—this is the work of genius! This is what the people love. They adore those who trample them under foot. Leave these poor men to themselves—they will plant their cabbages; their annals will be contained in two lines, like the moral of fairy-tales, *They lived long, were happy, and had many children.* With this fine system, what would history be? and wherewith would we teach rhetoric to our children?"

I was eloquent; I felt it. Truth, confounded, gazed at me with a peculiar air.

"Doctor," said he, "I do not like sophisms; but of all these witticisms, there are none more odious to me than the paradoxes of former times—falsehoods long since dead. They produce the effect on mè of an old courtesan who has forgotten to be buried, and who walks among the youth disgusted with her paint, false curls, and wrinkles. Washington has taught the world what an honest man is, governing a free people. The thing has been proved. The age of political egotism is passed; there is no longer room except for patriotism. Whoever does not comprehend this; whoever does not hear the voice of new generations; whoever does not feel that industry, peace, and liberty are the sovereigns of the moral world is only a dreamer and a madman. It is not to glory that he goes, but to ridicule."

"No more of that, sir!" said I, rising; and, despite myself, I carried my hand to the hilt of my absent sword. If I had had on my uniform of surgeon of the National

Guard, I would have forced this insolent wretch to draw his weapon, and, by making him bite the dust, would have proved to him beyond reply that America understands nothing of civilization, and that a Frenchman is never in the wrong.

CHAPTER X.

THE INFERNAL KITCHEN.

WHILE Truth, surprised at my transport of rage, cast on me uneasy glances, Humbug entered, carrying a bundle of proofs, which he placed on the desk.

"Quick!" cried he in his gruff voice, "the task begins. *Nunc animis opus, Ænea, nunc pectore firmo.* Doctor, help us; your right arm is at liberty; take this paper and prepare the bulletin."

"Write, *Defeat of the Federal Troops.* This will fill all our first column." And he threw a proof into the letter-box.

"Defeat!" said I, "are you going to announce to the country that it is beaten? Put, *Strategic retreat! Adroit manœuvre!* otherwise your imprudence will spread anxiety and dismay everywhere."

"Doctor, you are incorrigible," resumed Truth, "once more, the whole truth is due the country. Do you think that the Yankees are cast down by a reverse, and that, like children, they suffer themselves to be led by fortune? A victory would find us indifferent; a defeat would be equivalent to a redoubling of energy, soldiers and money. How many men are killed?"

"3,000 killed," said Humbug, "6,000 wounded, 2,400 missing."

Give the figures," returned Truth; "doctor, do not forget them on the bulletin. Now, what has been done in Congress?"

"In the Senate," said Humbug, "a long discussion on slavery. Mr. Sumner has effected the abolition of slavery in the Federal district of Columbia. It is a first step. Doctor, write, *Admirable speech of the eloquent senator from Massachusetts.* Here is our first page filled; we come to the next. Nothing of interest in the House of Representatives; three calls to order and time wasted in quarrels with the Speaker."

"According to custom," said Truth; "go on. Here is the political article; write, doctor, *Return to Law and Liberty, the Habeas Corpus reëstablished.*"

"What!" said I, astonished, "at the moment of a defeat, when it is necessary to concentrate authority and to govern *manu militari*, you reëstablish civil liberty with all its dangers! Know by experience that it is the moment to suspend all rights. Nothing reassures a people like feeling itself entirely in the hands of the ruling power. Truly, you understand nothing of politics."

"Despotism is not strength," replied Truth, "the freer a people is, the more it is gentle, obedient and resigned to sacrifices. If you wish it to sustain you, confide yourself to it. Let us proceed. *Exposure to the nation of Thefts in the Navy.* Write, doctor, and underline the words, that they may appear in relief on the bulletin."

"This is too great boldness," I exclaimed; "think of the interests which you will injure, of the complaints which you will call forth."

"Let the thieves complain," said Truth, "I am ready for them, I have proofs!"

"Proofs! who has furnished them to you?"

"Wherever there is a rostrum," replied Truth, "there

is some one to speak. Among a people on whom silence is imposed, the thieves act and the plundered are silent; among a people where every citizen is an active member of the nation and has a right to prosecute in the name of the country, the thieves hide and the plundered cry out and act. In Russia, twenty millions given to the police will not hinder thousands of millions from being stolen, the police will be bought cheaply; among us, where the police is the whole nation, one does not steal a penny without trembling. The suppression of swindling on a large scale is not the least advantage of liberty. Let us proceed to the foreign news."

"Here," said Humbug, "are the three correspondences from London."

"Why three correspondences?" asked I, surprised at this useless extravagance.

"There are three parties in England," replied Humbug; "we need, therefore, three echoes to repeat all the tones. First correspondence, colors of Old Pam: 'War against America—justice is a fine thing, but cotton is better—let us burn the world, to warm England.' Second correspondence, colors of Earl Derby: 'Old Pam trifles with the public; he cries, to arms! pockets fortifications and iron-plated ships, plays soldier, and desires but two things—to keep the peace and his place; give us the ministry; we will be as patriotic, and will cost less.' Third correspondence, colors of Bright and Cobden: 'John Bull, my friend, your government is fooling you; it is tickling your vanity to wheedle you out of the last shilling; be a man, imitate your cousin Jonathan, and attend to your own business; when people no longer suffer themselves to be taken care of by those ruinous charlatans styled diplomatists and great politicians, they will live like brothers; they will have peace and cheap living.' "

"I hope," said I to Humbug, "that in giving these three correspondences to the public, you append to them your opinion."

"Not at all," replied Humbug; "Jonathan is in the habit of forming his own opinions; he has too good eyes to use our spectacles."

The door opened abruptly. Three women, young and elegantly dressed, approached us; the oldest, who was under twenty-five, addressed us in a tone at once modest and self-reliant:

"Sir," said she to Humbug, "we are deputed by the lady coat-makers, to ask you to advertise that we are on a strike, and that we shall hold a meeting next Monday, to seek the means of shaking off the oppression from which we suffer; we wish to regain and secure our rights."

"The tailors are rich," said Humbug; "before bringing them to terms, you will eat up all your savings; have you a million to draw from?"

"Sir," said the youngest, with a stubborn air, "a hundred dollars' worth of advertisements will do the work for us. We will teach these gentlemen tailors, and the whole world, what five hundred women can do, who have taken it into their heads not to yield. It is a lesson which will do good to monopolizers and tyrants— a lesson which will make the despots of the Old World turn pale on their thrones. Oblige us only by inserting in to-morrow's paper the address to the public, drawn up and resolved on by our committee."

Upon this, our Amazon handed to the journalist a paper folded twice. Humbug read aloud this impertinent pleasantry, a memorable monument of feminine perversity and folly, in a country where the women themselves believe in liberty:

TO THE PARISIANS OF MASSACHUSETTS.

LADY COAT-MAKERS.

"To avenge our slighted rights and obtain justice, we, the lady coat-makers of the city of Paris (Mass.), have struck for wages; in eight days either our tyrants will yield, or we shall be out of employment. Who will give us work? We do not wish to stand with our hands folded, but we are determined not to work for nothing, for the profit of men who are able to pay. Who is in want of a helping hand? We know how to make hats, coats, puddings, cakes, and pies; we know how to sew, embroider, knit, wash, and boil; we know how to milk cows, make butter and cheese, tend poultry, and take care of the garden; we know how to clean the kitchen, sweep the parlor, make beds, split wood, kindle fires, wash and iron, and moreover we adore babies. In a word, every one of us would make an accomplished housekeeper. As to our wit and intelligence, inquire of our former employers. Speak quickly, gentlemen. Who wants black eyes, fine foreheads, wavy and curling hair, the charms and youth of Hebe, the voice of a seraph, the smile of an angel? Old gentlemen who are in need of a good housekeeper, handsome young men who are in search of an active and devoted wife, speak; the way is open. Going, going —gone! Who is the happy mortal?

"*Apply to the Committee of Lady Coat-Makers,*
"*No.* 20 *Poplar Street.*"

"Very well, ladies," said Humbug, "the advertisement will appear this evening in the paper, and we will put on the bulletin: *Tailoresses' Strike!* that no one may be ignorant of it."

Saying this, he made a profound bow, and showed out these silly jades with as much politeness as if a prefect had been in question.

"Is it possible," exclaimed I, "that in America women have the right to do as they please? Is not this to give the lie to experience and common sense? Meetings of tailoresses, unions of washerwomen, a strike of midwives! Revolution in coats is odious; revolution in petticoats is ridiculous."

"What is ridiculous," replid Truth, with his ordinary phlegm, "is that the coats ascribe to themselves the right to oppress the petticoats?"

"It is well," I answered. "Fill these foolish heads with the intoxication of liberty; you will see who will be the first victims."

"Doctor, you are dismal," said Truth; "at the least shock to your old-fashioned prejudices, you cry out that the world is going to end. Women, my dear sir, are one half the human race; this is a profound truth, verified by Aristotle, but for two thousand years no one has understood the philosopher except the Americans. If our women did not share our hopes and fears, they would make us share their weaknesses and caprices. We need wives, daughters and mothers who love liberty passionately, that the husbands, fathers and sons may never lose this holy love. These tailoresses appear ridiculous to you; for my part, I admire them, while laughing at their advertisement; I love generous souls that have faith in justice and defend their rights. It is from souls like these that a great nation is made; herein is the superiority of our beautiful country."

"Let us finish the paper," said Humbug; "here are the markets. Cotton, wool, coal, iron, wheat, grain, pork, mutton, beef, hay, leather, sugar, coffee. There is nothing special, except concerning wheat; choice brands are selling two per cent higher than common brands."

"What brands?" said Truth, taking up the list. "Colfax, Stevens, Pennington—these names must be underlined and printed in large type; you laugh, doctor, this is no trifling matter. Individual responsibility is the strength and life of republics. It is necessary that every one therein should bear inscribed on his forehead what he is or what he has done. To join to honesty reputation and fortune, to attach to rascality infamy and ruin, is the secret of morals and government—it is a problem of which no legislator has found the solution, and which the press resolves every day."

"A fine tirade concerning a barrel of flour!"

"And the application of which you will see in an instant; look here—Pork market, twenty barrels damaged, of the brands Thomas and Williams. To underline these two dishonest names is to drive them from the market."

"You will not do it," cried I; "you have not the right. Is it not enough for you to be the government, do you wish also to be the police?"

"You have said it, worthy doctor," returned Humbug; "we are the police, and still more—we are the public conscience. It is we that give honor and fortune. *Honestus rumor alterum patrimonium est.* Open your eyes wide if it amuses you, and make an outcry if it gives you pleasure. But, indeed, if you speak seriously, you must have been changed at nurse; you are not an American."

"You do not know," murmured I, "you do not know,

ignoramus, how near you are right; you do not suspect to what extent I despise a Don Quixote mad enough to take in hand the interest of others, the interest of the first comer, and this without mission or pay. See what a country is without functionaries! Every one there must meddle even with his own business. It is ridiculous! In France, an intelligent and compact administration frees me from all care. I am a king; I am waited on; I enjoy in peace a prosperity and greatness which costs me nothing but my money. It is the triumph of civilization, or I do not know myself."

"Here is the money article," said a young man, entering, out of breath from running.

"Anything new?" asked Humbug.

"Nothing but the Mexican loan."

"What do they say of it, Eugene?" said Mr. Truth.

"A complete fiasco, a swindle of old Little's."

"What! a swindle?" said I, reading the stock list; "the loan has risen a dollar above the rate of emission."

"Little has bought with one hand and sold with the other," said Truth; "it is an old trick, but it will never succeed with us. We are not such sheep. Mr. Rose," added he, addressing the new comer, "make me an article for to-morrow on this matter; see the stock agents and learn the whole truth."

"It will be ready this evening, Mr. Truth. I shall have more information than I need."

"Sir," said I to the young man, whose name announced him as a son of the apothecary, and, alas! a brother of my future son-in-law, "transactions must be very difficult to effect, with this fashion of throwing them open for the public benefit."

"Sir," replied Eugene, quite astonished, "transactions

are the easier, the better they are known. On 'Change, falsehood is ruinous, truth is wealth."

"Good!" thought I; "they all repeat the same nonsense. At Paris, the centre of intellect, the capital of wit, every one knows that the transactions to which the public rush are always those of which it understands nothing. What can a known transaction give? Five or six per cent at most, while the unknown promises fifteen or twenty per cent—therein is the secret of the banker. Here, value is truckled for value—a miserable trade; at Paris, one buys hope—it is the poetry of play, it is the charm of the lottery. What matters it to a Frenchman if he lose his money; this is prose. To feast on wealth in thought, to satisfy passions, caprices, ambition in dreams, this is the ideal; one pays for it, it is true, but can he pay too dearly for illusion?"

"Friend Humbug," said a squeaking voice, "here are two advertisements which I should like to have inserted in the body of thy journal; thee must throw off considerable, the times are hard."

The speaker was a little man in a long overcoat, with an immense hat; his face, gesture and costume said to every one—"Look at me, I am a Quaker."

Humbug took the two advertisements, and burst out laughing.

"They are droll," said he; "but I do not understand them." He read as follows:

"MONTMORENCY VILLA.—Seth Doolittle, proprietor of the Rose Hotel at Montmorency, has the honor to inform the public that, during the summer season, lovers who visit his house will be charged but half price."

"Why this exception?" asked I.

"Friend," answered the little man, crossing his hands on his abdomen and raising his eyes to heaven, "nothing is more beautiful or worthy of respect than love. Put a young man opposite a white dress and black curls fluttering in the wind, and he feels so celestial, so ethereal, that all the week he will never stoop to touch roast beef. It is nothing but robbery to make these angels of heaven, who never examine a bill, pay the common price; my conscience will not suffer this iniquity."

"The scruple does you honor," said Humbug, biting his lips. "Let us proceed to the next insertion."

"Friendly Counsel.—*Dinah D. L.*—You art entreated not to return. Your mother is in excellent health; nothing can be arranged; and your whole family has been much better since you quitted it."

"This is a family secret," said I, smiling. "There's no explanation."

"To the public, no; to thee, Dr. Smith, yes," returned the Quaker. "It concerns a sister, a giddy brain, whom, for her own sake and that of her family, and through care for the public morality, we have sent to California as a schoolmistress. There is reason to fear that the unhappy girl may stop on the way and wish to return to her evil ways. We, therefore, warn her charitably and in covert language, that she will do better to continue her journey; there is no room for her at home."

"This is admirable charity, Mr. Seth," returned I, shrugging my shoulders. "I regret not having sooner recognized so worthy a man."

"Thee would have had some difficulty in recognizing me," answered Seth, casting down his eyes; "thee has never seen me; but Martha has described her master and the terrible accident of yesterday to me with such fidelity, that I guessed who thee was at the first glance."

The virtuous hotel-keeper pronounced the name of Martha with a strange unction, which later recurred to my memory; I should have paid more attention to it had not a man, with a flushed face, entered the room abruptly, crying, "Great news, Mr. Truth; great news, Mr. Humbug: the mayor of the city has just been condemned. He was surprised in criminal conversation with an actress of the *Lyceum*, and has been sentenced to pay the husband ten thousand dollars' damages."

"Doctor," said Humbug, "take the pen and finish our bulletin; our paper is well filled, the sale is sure. Let us see:

Defeat of the Federal Troops.

3,000 killed, 6,000 wounded.

Admirable Speech of the eloquent Senator from Massachusetts.

RETURN TO LAW AND LIBERTY.

Exposure to the nation of Thefts in the Navy.

TAILORESSES' STRIKE.

CRIMINAL CONVICTION OF THE MAYOR OF THE CITY.

"Come," continued he, "this is a good day's work; we have barked well at the knaves. To press!" he exclaimed. "Work, boys, and in a quarter of an hour put up the bulletin."

CHAPTER XI.

ON THE CONSERVATIVE MAXIM: *Private Life should be immured.*

I SUNK into my easy-chair, reflecting aside on the sad spectacle which I had before my eyes. Devouring anarchy, general espionage, universal commotion, the government in the hands of everybody—such was this so much vaunted press! How form a people into an army with such an enemy in your rear!

"Well, my dear doctor," said Truth, in a soothing voice, "you know now how a newspaper is made. Are you tempted? Are you to be my successor in the paper?"

"Never! never!" replied I, drawing back my chair by an involuntary gesture. "What I see terrifies me; you play with all that I have been taught to regard as respectable and sacred. Let a minister or his deputies be attacked, it matters little, I am accustomed to it; from all time, ministers have served as a butt to pamphleteers; the most celebrated journalist is he who has overthrown the most. If there are countries and peoples whom this destruction amuses, much good may it do them! I wish them two or three revolutions to cure them of it. But private life, sir, should be immured; do you hear, sir, hermetically immured."

"Who says so?" asked Humbug, with a sly air, which only proved his ignorance.

"Mr. Humbug," replied I, "it is M. Royer Collard, a

great metaphysician, who has never had any ideas of his own, but who has cast in bronze and engraved on brass the ideas of others. It is he, this illustrious sage, who has uttered this golden speech, which should be posted up in every newspaper office—'*Private life should be immured.*'"

"Your great metaphysician talks nonsense," answered Humbug. "Can a man be cut in two? Is a man a knave in private life and a Fabricius in public life? What is private life? Where does it begin, where end? Is the cry of mad dog an attack on private or public life? If our navy is plundered by impudent contractors, do we attack private life when we denounce the thief? If the Honorable Mr. Little, enriched by the millions of others, wishes once more to despoil simpletons in behalf of his insatiable cupidity, is to tell Mr. Little that he is a cheat to attack his private life?"

"Sir," said I to this impudent fellow, "you have no idea of all that I could reply to you; a word will suffice. Here is the mayor of Paris, who has yielded to an unhappy weakness. Perhaps he has fallen into the snare spread by some siren of low degree; most certainly, he has not committed this fault in the capacity of municipal magistrate. What is the use of this noise, this scandal, this defamation of a man whose error, after all, does not concern you?"

"What is the use?" said Truth, with a frigidity worthy of Robespierre, "to make him resign. Do you wish us to preach respect for the conjugal bond and abhorrence of vice in our families in the face of adultery throned in the City Hall? This cannot be. It is the honor of private life which answers to us for public virtue; otherwise, politics are a comedy, in which each one wears a mask, plays a part, and amuses himself by talking of conscience, rights, and duties, without believing a word of what he says. Let childish peoples take delight in these dangerous farces, which always end badly—this may be; but in America, everything is in earnest. Let our debauchees go, if it seems good to them, to ruin their health and squander their fortune on the other side of the Atlantic; among us it is necessary to be respectable to be respected."

"Here is a letter from the mayor," said a clerk, "giving in his resignation."

"Mr. Truth," exclaimed I, "there is still time; stop the printing of the paper, strike out a condemnation which no longer concerns but a simple citizen, a sentence which is about to cause the dishonor of a man and the wretchedness of a family. Efface from your bulletin those odious words which brand with a new stigma which the law has not foreseen, a fault, doubtless excusable. Are there then only Catos in America? and, since you constantly quote the Gospel, is there none among you that has read the story of the woman taken in adultery? In Heaven's name, be humane!"

"I am neither humane nor cruel," replied Truth, with his icy tone; "I am not a person, I am a journal; that is to say, an echo, a photograph. The bulletin will remain as it is; I am sorry for the culprit, but I too have a mission to fulfill, I do not compound with the truth.

"But this mission," cried I, indignant, "you assume yourself!"

"Is it therefore the less holy?" returned the journalist. "Understand the part which I fill. In a community wholly occupied with its business and interests, and which, notwithstanding, governs itself, how is liberty maintained? how are generous ideas maintained and developed? how is right respected by all, virtue esteemed, services rewarded? Thanks to the press, an invention still more admirable than steam and electricity. We journalists, we are the echo of society—a formidable echo, a sounding trumpet, which swells every report, spreads it to the ends of the land, and goes to awaken the most torpid conscience. Good or evil, everything serves us—the good to make all hearts beat with joy and emulation, the evil to arouse them to indignation and disgust. Yesterday you accomplished a heroic act. In Russia or Spain, who would have known it?—A few friends, a few neighbors, a city. Here, thanks to us, thirty-one million men are about to repeat the name of Dr. Smith; three million youth will envy your courage and resolve to imitate it. This is the work of these pamphleteers for whom you seem to have little esteem. To-day there is a scandal made, a fault committed by a magistrate. The law has condemned the man, the press condemns the crime, and makes it hated and detested by the whole nation. The greater the fall, the stronger the lesson. Our harshness will grieve a family and wound a few timid souls; it will save from a like weakness millions of men who would be emboldened by impunity. Doubtless, our rigor will cost us mortal enmity. What does it matter? Shall we weigh our duty against our interest? Doctor, be less severe on us. How many statesmen would be able to fill the qualities demanded by the vocation of journalists? how many would resolutely accept our dangers and obscurity?"

"Bravo, Truth!" cried Humbug; "you talk like a book, my good friend, and like a book which tells the truth: *rara avis in terris, nigroque simillima cycno.*"

"There is such a thing as hidden ambition," returned I, furious both against Truth and myself (the words of the sophist had shaken me). "Some men believe themselves virtuous in making a show of severity, who, at the bottom, without knowing it, are the dupes of their own interest, and pursue after fortune."

"Fortune," said Humbug, "is not made for journalists. Doctor, my friend, the world is a stage, on which three sorts of persons figure—spectators, actors, and authors. The spectators are you, Green, Rose, all those good people who have neither vices nor virtues, and live in the shade of their own vine and fig-tree. The actors are a jealous set, resembling all troupes of comedians. The ambitious man, the fine talker, the miser, the poltroon, the tyrant, the valet, play their part in the farce, to the great pleasure of the public, who often applaud, sometimes hiss, and always pay them. Their chief singers must have fine clothes, palaces, gold, plenty of gold. They know the whim of the crowd and take advantage of it. As to the authors—as to the poet who has created the saying of the day, written the air in vogue, inspired the tirade, they throw him a crust of bread and pass him by in disdain. What is the idea to the shrewd? Nothing but a cockade: the thing is to use it at the right time. Cry for twenty years that liberty is the salvation of peoples—you are nothing but an echo, odious to those who rule, importunate to those who serve. Let the day come when the wearied people wishes to shake off the burden which crushes it—the first rash man who dares inscribe on a banner the motto which you have repeated twenty years will be the chosen of the crowd—honor, money, power, all will be his. An hour will make the fortune of this first actor; but he will not find contempt enough for the obscure journalist, who, by twenty years of sufferings and dangers, had paved the way for his triumph. The people will judge like the actor. Do you wish a moral to my tale? Paris is about to choose a mayor; be sure that every one else will be thought of except the only man who would do honor to the office; namely, Truth. On the day that he perishes, if I am not there, there will not be two lines of eulogy in his own journal. This is the way that civic virtue is recompensed in America! Yet we are the first people on earth. *Ab uno disce omnes.* Judge now of our ambition!"

"Humbug, my friend," said Truth, "do you count as nothing the honor of being loved and praised by you?"

"The door opened, and, for the second time, a weasel's paw was seen extended, which could belong only to Mr. Fox. It was he, more smiling than ever.

"Mr. Truth," said he, in his softest voice, "will you have the kindness to announce, in your excellent paper, that the Honorable Mr. Little has just given ten thousand dollars to the Child's Hospital, five thousand dollars to the poor of the city, and five thousand dollars to the city library?"

"The Mexican loan is doing well," said Humbug. "Little is a pious Jew, who pays his tenth to the Lord."

"The Mexican loan is abandoned," replied Fox. "Mr. Little has satisfied himself that the guarantees offered by the Mexican government are not secure."

"Whence comes this suspicious generosity?" asked Humbug. "There is some fearful speculation under this. Here are twenty thousand dollars which will cost us dear."

"Always suspicious," interrupted I; "and why?"

"Because I am an old journalist," replied Humbug. "I believe in the virtue of bankers as in the simplicity of Quakers."

"We will convert you, old sinner," returned Fox, laughing.

"Great news on 'Change!" said Eugene Rose, entering.

"The Mexican loan is withdrawn," answered Humbug; "we know it."

"But you do not know that the mayor has resigned, and that Mr. Little is a candidate for his place."

"Really," said Fox, "it is impossible. Mr. Little has not said a word to me about it; I doubt even whether, with his multiplicity of business, he could accept this important office."

"Excellent Fox!" exclaimed Humbug; "he is as innocent as a lamb! You will see, honest attorney, that Mr. Little will make up his mind to this great sacrifice."

"But we are modest people," said Truth; "and, on our part, will not impose on him so heavy a burden; we will oppose his election."

"And why?" exclaimed Fox.

"That," said Humbug, "is the secret of the play; you are not to ask it."

"So, then," resumed Fox, "we always find you against us, virtuous Puritans, proud and unsociable race; but, damn me, if I do not some day burn out your nest, you useless hornets, who know how to do nothing but tire our ears with your detestable buzzing."

"Fox, my friend," said Humbug, "do not put my patience and hands to the test, or I shall throw you out of the window."

Fox did not await a threat, the execution of which

was certain. For my part, I left, moved and troubled by all I had heard. Reason and education told me that the press is a weapon aimed at power and society; twenty times the wisest ministers had inoculated me with this precious truth. But, on the other hand, I was struck with what was great and generous in the conduct of Truth, brave and decided in the character of Humbug. To take in hand the cause of honest men against all the knaves with which the world is overflowing, to be daily on the chase, and unrelaxingly to pursue theft, injustice, and falsehood, is something, notwithstanding. A people that numbers such men is not a common people.

"Bah!" said I to myself, driving away vain scruples, "this is an exception. The wisest course would be to suppress the journals. It is said that this is to suppress the remedy and not the disease; but, when the disease is without remedy, we resign ourselves to it, and if we die, at least die without complaining. It is a great advantage—to the physicians."

I had arrived thus far in my reflections, when a voice called me from the middle of the street—the voice of Susan. She was approaching in a two-wheeled gig, driven by Martha. The horse was sure-footed, and Martha was a prudent woman, who used the rein more freely than the whip; but, at the corner of the *rue Taitbout* and *rue Helder*—I am wrong—at the corner of Seventh and Eighth Avenues, there was a terrible little paving-stone, laid down, I suppose, by some interested veterinary; for, during ten years, a day had not passed that horses had not stumbled on it. Martha's courser was predestined; on nearing me, the poor animal suddenly fell on his knees; Martha was flung over the horse's head, while Susan fell into my arms, throwing me down by the shock, and rolled on the ground with me

I rose, furious, and covered with dust; Susan's face was scratched; Martha was bleeding.

"Are you hurt, Martha?" I exclaimed.

"No, sir; it is nothing," said she; "the right hand of the Eternal sustained me; nothing was hit but the end of my nose."

We both busied ourselves with ungirding and raising the horse.

When the animal was harnessed, "Good heavens!" I exclaimed, "it is a shame that the city government should suffer for ten years such a break-neck trap at my door, in the most frequented street of the city." And I re-entered the newspaper office in a rage.

"Doctor, what is the matter?" said Humbug, still laughing. "Have you already commenced the electoral struggle with Fox? Judging from your coat, you have not had the best of it."

"The matter is," said I, "that it is abominable that a pavement should have been left for ten years in such a condition; that my horse has just fallen; that my daughter's face is hurt; that my cook has been nearly killed. I am in a rage; I wish to make complaint; I demand justice. We are in Paris in America, I shall obtain it. Publicity will bring every one on my side. Give me a pen and ink; I wish to address a severe letter to you, in which I shall treat the administration as it deserves."

"Here is what you desire," said Humbug; "and here besides is a dollar."

"A dollar! For what?"

"We always pay a dollar to whoever brings us an *item*. Don't be nice, doctor; keep it, and frame it, with

the date. It will remind you that the press is the voice of all, and that you comprehended this great truth on the day that you yourself suffered."

"Humbug," said I, "these words, which you throw to the winds with your usual lightness, have more scope than you think; I will not forget them. On reading my morning's paper, each complaint will recall to me a suffering which to-morrow, perhaps, will be mine, an evil which I can succor or prevent by joining in the public outcry."

"Bravo, doctor; you are a great philosopher. When your eyes are opened, you cry, *Et lux facta est.* No matter; you will ere long perceive a no less important truth; namely, that in the end the liberty of the press is of little profit to any but honest men. This will suffice to teach us what are its enemies."

CHAPTER XII.

A NOMINATION IN AMERICA.

ALL these discussions had disturbed me. Of course, I had not the weakness to deny the political faith which the masters of my infancy had given me—I abhor renegades. When one is born in error, if conscience commands him to depart from it, honor commands him to remain in it; and a Frenchman always listens to honor. I would have been hewn in pieces rather than acknowledge publicly that these Yankees were not wrong. But in my soul I felt that I had lost my first innocence; I had made use of the press, and I had no longer the strength to blush at it. Dissatisfied with myself, I slept a restless sleep; when I awakened, it was still dark. The sophisms of Truth and Humbug had entered into my spirit like arrows into the flesh. I was seeking in my bed replies which I hardly found, when all at once, in the midst of the obscurity and silence, I heard a voice in the street calling me. It was my daughter's voice; a father cannot be mistaken.

To throw on my dressing gown and run to the window was the work of an instant. I leaned forward to look into the darkness, when my head encountered some strange obstacle which gave way. Directly a splendid sun dazzled my eyes; joyful shouts greeted my appearance. The street was filled with people, an immense placard covered the whole house, and my head wedged in a gigantic O, presented a ridiculous spectacle to the passers. "Papa, stay there," cried Susan, dancing up and down and clapping her hands, "all Paris will read the placard."—"*Green for ever!*" repeated the Yankees, as they ran. "A very good trick," added they, laughing and showing their great teeth.

I dressed myself hastily and went down into the street; Paris was no longer but an immense placard; candidates of all colors, blue, red, white, yellow, green and pink, displayed on the walls their vices and virtues. My house was devoted to green. The name of Green was lengthened out in capitals three feet high; opposite me, the printing office had raised to the sky an immense placard, on which was read:

CITIZENS

OF THE FIRST CITY OF THE WORLD.

No bankers!

No lawyers!

No tricksters!

ELECT THE SON OF HIS WORKS.

The generous patriot!

The adventurous merchant!

The good father!

The child of Paris!

ELECT THE HONEST AND VIRTUOUS GREEN!

This democratic farce amused Susan; Alfred Rose was by her side with the venerable apothecary and his other eight sons. Henry danced for joy like a child enchanted by the uproar. For my part, I have little taste for popular orgies, they may be summed up in one sentence—*a great noise for nothing.*

"Neighbor," said the druggist, "here is our captain going to battle; I hope you will lend a helping hand; the cabal is powerful, and we shall overcome it only by dint of words and action."

"My dear Mr. Rose," answered I, "with your permission, I shall stay at home. In all this I have no interest. I am a nobleman with numerous stewards to manage my affairs, whom I pay without even having the trouble of choosing them; what happens among my men does not concern me. What is a mayor of Paris? A gentleman in an embroidered coat who marries old maids and inconsolable widows, and who twice a year goes in state to call on the prefect and dine at the Hotel de Ville. These are great honors, they cannot be too dearly bought; but in what do they concern me—me a simple citizen, that has no other privilege than that of paying expenses which I do not vote? I do not know who a mayor represents, but assuredly it is not those under his administration. Choose whom you like; I am a physician and never trouble myself about anything."

For his sole answer, Mr. Rose took my hand and felt my pulse.

"Terrible doctor," said he, "you make me shudder with your everlasting jests; I should think your brain disordered. The citizen of a free country, do you need to be told that our most important interests are to-day at stake? Is not the mayor the first personage of the city, the representative of our ideas and desires? Police, markets, streets, schools—does not the mayor, assisted by our councilmen, regulate everything by the sovereign authority conferred upon him by our vote? If he have superiors in the State, has he any in the city? Does he receive orders from any one? Is he not our right hand, our organ, our minister; is it not to us alone that he is answerable for his actions and expenditure? Yet you wish that such an election should find us indifferent? For my part, I trouble myself little enough about what is done at Washington by the fine talkers of the West and South; but Paris is my property, my fact, the tomb of my father, the cradle of my children. I love everything in Paris, even to its blots and excrescences. I love its old streets where I have played in my childhood; I love its new avenues, broad arteries of civilization; I love its Gothic churches, which tell me of the past; I love its railroads and schools, which tell me of the future. For me, forty generations have enriched this corner of the globe; here is a heritage which I have received from my fathers, and which I wish to transmit to my children after having embellished it. I do not mean that a stone or an institution of my beloved city, of my true country, shall be touched without my consent. I am a Parisian, Paris is mine!"

"Rose, my friend!" exclaimed I, "you are the Cicero of apothecaries; but eloquence is privileged to say the opposite of truth. You do not surely speak in earnest of entrusting to one of ourselves, to a simple citizen, the police of such a pandemonium. This needs a firm and independent hand which rules us despite ourselves."

"Papa," said Susan, "why do you tease good Mr. Rose? You know very well that it is the mayor who chooses the policemen; you yourself secured the appointment of the one that guards our street."

"Perhaps also," added I with an air of pity, "your city taxes are voted by those who pay them?"

"Doubtless," said Rose, "who has the right to vote for an expense if not he who bears it?"

"You will have a pretty budget! This is a fine way of calling in millions! And when you open new streets, you consult the inhabitants perhaps, in order to conjure up against you the selfishness of private interests?"

"Whom should we consult?" asked the innocent apothecary; "these streets are made for us, I presume, and our private interests summed up are the general interest."

"Perfect! perfect!" exclaimed I, laughing; "they have all sucked the milk of the same ass! Good God! that it should be necessary to hammer into these narrow brains the great ideas of civilization! Could they see the miracles of centralization, they would comprehend at length that our business is never better done than when it is committed, without our consent, to the hands of those who have no interest in it! And the schools," added I, "perhaps it is also the fathers of families who vote the tax and fix the amount of expenditure? I would like to see the total."

"The expense of the schools," said Alfred, eager to make a display of his wit; "is voted by the whole people; education is the common debt; each one glories in contributing to it. The day before yesterday, the tax was fixed for 1862; it is two dollars per head for every inhabitant, without counting what is given by the State."

"Sixteen million francs voted by the sixteen hundred thousand inhabitants of Paris for the schools of this great city," exclaimed I; "such a thing never has been, and never will be seen; it is impossible."

"Papa," returned Susan, sharply, "since Alfred says it, it is true."

5*

"Come, my dear friends," said I in my turn, "we must howl with the wolves. If our affairs be really our affairs; if Paris be ours and not the State's; if we vote and spend our money ourselves, all things incredible, enormous, and contrary to experience and good sense, I yield to the common madness! A Parisian who is not a stranger to Paris, a Parisian who has a voice in the municipal chapter, a Parisian who speaks and is listened to, is a phœnix which is seen only in America. Let us go vote. Hurrah for Green, mayor of Paris—in Massachusetts!"

"Hurrah for Green!" cried all the company, directing their steps towards the shop of the grocer.

"Papa," said Susan, "kiss me before you go. You know," added she in a whisper, "that your name is on the list."

"What list, my child?"

"The list of municipal officers. The Nominating Committee proposes you in the *Paris Telegraph*, as inspector of streets and roads, by the side of Mr. Humbug, whom they wish to make justice of the peace. Look, papa!" and Miss drew the paper from her apron pocket. What a country, where a girl in love reads the newspapers and is interested in elections!

I took the *Paris Telegraph;* my name, printed in large characters, and accompanied with a fitting eulogy, figured at the head of the list. It had a strange effect on me. To criticise the ruling power, do as it may, is to me a matter of course; I am a Parisian. To blame and make songs on our masters is the only part of liberty which the great monarch himself was not able to wrest from us; it is the vengeance and consolation of our political leisure. But to administer and command, to act instead of complaining, to emerge from the opposition to encounter it before one's self and to reduce it to silence by dint of zeal and success, was to me an unknown and charming prospect—already ambition glided into my heart. I reflected that on the night before I had been harsh with Humbug (a journal is an influence!) and that perhaps I had spoken too rudely to Rose and his children—there were ten voters! I hastily embraced Susan, therefore, and running after the apothecary, entered into a confidential conversation with him on some admirable pills of my invention—pills destined to revolutionize practice no less than to make the fortune of the physician who had invented them, and the druggist who should sell them. A concentrated extract of camomile is a heroic remedy which cures in a week the incurable and painful malady of men of intellect—dyspepsia. I had been keeping the first fruits of this marvelous discovery for the Academy of Medicine; my memoir had been commenced six years before; but when ambition seizes us, adieu to prudence! The academic glory ceased to dazzle me; the inspection of the streets opened to me a political career. I was a candidate.

CHAPTER XIII.

CANVASSING.

WERE you ever in love, dear reader? do you remember, in those happy days, how light was your heart, how ardent your glance, how buoyant your life? You know then what it is to be a candidate. Fifty paces off, despite my bad sight, I recognized voters whom I had never seen; I found stored away in my brain the history of a host of people with whom I had never spoken; and not only their history, but that of their wives, children, fathers, grandfathers and distant cousins. Right and left, I flung promises and shakes of the hand. Familiar with the small and modest with the great, I would redress all the wrongs and repave all the streets. Cicero, imploring the consulship, was surely neither more eloquent, nor generous, nor affable than I.

Green joined our train; he was, believe me, a poor enough candidate. The Committee that had put him forward had been unfortunate; without going out of their street, they might have easily made a much better choice. A grocer does not receive that high social education which permits him to play with men and things. No flattery to the crowd, none of those promises which remain at the bottom of the ballot-box, none of those pleasing falsehoods which are the necessary fireworks of all elections. Green was cold and timorous as a merchant transacting business and weighing every pledge.

When he had shaken hands with a voter and said to him, "*I will do my best*," or "*It is a difficult position*," or "*Vote for Mr. Little if you think him more capable*," it seemed to him that he had done his part. To the kindly reproaches which I addressed to him, he replied, in a frigid tone, "My conscience forbids me to do more; I cannot promise more than I shall fulfill." Conscience in a candidate! it was a grocer's scruple. When a man is seeking to make his fortune, he draws a double bolt on his conscience the day before election, and does not always remember to withdraw it on the morrow. In France, every one knows this.

I should have died of ennui in this electoral procession, if the enormous, merry Humbug, had not accompanied us. Always on the alert, always ready with repartee, his trace was marked by the roars of laughter which he left after him. The welcome which he received was not always gracious; in his hatreds, as in his friendships, the Saxon carries a rude frankness; American salt is not Attic salt. But Humbug was an admirable tennis player; there was not a jest that he did not receive and send back in first-rate style. Once hit by him, the attack was scarcely repeated.

"Green a candidate! it is a shame," said a stock-broker, with pale face and distorted features. "Imagine the grocer in the city council! When the bell rings, he will answer, '*Look sharp there! make yourself useful.*' Let him go to h—, he and all his crew."

"To h— ?" said Humbug. "What shall we tell your father, the bankrupt—that you have had three failures and are expecting the fourth?"

"Green a candidate!" repeated a dry-goods' clerk, a dandy in varnished boots, who cleft the air at every word with his harmless whip; "Green, a shopkeeper, who doesn't know a horse from a donkey."

"Don't be afraid, my boy," said Humbug; "he would know you among a thousand."

"A fine answer, and worthy of a man who lives on his wits."

"If you had no other capital to live on, my boy, you would be thinner than I am," replied Humbug, continuing his route amidst the laughter of the crowd.

We entered the Union Hotel; the proprietor had been pointed out to us as one of the most influential voters of the city. But if the honest man held the reins in the household, it was his wife that guided them. At Green's first word, the irascible matron cut him short.

"Down with politics!" said she.

"Down with hotels!" answered Green, making the lady a profound bow.

"Joseph!" exclaimed the imperious Juno, "your wife is insulted, you are outraged, and you stand there like a stick. Are you so chicken-hearted?"

At this terrible voice, Joseph stopped short, opening his eyes wide. I believe that in the street the honest hotel-keeper would have gladly shaken hands with us; his broad face, hanging lip and big belly did not indicate a thunder-clap; but, under the eye of his wife, he deemed it prudent to fly in a rage. To carry the war outside was the means of keeping peace at home.

"Let this fine candidate come on," cried he, in a coarse voice which he vainly strove to render surly; "I have a halter ready to hang him."

"Many thanks, my good friend," said Humbug, in an affectedly soft voice, "we have scruples about depriving you of a family piece of furniture."

Laughing heartily, we were about to flee the cave of Polyphemus, when behold! the retreat was cut off. On the threshold of the door, the lady, erect as a sentinel under arms, stopped Humbug, and, trembling with anger, said:

"Do you know who I am?"

"Who does not know and admire you?" returned he, bridling up with a rakish air; "you are a charming child that has not yet reached the age of discretion."

Upon this, he bowed, leaving the worthy matron more mute and confounded than Lot's wife on her transformation.

These were merely skirmishes; there were public meetings where the claims of the candidates were discussed; there the battle was waged and the victory decided. The moment had come for us to separate; it was necessary that each one should show himself in these. The *Lyceum* was assigned to me. I entered the immense hall, where a restless crowd was waving to and fro. I was recognized and called for, all eyes were fixed on me; I was seized with a sudden panic, and would have gladly renounced this fatal nomination, which delivered me over to the public. Alas! it was too late.

In front of me, a man, mounted on a stage, was speaking and gesticulating with the greatest eagerness; the crowd listened in silence, then suddenly burst into terrible huzzas and groans—the way they applaud and hiss among the Saxons. This popular orator, who aroused at his will the passions of the crowd, was the lawyer of Banker Little—it was our enemy, Fox.

While execrating the rascal, I was forced to recognize

in him a certain talent which he abused. By turns serious and mocking, he had a way of praising his adversaries so as to render them ridiculous, and of jesting on his candidates so as to raise them in all eyes. He ended by a rapid enumeration of the wealth which the banker would diffuse in America. Little became a Jupiter, falling in showers of gold into the lap of a new Danæ. At the voice of the lawyer, railroads, canals and steamboats ranged around the banker in an electoral cortège, while, with a disdainful gesture, the haranguer showed us the grocer drowned in his molasses, or swallowed up in the account of his herrings and sardines.

"Friends of peace!" exclaimed he, in closing, "will you choose for the head of the city this manufacturer of lucifer matches, whose merchandise is at the bottom of every conflagration? Friends of liberty! will you elect this dealer in salt cod, who feeds the slaves of the South, and who would become bankrupt to-morrow if his customers, freed by our money, should leave his corrupt merchandise on his hands? No, never will you descend to this shame. For my part, a pure-blooded Yankee, a friend of the country, proud of all our glories, rather than give my vote to this man, I would cast it for"—he paused, winking his eye and lowering his voice—"for him whom, in their universal pity, our women call a *poor fallen angel*—I will not utter his name."

A thunder of applause greeted the orator. He descended from the platform, showered with compliments and promises. In every assembly there is always a flock of simpletons that bleat after the last speaker. His success was not sufficient for the traitor; he came straight to me, extended me a hand which I dared not refuse, and said, in a voice which resounded through the hall:

"Dr. Smith, it is your turn now; fair play for all is the motto of a Yankee."

I rose in a cold sweat. The cry rung from every part of the hall, "*Hear! hear!*" The noise, the eyes fixed on me, the silence which ensued, all turned my brain; a red cloud passed before my eyes, my voice stuck in my throat, and my whole body shook from the throbbing of my heart. What would I not have given to have purchased the loquacity of this wretch! I had nobler ideas than his—a more sincere patriotism; but the lawyer had the habit, the trade; and I, the citizen of a free country, had not even been taught to speak. I was vanquished, and vanquished without a struggle.

I was about to swoon with anger and shame, when suddenly my son Henry, who had seen me turn pale, leaped on the platform and made a sign that he wished to speak. His body upright, head erect, feet square, and left hand buried in his buttoned coat, he gracefully waved his right hand, and waited till the tumult should subside.

"His son! his son!" the murmur ran on all sides. "*Hear! hear!*" Every one looked at the child with curiosity. There was a profound silence; one might have heard a fly buzz.

"Citizens and friends," said he, in a clear and piercing voice, "I do not come to fight the terrible Goliath of Banker Little. Not that I lack stones: the Philistine has thrown only too many into our garden; but I have nothing of David but his youth. I have not strength to cope with this too practised adversary; all that I shall attempt is to defend my father and my party; and I am sure that there is not one among you, noble-hearted men, but will say, 'This young man is right.'"

"Hear! hear!" the shouts rung on all sides; "he speaks well."

"The honorable lawyer," continued my son, emphasizing the first word, "does not like the grocery business. This surprises me. He spends so much for coarse salt that we would be glad to have his custom. If he will give it us, we will supply him, into the bargain, with the sugar which he lacks. Sugar allays the bile; without it, a man looks on things with a jaundiced eye, and is unjust to his friends and companions in arms."

I know not where my son found this low cast of eloquence, but it suited the taste of the ignorant crowd: they laughed, they applauded, the women waved their handkerchiefs. Henry replied by a smile; the assembly was his.

"I shall not speak ill of the bankers," continued my orator of sixteen. "Bankers are like dentists—we must not make enemies of them; who knows whether we may not need them to-morrow? But is it into their hands that we are to commit the interests of the city? I remember that my grandmother, a sainted woman of Connecticut, a grand-daughter of our pilgrim fathers, often used to repeat to me, that she had heard her virtuous sires say that the banker sustains the State as the cord sustains the thief—by strangling it."

"Three groans for the bankers!" cried a shrill voice—the voice of some stray debtor in the crowd. The cry was echoed; the hall shook with these howls, which tickled my paternal ear as if they had been a sonata of Beethoven.

"My grandmother," continued the child, excited by these huzzas, "used to set us riddles to amuse us winter evenings in the chimney corner. 'If a banker, a lawyer, and a tailor be put into the same bag,' said she, 'and one drawn at random, which will surely come out?' "

"A thief!" repeated the audience, delighted to recognize a memory of childhood.

Henry approached the edge of the platform, laid his finger on his lip, and said, in a low tone:

"That is the word which grandmother used, but to-day we say, 'A successful millionaire.' "

"Indeed," added he, "I have no spite against fortune; I hope to make my way as well as others."

"And you will go far, my little giant," cried a coarse voice, which stirred the assembly.

"Show me," added my son, animated by this suffrage, "show me a fortune honorably acquired; ships sent to the East Indies, Newfoundland, and the Moluccas. I will greet in the person of Green twenty years of labor, calculation and economy; but these chance riches, these millions gained at play in a day, do not tell me of them; they are the property of others passed into the pocket of a more adroit trickster. A fortune without labor is a fortune without honor! (*Hear, hear!*)

"And besides, my dear fellow citizens, is it fortune that you reward? Is it not courage and devotion? Was not Green the noble captain who entered a burning house to save your wife or daughter, perhaps? Have you not all adopted the child that my father snatched yesterday from the flames? Oh ye, our conscience, ye stars of our souls, mothers, wives, daughters, sisters! speak, ladies! for whom are we to vote? (*Hear, hear!*)

"I love brave men, who are not afraid to enter the flames," continued my young Gracchus, "I have no taste for those who live in them eternally. Let the nameless gentleman of whom my opponent speaks have all the sympathies of our adversaries, I am not surprised at it. It is natural that Mr. Fox should choose his representative from his family or friends. We, who have less illustrious connections—what we wish at the head of our affairs is an honest man. This man's name we have not to hide: it is the son of his works, it is the child of the city, it is Green!"

"Hurrah for Green! hurrah for Smith!" cried all the crowd, carried away by emotion. The victory was ours.

In the midst of this uproar, Henry sought my eye. He was about to escape from his rising glory when a robust Kentucky hunter, one of those giants who boast of being half horse, half alligator, carried off my son by force in his arms, and made the round of the hall. The thunder of applause that ensued well nigh brought down the walls. All the men shook the young prodigy by the hand, all the women embraced him. I wished to cry, "I am his father!" but a second time fear choked my words, and I sighed, saying in a whisper, "Alas, that I am not my son!"

CHAPTER XIV.

VANITAS VANITATUM.

When the crowd had dispersed, bearing afar the glory and name of the future Webster, I embraced the orator at leisure, and we set out for home together. Ashamed of the mute part to which my timidity had condemned me, I could not resist the wish to tease the Cicero in embryo.

"Come, you dog," said I, "where did you get this facility of chattering, and this assurance which is disturbed at nothing? To improvise, declaim, wed the gesture to the word—where has this art, lost since the ancients, been taught you?"

"At school," replied Henry. "You must know, papa —you, who have so many times made me recite my Enfield.* Did I stand erect? Did I not carry my arm above my head? Are you satisfied with me?"

"And do all your comrades chatter like yourself?"

"Of course, papa. A nation of mutes would be fine citizens! To speak and gesticulate is as necessary to us as to read and write. There is not one among us that will not be something in society, the county, the state.

* "Enfield's Speaker" is a collection of the finest pieces of poetry and eloquence in the English language, and is used in American schools to teach children to recite by heart, or rather to declaim. The work is preceded by a treatise on mimicry and gesture, with plates, giving the position of the body, head, and hands, for each passion to be expressed.

Members of a meeting or an association, voters, candidates, magistrates, senators—we will all find it necessary to address the public; we are, therefore, accustomed to it at school. To improvise is not difficult, and is very amusing. It is our delight, in our play hours, to argue; I have already made a hundred speeches to my future voters. But my forte is gesture. 'Action!' says Demosthenes, in my Enfield, 'action! action!' Look at me, papa."

And behold! my scamp strode up and down, declaiming some speech of Lord Chatham against the American war. He advanced, paused, raised his eyes to heaven, clasped his hands, clenched his fist, placed his hand on his heart, and ended by leaping on my neck with shouts of laughter; while I, his father, incapable of saying a word or lifting a finger, stood confounded before this exhibition of a precocious perversity, the fruit of an unhealthy education. My son was not a prodigy, he was only a Yankee, too skillfully trained.

"Unhappy child," said I; "since you are going to the East Indies, of what use will this histrionic art be to you? It would do, if you were a lawyer."

"I shall be, some day, papa," answered Henry. "Let me earn ten thousand dollars there; on my return I shall study, and enter into partnership with an experienced master."

"And then?" asked I, dismayed at this youthful ambition.

"Then, papa, I shall get myself chosen representative for the State of Massachusetts, and afterwards senator."

"And then?"

"Then, papa, I shall be sent to Congress, and later, made United States senator."

"And then?"

"Then, papa, I shall be Secretary of State, like Mr. Seward; or, if I cannot succeed in that, President, like Mr. Lincoln."

"And then," exclaimed I, "you will doubtless take the place of Lucifer; for you have the ambition and pride of a demon!"

"Papa," returned the child, troubled at my vivacity, "all my companions do the same. Our masters have always told us that we are the hope of the country, and that the republic stands in need of us. To enter the political career is not ambition, but a duty. The citizen who advances furthest in it is the one who best serves his country."

"Oh, the heathen! the heathen!" I exclaimed; "behold us returned to the scandals of Athens and Rome! The first duty of a Christian, sir, is to remain in his humility, to shun politics, and never to meddle with the affairs of his country, unless compelled to do so by the sovereign power."

"Papa, this is not what is taught us from the pulpit. Last Sunday, a Pope—Pius VII., I believe—was cited to us, who said—when he was only a bishop, it is true—'*Be good Christians, and you will be good republicans.*' All our liberties come from the Gospel. It is repeated to us without ceasing, that the morality of Christ leads to democracy; that is, to fraternal equality, and respect of the most obscure individual. *Love each other.* What does this mean, if not that the stronger should aid the weaker, with his fortune, counsels, and devotion?"

I seized Henry's arm:

"Poor child, blinded by the folly of thy masters, see," said I, "whither the democracy is going!"

Before us walked, with measured steps, a man encased in a wooden frame. On this ambulating placard was written, in large characters:

THE LYNX.

The Journal of the Democracy.

—

CITIZENS!

BEWARE OF INTRIGUERS AND FOOLS!

GREEN,
SMITH,
HUMBUG, } or the ridiculous trio unmasked.

"Give me the *Lynx*," said I to a newspaper vender.

"Here it is, sir," said the man in a jeering tone; "but, if you want to laugh, I advise you to take the *Sun* and the *Tribune*. There you will see the *trio* lashed in fine style."

The *Lynx* was enough for me. I opened the execrable sheet. Green was keenly satirized; coarse truths were told of Humbug; but I! great God! how was I treated? What falsehood! what abuse! what abomination!

I crumpled the wretched paper, and was about to throw it into the gutter, its true place, when, at the threshold of my door, I met the jovial and impertinent smile of Humbug.

"You are triumphing, Mr. Journalist," said I, thrusting the *Lynx* in his face. "Elections are your festivals; they are the saturnalias of calumny!"

"Calumny," said the fat man, shrugging his shoulders,

"is like the small pox; when it comes out, we are cured; when it strikes in, we die."

"It is only in your democracies that such infamous things are printed."

"I believe it," replied the sophist, happy to seize a new paradox on the wing. "In the monarchies of the Old World, men take care not to print calumny—they whisper it; it is a more perfidious and surer way. They do not attack men in the face, lest they might defend themselves; they stab them in the back. There, intrigue and falsehood rule without diffusion; and there the prince is the first victim of that poison, whose exhalation he prevents. *Summa petit livor.* Calumny, doctor, is the scourge and chastisement of despotism; in a free country, it is like the sting of a wasp—it is forgotten on the morrow."

"Mr. Philosopher," said I, drily, "read this journal; you are in question in it."

"Another reason for not reading it. It is always the same theme, with six or eight substantives, pretentious epithets, to vary the chorus. Have you the audacity not to follow the docile sheep which are drawn along by adroit leaders? dare you have an opinion and will of your own? you are a *proud visionary* and an *ambitious fanatic.* Do you tell the truth to your fellow citizens, do you seek to enlighten them on the conditions of liberty, to warn them against the dangers of anarchy? you are an *infamous aristocrat*, a *servile admirer of perfidious Albion.* In other words, to open the eyes of the people, is to ruin the trade of the leaders of the blind, and to throw out of employment honest men, who are far from pardoning it. Do you speak frankly and call by their name abuses and those who live by them?

you are a *flatterer of the crowd* and a *cowardly demagogue.* Ironical eulogies if your nomination be defeated, gross and stale abuse if it succeed—such is the eternal song of journals and journalists without self-respect. We are made in this like street organs. It is the pleasure of the envious, of gossips, of good people with a false ear. We must be indulgent to the petty miseries of humanity."

"Read the article," returned I, impatiently; "we will see how far your placidity will go."

Once entered into the parlor, where happily we were alone, Humbug burst into laughter at the insulting diatribe, while Henry ran to learn the news.

"Green has no cause to complain," said the fat journalist, laughing. "From the rough manner in which he is treated, it is evident that his stock is rising. Mine is not bad. *The shameless Falstaff*, is fine; *the tipsy Silenus, who does not even lack his ass when the doctor is by*, is from a mythology which does honor to the erudition of the writer. All this is the *telum imbelle, sine ictu*, of a party at bay."

"Why are these wretches not hindered from speaking?"

"Doctor, have you found the philosopher's stone? To know in advance what people will say is a secret which is still sought; the only way to avoid the scandal which terrifies you is to gag the whole world—a heroic remedy, which kills men to prevent them from leading an ill life. Is this the medicine which you practise? These scoundrels, you say, are paid to carry on an ignoble trade; they abuse liberty, they prostitute it; I grant it you, but this abuse preserves us the use of our rights. There are women who abuse the right of walking the streets; shall we shut up our wives in a harem? There are people who kill themselves by gluttony and drunkenness; shall we put ourselves on the diet of Sancho Panza in the island of Barataria? Through fear of a conflagration, would you forbid tinder-boxes and matches? Through fear of an assassin, would you take from us one of the first rights of a free people, the right to have arms? Every liberty involves in its train a possible abuse; every power and every instrument does the same. To suppress liberty in order to prevent abuses, to prevent good in order to prevent evil, is to arraign God himself and to prove to him that he understood nothing at Creation."

"If you cannot prevent calumny," exclaimed I, "punish it; invent fearful tortures; chastise him who takes away my honor as you would him who takes away my life!"

"The courts are open to you," answered Humbug; "but contempt is a speedier and surer justice. Is it certain, moreover, that we are calumniated? For my part, I do not feel hurt."

"I do not know what you have in your veins," said I, snatching the paper from his hand. "Hear how an anonymous coward dares treat a man of my rank and age; I will show you then how to punish such infamies."

And in a voice trembling with rage I read as follows:

"The doctor is a triple fool. He is a fool by birth; thirty years' study have rendered him still more foolish; and he lacked nothing but a grain of ambition to lose the little sense which labor had left him. We all know the folly of the simpleton, who sees no further than the end of his nose. The stupid admirer of the past, Old Europe is his ideal; he sees nothing to admire outside those decrepit societies where Roman tradition, where the despotism of the administration stifles all independence and vitality. The learned Smith, the glory of twenty unknown academies, is one of the tremblers who would have cried on the day of creation, 'O God, stop! you will disturb Chaos!' He is like the railroad conductors, who turn their backs on the train which carries them along. He sees nothing, he admires nothing but what is fleeing and disappearing in the shadow of the past; he does not feel that behind him is rising a new sun and world—the reign of the individual, the triumph of liberty. Let such a mummy remain in his museum and receive the adoration of idlers; we will not go thither to disturb him; but what would these dim eyes, these mute lips, this powerless aim do in the broad daylight of public life? What our young and glorious republic needs are men of our times—bankers, to advance civilization by daily creating new enterprises and stocks; orators, to guide us towards the magnificent destinies which the future has in store for us. Leave the dead to bury their dead; ours are hearts open to all the great social aspirations, heads alive to the palpitating questions of the present moment. Let simpletons and poltroons vote for their old fetiches; our candidates are men whom Europe envies us; the able and generous banker, Little, the eloquent and celebrated lawyer, Fox!

"To-morrow, the voice of the people, issuing from the ballot-box like the thunder from the cloud, will proclaim through all America the victory of the chosen of the Democracy. Hurrah for Little! Hurrah for Fox!"

"Bravo," said Humbug; "doctor, you are hit. This is a pretty article—nothing that attacks your character; pleasantries somewhat strong, it is true, but at the same time spicy, spirited, ingenious and observant, to say nothing of their fine style. The fellow who wrote this tirade is no fool."

"Come with me to the office of the *Lynx*," said I, in my turn, "and you shall see how a triple fool boxes the ears of a witty fellow; the gentleman is in need of the lesson."

"Are you mad?" cried the burly journalist, springing from his seat. "If any other than I heard you, you would be made to give bail for ten thousand dollars, or be sent to the penitentiary. Do you take us for red-skins? Are you a Christian? It is in the wilds of Arkansas that men argue with fists and revolvers; in Massachusetts, there is no vengeance but that of the law. Among a civilized people, men talk much and quarrel sharply; but they do not assassinate a rival—no more do they fight him."

"Savages!" exclaimed I, "who do not even know a point of honor."

"Savage, yourself," answered Humbug, laughing. "Really, doctor, the bleeding renders you ferocious. In what can it avail the cause of justice and reason, to kill men or be killed by them? A duel profits no one but the physician or grave-digger."

"What do you do, then, sir, when you are meanly insulted by a pamphleteer?"

"My dear doctor," replied the tame-spirited candidate, "I repeat to myself or aloud a Turkish proverb, the profound wisdom of which I commend to you:—'*He who stops to throw stones at all the dogs that bark at him, will never reach the end of his journey*'—upon which, I go to look after my election and yours; do the same on your side, and you will soon forget the *Lynx* and its rhetoric. '*Tu ne cede malis, sed contra audentior ito.*' Adieu."

CHAPTER XV.

A SOUVENIR OF THE ABSENT COUNTRY.

The arrival of my wife and children softened my ill humor; the news was good. Alfred and Henry had been through all the meetings, and had received cheerings and promises everywhere; Jenny and Susan had seen all their female friends. Two hundred ladies, the most important in the city, were wearing my photograph in a medallion on their neck; the election was certain.

The gaiety of our modest dinner completed the cure of my wounds. We were all of one heart and soul. My Jenny was more animated than at the baptism of her first born. I have always remarked that women are naturally ambitious; a young and handsome husband, who is nothing, will never have the art to please them long; an old husband will receive their sweetest smile, should fame or fortune crown his white hairs. When love is joined to this legitimate ambition, the wife then becomes our veritable half, in all the beauty of the word. We see, we think, we dream double; it is perfect happiness on earth; a happiness almost unknown in France, where the fashion interdicts to women serious tastes and generous passions; a happiness common in the United States, where public opinion invites women to take part in them. Susan was still more ardent than her mother—it was my blood! She talked of nothing but my election. It is true, that she had made Alfred one of my principal supporters; to occupy herself with me, was to occupy herself with him.

In the evening there was a new demonstration. All the firemen, in full dress, and each carrying a torch in his hand, defiled under our windows, with music at their head. The young men of the city, dressed in uniforms and varied costumes, accompanied them with long poles, surmounted by Chinese lanterns. In the midst of the procession an immense banner, with a lighted transparency, showed to the amazed crowd two species of black devils, emerging from the flames, with white bundles in their arms. The names Green and Smith, written under these figures, gave a human meaning to this infernal scene, which was applauded as it passed. The woman and child whom we had rescued were drawn in an open carriage by four white horses, the whole adorned with lanterns and inscriptions. It was a triumphal march—a procession worthy the palmy days of Eleusis. Shouts and cheers burst forth on every side, and sometimes also a few groans, which were quickly drowned by huzzas. The opposition was conquered and put to flight by the beauty of our inventions. It was difficult for Little to rival our marvels. What could he parade through the streets? Ruined stockholders? A people is not allured by this daily spectacle.

At ten o'clock, Jenny read the Bible to us. We left off at the fifth chapter of Daniel; that is, the story of King Belshazzar and the avenging hand which wrote on the wall the death sentence, *Mene*, *Tekel*, *Upharsin*. It was a fine opportunity for Martha to prophesy; she did not miss it. Whether I would or no, she compared me to Nebuchadnezzar, and condemned me to *remain with the wild asses and eat the grass of the field like an ox*, if ever I should forget that the Most High has a sovereign power over men, and that he sets on the throne whom he pleases. The lesson seemed to me a little emphatic for a future street inspector; but perhaps it is not necessary to be a king, to have the pride and insolence of Nebuchadnezzar. Who knows whether the Assyrian clerks were not already more impertinent than their magnificent sovereign?

I laughed at the sibyl; nevertheless I was excited by this nomination, and too much excited to find sleep. On going to my room, I filled a pipe with excellent Virginia tobacco and, seating myself by the window, endeavored to soothe my agitated senses.

The street was deserted; the moon, illuminating with its pale light the mute and closed houses, added to the mystery and calm of the night. All was sleeping in the distance; all was silent. The only sound that disturbed this universal silence, or rather that made itself felt, was the ticking of a wooden clock at the foot of my bed. Lulled by this monotonous sound, and stupefied by the fumes of the tobacco, I gave full rein to my reveries, when suddenly the clock became animated. A grating of wheels and groaning of cords and pulleys announced that the hour was about to strike. I rose to admire this masterpiece of German clockmaking. On reaching it, a cock of painted wood, perched on the top of the clock, flapped his wings and uttered three shrill cries. A door opened abruptly below the cock, and showed me Paris, the Seine, and the Hotel de Ville in 1830. Lafayette, in a blond peruke, blue coat, and white pantaloons, was embracing at the same time a foot soldier, a gendarme, and a tricolored flag, on which was written, in letters of gold, LIBERTY AND PUBLIC ORDER. Eleven times the clock struck, eleven times the brave Lafayette shook his head and waved his flag; then the door closed, the Gallic cock flapped his wings and crowed more shrilly than ever, and the vision disappeared.

This lost souvenir, this motto, long since forgotten, awakened the golden dreams of my childhood. How our hearts beat in 1830! Poor, ignorant beings! We did not know then that liberty, like all mistresses, ruins and betrays those who love her. *Liberty and public order!* terrible words—the *Mene, Tekel, Upharsin* of modern times! This is the enigma which, every fifteen years, the Sphinx of revolutions proposes to France, always ready to devour the Œdipus that does not divine it. *Liberty and public order!* One might style them two immortal enemies who, by turn, conquering and conquered, wage against each other an endless combat, of which we are the stake. One day liberty prevails—the sky resounds with joy and hope; but, lo! under the mask of this serene divinity, anarchy triumphs, drawing after it civil war, attacking all rights, menacing all interests, making a frightened people recoil in horror. The next day public order is installed, sabre in hand, giving peace, imposing silence; ere long breaking all barriers, and, by its own weight, gliding into that abyss where falls every power which nothing counsels or restrains. Whence comes this perpetual shipwreck? Whence comes it that for seventy years past an honest, brave, ingenious people has built naught but ruins, always discontented, always declining?

How is it that in the United States, where all heads are turned by liberty, where no one speaks of public order, the internal peace is never disturbed? In this turbulent democracy, in this crowd abandoned to itself, without police and without gendarmes, why are there neither riots nor revolutions? America has not, like us, a hundred thousand functionaries ranged in battle array, an admirable administration, which prescribes everything, anticipates everything, directs everything, and regulates everything. It has not, in the face of this compact organization, a docile, commanded, repressed, directed, and regulated people; yet, notwithstanding, it is tranquil and prosperous. Liberty, guarantied in its full exercise by law, punished in its excess by justice—this is public order to the Americans. Their narrow intellect has never risen to that tutelary centralization which makes our unity and glory. Among this primitive people, public order has not been separated from liberty; it has not been personified; it has not been surrounded with formidable ramparts and ever-loaded cannon. No hierarchic administration, no repressive police, no inviolable functionaries, no privileged tribunals; nothing of that scholarly mechanism which, among civilized nations, breaks all resistance and crushes all individuality. The law all-powerful, the citizen master of and responsible for his actions, the functionary reduced to the common law, the administration amenable to the courts—this is the whole system. It is of ridiculous simplicity. Nothing but laws and judges in this embryo government; yet, notwithstanding, peace and wealth everywhere. Strange derision of fortune which our great politicians have not yet explained to us. Why has it not yet been proved to the Americans that they are happy contrary to all rules, and that they ought to envy us our revolutions?

With these fine reflections I fell asleep.

I know not how long I had slept when I felt myself abruptly shaken by a muscular hand. By my side, on my bed, was a corporal of the gendarmery. The sight gave me pleasure. A gendarme! I was in France, I had regained my country!

"Up! up! M. Lefebvre," cried the corporal, with a Gascon accent which smelt of garlic half a league off.

I looked closely at this amiable messenger; his face was not unknown to me. This eye, this voice, this sardonic laugh—it was the terrible medium, Jonathan Dream, my enemy. At the sight of the traitor, my joy changed to terror.

"Who are you? What do you want?" asked I. "By what right do you enter by night into the dwelling of a peaceable citizen? My house is my castle."

"Silence, citizen," returned the gendarme. "Do not be so unreasonable as to reason with the government which does not reason because it always has reason upon its side."

Upon this he opened his cartridge box, and took from it a file of stamped paper.

"Number one," said he. "To the Sieur Lefebvre, or one styling himself such. For having had the impertinence to criticise the municipal authority in a public sheet, with respect to paving the street, a reprimand, until further judgment."

"This is extraordinary," exclaimed I. "Instead of reprimanding me, the authority had better offer me apologies and mend the pavement."

"Silence, citizen," returned the gendarme. "As a private individual, I do not deny that the pavement is bad, I have just picked up two animals which had stumbled on it before the door; but as a gendarme, I declare your complaint as indiscreet as inopportune. If my colonel should say to me, 'Corporal, to-morrow it will be dark at noon-day,' I would answer, 'Very well, colonel,' and would put the first street boy into the guard room who should take it into his head to see clearly. The instructions say that the pavement is good; therefore, it must be good, and none but evil-disposed persons come expressly through guilty malice to break their necks on it."

"What!" cried I, indignantly, "have I not the right to criticise the authority when it does not do its duty?"

"On the contrary, citizen," returned the gendarme, "prefer your complaint; the French government is quite willing to be censured; but it is necessary to be polite with it. You have not asked its permission to criticise it. You have been rude, my dear friend."

"My good fellow, I respect you, but you reason like a cartridge box. The government is made for us, I suppose, not we for the government."

"A colossal error, my good sir," returned the gendarme, with an air of contempt which roused my indignation. "Those who obey are made for those who command; those who command are not made for those who obey."

"But we are France—we are the country."

"The country, my good sir," returned the impassive gendarme, "is composed of marshals, generals, colonels, captains, lieutenants, prefects, mayors and other embroidered coats that I respect; the rest is a heap of conscripts and tax-payers whose duty it is to pay and be silent"——

"Without murmuring; is it not? I know this song. Ah! if we had justice!"

"You would not have the administration, citizen; you would be an Iroquois, like the Englishmen and other cannibals who do as they please. You would not have the honor to be a civilized man and a Frenchman.

"Number two," continued he. "To the Sieur Lefebvre, for having had the audacity to parade his lugubrious person from door to door—a notice from the prefect, who deprives him of his free functions as member of the charitable board, until further judgment."

"All nominations are free," exclaimed I.

"Doubtless," answered the gendarme, "they are free, but with the authorization of the authority.

"Number three. To the said Lefebvre, for having distributed, or caused to be distributed, electoral ballots bearing his name or that of certain persons by name unknown, equally obscure and scandalous—a summons to appear this day week before the president and judges composing the tribunal of correctional police, to answer for the offence of the distribution of unauthorized printed matter."

"What! Cannot I distribute to my voters the ballot bearing my name?"

"You can do everything, my good sir," returned the gendarme, "but with the authorization of the authority. Well, if you do not admit it, do you imagine that the authority will suffer idlers to commit a folly which would degenerate into opposition? Would that I were the government! I would lock you up properly, until further judgment.

"Number four. To the aforesaid Lefebvre, for having joined himself publicly to a band of persons unknown, assembled in a so-called electoral assembly, which constitutes a club, if not a secret society—a summons to appear before the aforesaid tribunal, to see himself condemned in virtue of Article 291 of the penal code, to prison, until further judgment.

"Number five. To the said Lefebvre, for having incited his minor son to hold in the aforesaid club an incendiary speech against the honorable and discreet person of M. Petit, the candidate of the government—a summons to appear before the aforesaid tribunal, as abettor and accomplice of and moreover civilly responsible for the said offence, until further judgment."

"What, have I not the right to assemble my constituents, and have they not the right to know the opinions of their representative?"

"They have all the rights, my good sir;" answered the gendarme, "but always with the authorization of the authority. It would be a fine thing if the soldiers in a barrack were left to assemble together, and raise an outcry, without permission!"

"But we are not in barracks."

"A foolish question needs no answer," returned the gendarme; "nevertheless, citizen, I will condescend so far as to enlighten your profound ignorance. Every Frenchman is born a soldier, and made to await the word of command. The more he is ruled, the better he is contented. Let no one disturb the obedience which makes his joy. If I were the government, I would hang all the loungers, while awaiting further judgment.

"Number six. To the aforesaid Lefebvre, for having covered the walls, or suffered them to be covered, with unmeaning and criminal placards; *item*, for having organized, or suffered to be organized, a revolutionary procession, and having paved the way for an improper riot, which would have broken out, had it not been for the precautions and vigilance of the police, whose eye is always open—a summons to appear before the aforesaid tribunal, to see and hear himself condemned to the penalties prescribed by the law, until further judgment."

"Thanks, corporal," exclaimed I; "thanks, M. Gendarme; I am the victim of an error. In France, doubtless, I should be a great culprit; but we are in America; I am innocent. What is a crime in France is a right in the United States."

"Spare me your thanks," answered the inflexible gendarme, taking from his pocket something that looked like handcuffs. "As a private individual, I flatter myself that I have not an unfeeling heart, but at this moment I am the organ of the law."

"Then the law is gasconade."

"Silence, rebel; enough talk. To hear them, they are all as innocent as a new-born child. Innocent or not, my fine fellow, I suspect you of being suspected, and through precaution, I shall lay hold of you."

Saying this, he grasped my arm with such force that I uttered a cry of pain. The cry awakened me. Thank God! I was dreaming.

To shake off this abominable nightmare, I lighted the gas. Horror! At the back of the bed I perceived the shadow of a menacing arm, and that cocked hat and tuft which make the boldest turn pale.

Frozen, with trembling heart, I remained motionless, like a criminal awaiting the sentence of death. At this moment, the cock of the wooden clock crowed—the cock which puts to flight the evil spirits of the night; I turned towards the wall, and—burst into a fit of laughter. The arm which had terrified me was my own; the cocked hat was nothing but the shadow of a few disordered hairs; and the terrible tuft was only the tassel of my—through respect for the modesty of my lady readers, I will not finish.

I extinguished the light, and, falling back into my bed:

"Oh, gendarme!" I exclaimed, "brave and loyal soldier, simple and generous heart, no one better than thou represents public order among a people that knows authority only in uniform, and peace only with a sword in hand. The terror of the mendicant and vagrant, the remorse of the poacher, the conscience of the innkeeper and wine merchant, the religion and morality of the citizen, the right hand of the mayor, the organ of the prefect, oh, gendarme, I respect and love thee! but pardon the temerities of my fancy; I would have misery some day no longer a crime; I would not have the police repress the good which is superabundant, in order to prevent the evil which is only the exception; I would have liberty, restored to all citizens, banish from our laws offences which are not such; I would lastly (oh, minister of the government, do not shrug thy shoulders) I would have the courts alone give the orders, and thy avenging mission limited to pursuing knaves and arresting villains legally denounced! I know, oh, corporal, how thou wilt smile at this American Utopia, but I bequeath it to the twenty-first century, as the thought which will one day immortalize my name. Then, I ask that, in my native city, in the midst of the square that will replace my street and house, an imaginary bust shall be erected to me over a fountain without water, and that on it shall be engraven the following inscription·

TO THE DREAMER,
WHO,
IN 1862,
DEMANDED THAT THE COURTS
ALONE
SHOULD HAVE THE RIGHT TO ARREST CITIZENS,
AND ONLY UPON LEGAL DENUNCIATION,
BY THE GRATEFUL GENDARMERY,
JULY 14, 2089.

"And I bequeath my last five-franc piece to the Academy of Inscriptions and Belles Lettres, with the compound interest thereon for two centuries, in order that it may write out, in Hebrew, Coptic, Sanscrit, and Syriac, an idea which the Frenchman, born *malin*, has never comprehended, and which his language is powerless to express, *sub lege libertas*."

CHAPTER XVI.

THE ELECTION—THE SABBATH.

At length the day arrived—that famous Saturday, April 3, which was to make a Parisian of the Chaussée d'Antin a member of the municipal administration of Paris, in Massachusetts. At seven o'clock in the morning, in glorious weather, a hundred and twenty ballot-boxes were opened amidst a solemn calm. At the door of every poll were seen two long files of voters, who, with a patience and decision wholly Saxon, awaited the moment to exercise their sovereign right. The quarrels had ceased; the enemies of the night before were exchanging jests and shaking hands. Each one bowed in advance before the decree of the majority, while awaiting his revenge at the end of the year.

At noon, the ballot-boxes were emptied and the election proclaimed. Green received 116,735 votes against 78,622 given to Little; Humbug obtained 146,327 votes, while the unlucky Fox had but 18,124; lastly, despite a few ballots contested by envious scrutators, I was elected by 199,999 votes. Never had street-inspector been proclaimed by a more imposing majority. The effect was great in Massachusetts, greater still in England. As the price of cotton had just risen, the *Times* declared that the Yankees were savages, whose ballots were ruled only by bullets, and thence concluded that the democracy was ungovernable Old Pam resumed the theme in Parliament. He proved to the English that they were the first people on the globe, and that, in default of a hereditary aristocracy, Jonathan did not reach to John Bull's knee—a somewhat harsh truth, which honest John Bull will digest with his usual modesty, while voting his largest budget.

The amiable Truth informed me of my election. He greatly regretted, he said, being unable to announce this good news to the public; but, the day before, he had sold his journal to Eugene Rose, and retired from politics.

"You do well," said I. "Rest, and for a long time; you are in need of it."

"To rest is not an American word," replied he, with his gentle smile. "Young or old, sick or well, a Yankee works till death. It is the duty of a man and Christian. I have followed the advice of Humbug and returned to the studies and tastes of my youth. The Congregationalist Church in Acacia street has called me to be its pastor, and I have accepted. To-morrow I enter upon my functions."

"A journalist yesterday, a pastor to-morrow—you are a universal man: you change your profession like your coat. In six months what will you be?"

"What God pleases," replied the new minister. "If Humbug were here, he who has been by turn a planter in the West, a soldier in Mexico, a lawyer in Philadelphia, a journalist in Paris, and who to-morrow will be a magistrate, he would tell you, in one of his favorite quotations:

'Homo sum, humani nihil a me alienum puto.'

You yourself, doctor, were a scholar the other day, a fireman the day before yesterday, a candidate yesterday, an inspector of the streets to-day: on Monday you will be a physician. It seems to me that you change character with sufficient facility. Herein is one of the great virtues of our glorious country. In Old Europe, one is born and dies in the skin of a comedy actor. All his life, he is soldier, judge, lawyer, merchant, manufacturer—never man. He has only the narrow ideas and prejudices of his trade. Here the occupation matters little; it is an overcoat put on and taken off, according to the occasion; one is a man before all, and everywhere. In this is the root of that equality which makes our strength and glory. Clay was a Kentucky miller; Douglas and Lincoln were Illinois farmers; General Banks, *the Bobbin Boy*, was a cotton tyer. All have become men because they have labored and suffered. He who has not struggled with life does not know what it is worth. The struggle against realities makes the education of the will and the wisdom of the heart. The aristocracy will produce delicate, sickly souls; the empire of the world belongs to the *parvenus*. The future is ours."

"Truth, you preach marvelously. When you are speaking, I feel that you are right; but when you are gone, and I collect my memories, your theories appal me. If I had the weakness to listen to you, you would make me unlearn all that my masters have taught me. No matter, we will go to hear you to-morrow. A simple Christian addressing his brothers, and expounding the Gospel to them in every-day language, will be original. I have no idea of republican Christianity."

Just as Truth quitted me, I was sought for to be installed into my new functions. Jenny, Susan, Alfred, and I seated ourselves in a beautiful open carriage, with Martha, who was anxious, doubtless, to watch over my pride. Henry sat with the coachman, and Sambo climbed behind the carriage. Two vigorous trotters, such as are seen only in America, bore us to Montmorency, the extreme limit of my jurisdiction. We were forced to stop more than once. Every road laborer was at his post, awaiting the new inspector. I assured these honest men of my good will, while my wife and daughter lavished on them their most gracious smiles. We were born to be princes. The only thing that annoyed me was to find toll-gates at intervals. I recognized here that democratic meanness, which causes service to be paid for by those who profit by it, to release those to whom it is of no advantage. I promised myself to correct this abuse, unknown in old Europe, and to establish everywhere a triumphant equality. Moreover, this annoyance did not hold out against the magnificent bouquets which the gatekeepers and principal roadmakers offered to Jenny and Susan. The carriage was a basket; we were buried in flowers. We were harangued like kings. Good people, who certainly had no knowledge of Hebrew, did not fail to compare my Susan to the lilies of the valley. Jenny, blushing with pleasure, looked like a full-blown rose. As to Martha, she was a peony: it seemed as if the blood would gush from her crimson cheeks. She panted like an ox at the end of the furrow. Oh, woman, your true name is vanity! For my part, indolently reclining in the corner of my carriage, I did not suffer myself to be intoxicated with the fumes of this new-born popularity; but in my soul and conscience, I found the roads admirable, and bore malice towards the wretched jade which the day before had stumbled on a pavement kept in order by such gallant roadmakers.

On reaching Montmorency, the coachman, without orders, drove us straight to the Rose Hotel, the house of Seth, the Quaker landlord. Alfred and Susan found no grace with this friend of lovely youth. Instead of treating us as lovers, he made us pay double for a very bad dinner. I protested; but, to his natural avidity, brother Seth joined the most insupportable of the vices produced by civilization—the rascal was an economist. He preached me a sermon in three heads, to demonstrate to me that to live well and cheaply is the calamity of peoples without commerce and industry, while dearness is the token of the most advanced civilization—population reducing the supply, and wealth raising the demand. The day would come when the last of the Rothschilds alone would be in a condition to pay for an egg; this day would mark the apogee of universal prosperity. To economise time and words, at least, I paid him. Heaven preserve me from arguing with these fanatics, who have but one idea! I know these pilgrims. France, its arsenals, its marine, its armies, its glory, its rights,—they would yield them all to the Grand Turk, should he promise them in exchange freedom—of the shambles.

It was four o'clock when our caravan resumed its way to Paris. To my great surprise, they were closing the shutters and doors of the hotel with iron bars, as if there had been mourning in the house. It was a strange fashion of celebrating the approach of Sunday; but in this country, the opposite of all others, it is wise not to be astonished at anything. Friend Seth accompanied us to the city, mounted on a fat horse, which he overshadowed with his immense hat. By his side, on a grey mare, with broad neck and shoulders, trotted Martha, tall, erect, rigid, and majestic as a carabineer. They were a couple of scouts marching before us to announce to all the passers our triumphal entry.

At the first toll-gate, I found the pacific Quaker in a quarrel with the toll-gatherer.

"I tell you," cried the last, "that you cannot pass till you have paid the toll. There are two of you; I must have twenty-four cents, not twelve."

"Friend," returned the innkeeper, "thee does wrong to heat thy blood; it is neither like a reasonable man nor a Christian. Look at thy rate of toll, and do not ask me what the law does not permit thee to exact, otherwise thee will render thyself guilty of the crime of extortion."

"Here is the rate of toll," returned the gate-keeper, furious; "read it yourself, insupportable chatterer: eight cents per horse, four cents per man. Is this clear to you?"

"Very clear," said the Quaker; "and I call these respectable persons to witness that I have paid thee thy twelve cents."

"And this woman?" said the gate-keeper, pointing to Martha, who trotted forward.

"Well," returned Seth, with his imperturbable gravity, "this woman is not a man, her mare is not a horse; therefore, she owes thee nothing."

Upon which he set off on a gallop, leaving the toll-gatherer dumbfounded.

"I hope," said I to the gate-keeper, "that you will institute proceedings against this impudent fellow."

"No, Mr. Inspector," said he, "we should lose the suit. He is one of those cunning rascals who would drive a coach and four through our laws, without ever being caught in them. He has the letter of the toll-rates on his side."

"The spirit of the law condemns him," returned I. "His pretence is absurd."

"Among us, sir," replied the good man, "the law has no spirit. We know nothing but the text. If the judge should interpret the law, it is said, he would be the law-maker; the right and honor of the citizens would be no longer guarantied."

"The ignorant beings!" I exclaimed. "Have they not, then, been taught the alphabet of all legislation? When there is a doubt in an affair between the public treasury and the private citizen, is not the doubt on the side of the treasury, which represents the general interest?"

"Never, sir," answered the gate-keeper; "the decision is always in favor of the citizen. The treasury must be doubly in the right to gain its suit."

What was to be done amidst such barbarism? I shrugged my shoulders, and bade the coachman drive home.

On entering the city, I thought that it had been transformed in my absence. The streets and squares were deserted; large chains were stretched behind us to arrest travel; the windows offered a strange spectacle; on all the balconies were seen boots, ranged in battle array, and presenting the soles to the passers, had there been any. On following a pair of these boots with my eye, I finally perceived human legs, then a body thrown backwards, and lastly a cigar, whose bluish smoke mounted to the sky. I was at a loss to explain to myself what offence deserved this cruel punishment. Sambo, whom I questioned adroitly, informed me that it was the fashionable amusement. Every Saturday evening the Yankee endeavors to give himself a fit of apoplexy, in which he sometimes succeeds. How much wiser are we Frenchmen, who never expose ourselves in our play-houses to anything more than the beginning of asphyxia

Once at home, I had a desire to finish this happy day gaily, and entreated Susan and Henry to sing me my favorite air, *Là ci darem la mano*, from Don Juan. Susan looked at me, and turned pale.

"What is the matter, my dear child?" I exclaimed. "Are you ill?"

"Father," said she, "I am frightened at your request. Would you raise the city about our house? Would you destroy our reputation? Do you forget that the Sabbath has commenced, and that nothing should disturb the rest of the Lord?"

"Good God!" thought I, "in transporting us to America, has the traitor Jonathan transformed us into Jews? Forgive me, my child," said I to Susan, "I was absent-minded; the events of the day have made me lose my memory. Go bring me my large Hippocrates from the library; I shall not be sorry to rest my brain by reading a little Greek. There is nothing more refreshing."

For her sole answer Susan seated herself on my knee, passed her hand over my forehead, and kissed me.

"Poor papa," said she, "how tired he is! See, mamma, he forgets that on the Sabbath eve we read nothing but the Bible."

Decidedly, I was a Jew without knowing it. What, nevertheless, gave me some doubt was that on opening the family Bible, I found there the New Testament, and was able to read in St. Mark that *the Sabbath was made for man and not man for the Sabbath.* This saying made me reflect; but not wishing to wound any one, I kept my meditations to myself, and leaving the whole family absorbed in their pious reading, I went down into the garden.

The evening was beautiful, the trees displayed the freshness of their young verdure, the sun was setting in a golden cloud—everything invited revery. I was weary, I entered the Chinese kiosk, threw myself on the divan and lighted a cigar. There was a rustic chair by me which was standing idle; I placed my legs on the back and perceived, to my shame, that the American fashion had its advantages.

Concealed behind the blinds of the kiosk, I reposed, my eyes mechanically fixed on Sambo, who was pounding sandstone in a corner of the garden to clean his knives. The poor fellow was wholly absorbed in his task when Martha darted from the kitchen like a spider pouncing on a fly.

"Son of Ham," said she, snatching the hammer from his hands, "what is thee doing here?"

"You see, Miss Martha, I am breaking stone."

"Wretch!" exclaimed she, "thee is breaking the Sabbath."

Sambo fled with a piteous air; he passed near my retreat, sighing; then suddenly, perceiving the house cat which had just caught a mouse:

"Take care, Pacha," sung he, "if you chase rats on Sunday, Martha will hang you on Monday."

I was still laughing at the grotesque face of the negro, when two persons seated themselves on a bench placed in front of the kiosk, and so near me that I did not lose a word of their discourse. I recognized the amiable

Seth, who was profiting by the solitude, Sabbath, and evening, to preach a sermon to the fair Martha.

"Beloved sister," said he with a grotesque gravity and listening to each of his words, "there are three things which astonish me greatly—The first is that children should be foolish enough to throw sticks and stones at the trees to knock down the fruit; if the children remained quiet, the day would come when the fruit would fall of itself. My second astonishment is that men should be mad and wicked enough to make war and kill each other; if they remained quiet, they would die a natural death. The third and last thing which astonishes me is that young men should be so unreasonable as to waste their time in running after the girls whom they wish to marry; if they stayed at home and made their fortunes, the girls would run after them. What does thee say to it, Martha?"

"Seth, I say that thee has the wisdom of King Solomon, as well as his vanity."

"Martha," exclaimed the Quaker in a softened voice, "thee has as much wit as beauty."

"Seth," answered Martha, still panting for breath, "thee does not mean what thee says."

"And thee, Martha," resumed the other, "does not say what thee thinks."

"Bravo!" said I to myself; "people make love in America. It is a use of the Sabbath of which I had not thought. This shop-keeping nation, which calculates everything and lives but to grow rich, condemns itself to compulsory repose on one evening in the week in order to pay at this time the debt of youth and love. Let us see how Mr. Seth will make his declaration."

After a thousand circuits, the amorous Quaker arrived

at the speech, which, according to all appearances, had been long expected.

"Martha," said he, drawing a long sigh, "Martha, does thee love me?"

"Seth," replied the good Christian, "is it not commanded us to love one another?"

"Yes, Martha, but what I ask thee is whether thee experiences towards me something of that particular feeling which the world calls love?"

"I do not know what to say," stammered the timid dove, "I have always tried to love all my brethren alike, but if I must confess it, Seth, in communing with myself, I have often thought that in this general affection, thee had much more than thy share."

The confession was made, it could no longer be withdrawn; I heard, I think, a loud kiss which sealed the betrothal; when suddenly Martha uttered a terror-stricken cry, and sprang upon the bench. An enormous Newfoundland dog had suddenly dashed athwart the amorous *tête-à-tête*. I rose and perceived in the shadow, the white teeth of Sambo. The rascal was bursting with laughter; to avenge himself on the Quakeress, he had opened the door of the house and let loose upon Martha the importunate third party which had terrified her.

I had little liking for the Quaker, but I could not help admiring his firmness and gentleness. Far from being afraid of the dog, he called him, and taking from his pocket a lump of sugar, offered it to the animal, who readily suffered himself to be allured and caressed.

"Friend," said the holy man, speaking to the dog, which was looking at him, wagging his tail, "thee has disturbed me in the sweetest moment of my life; another than I would have beaten or killed thee; he would have been justified in doing so; but I will show thee the difference between a Quaker and the generality of mankind. For my sole vengeance, I will content myself with giving thee a bad name."

And, flattering the dog, which sprang after him to obtain a new lump of sugar, Seth politely conducted the animal to the gate; then, suddenly closing the grating, he cried at the top of his voice:

"Mad dog! mad dog!"

In the twinkling of an eye, there were no more boots at the windows; thousands of heads looked out, and menaced the enemy; stones, sticks, and utensils rained like hail on the animal; a pistol-shot struck him before he reached the end of the street, and he fell to rise no more, uttering a howl which pierced me to the heart.

Furious, I seized Seth by the collar, and flung him out of the gate.

"Wretch!" said I, "I know not what restrains me from crying 'Mad Quaker,' to have thee knocked down like this poor animal."

"Friend Daniel," returned master Seth, picking up his hat, "I will meet thee again."

And he departed coldly.

"Go to your room, miss," said I to Martha. "What are you doing, at this hour, in the garden?"

"Bless me!" said she, sobbing, "I was doing no harm; I was only looking for a son-in-law for my mother!"

I was stifling with anger. "Ah!" I exclaimed, "how many men call and perhaps believe themselves virtuous, who act like this cowardly hypocrite! They admire themselves as honest men and saints, because they do not lay hands on their enemy, but they rid themselves of him by giving him a bad name. Calumny! calumny! thou art only the form of assassination among a people which is vain of its civilization. Shame on the wretches who make use of this venomous weapon, were it only to kill a poor dog."

Tired of my solitary eloquence, I betook me to bed, but not without thinking of the dismal day which the first pleasures of the coming Sabbath promised me for the morrow. How much I regretted the free gaiety of the Parisian Sundays! "Frenchmen!" I exclaimed, "amiable and chivalrous people, let rude nations glory in their feverish industry and tiresome liberty! Drive far from thee these savage democrats, these melancholy dreamers, who, shouldst thou listen to them, would make thee the rival of the English and Americans. Friend of wine, glory, and beauty, thy lot is the best. Leave the empire of the world to these wan laborers, who take life in earnest; keep thy incorrigible tone and charming lightness. Amuse yourselves, Frenchmen. Make war and love; forget the world and politics. If ye should reflect, ye would laugh no longer."

CHAPTER XVII.

JOURNEY IN SEARCH OF A CHURCH.

THE next morning I rose at daybreak. A public man should set an example, and I was not sorry to let the Yankees admire the zeal and vigilance of their new edile. My morning walk was long; the pavement belonged to me. I followed, with a jealous eye, all the passers who dragged their feet after them like ducks, and wore a furrow in my side-walks. Anarchy reigns in the streets; each one goes where he likes and as he likes; it is scandalous; I do not understand why a law is not made to oblige men to walk according to the pleasure of the government. To France, the queen of order and propriety, would belong the honor of correcting a last abuse.

On approaching the house, I perceived Sambo, dressed in black like a gentleman, with waistcoat, cravat, gloves, and stockings of dazzling whiteness. He looked like a magpie. As soon as he recognised me, he ran to meet me, waving his hand impatiently.

"Massa," he exclaimed, "everybody is at service; make haste; I am waiting for you."

And he put in my hands a thick book, bound in shagreen, and fastened with silver clasps.

"Are the ladies at mass?" asked I.

"At mass!" said he, with an air of astonishment. "My mistress is a Christian."

"Fool! Are the Catholics Turks?"

"Massa, they say that the Catholics are like the heathens of Africa; they have *vaudous*."

"What is a *vaudou?*"

"Massa, it is a little god which one makes himself, and which is not the true God."

"Are you stupid enough," exclaimed I, "to believe that the Catholics adore a fetich? This will do for your savages of Senegal."

"Massa," said he, opening his eyes wide, "the Papists pray to statues; I have seen them on their knees before them."

"And you did not understand that what they invoked was not those stones, but the saints of whom the statues are the images?"

"I am not a scholar, massa," returned the negro, with a contrite air, "but the minister, who knows everything, often warns us not to do like the Papists, who worship idols."

"Oh, preachers!" exclaimed I, "you are everywhere the same! Nothing is easier than to know the Catholic faith; it is only necessary to open a catechism; but hatred does not wish to be enlightened; what it needs is to outrage the greatest communion on the globe. Continue this abominable work, worthy of your father, the devil. We Catholics—we, your victims—will not employ towards you this terrible retaliation of calumny. The truth suffices us. Every one knows that Luther and Calvin were two villains who, through ambition and covetousness, destroyed the human mind by intoxicating it with pride and liberty. Falsehood brought forth the Reformation; the Reformation brought forth philosophy; philosophy brought forth revolution; revolution brought forth anarchy; anarchy brought forth"——

"Massa," said Sambo, incapable of comprehending anything of my just indignation; "if the Papists are Christians, so much the better, I am very glad of it."

"Why so much the better?"

"Because Jesus Christ died for all who call upon him; he will save the Papists like the rest of the Christians."

'Sambo, my friend," said I with supreme disdain for so much simplicity, "you will never be a theologian. Go to your church; I will keep you no longer. Where are the ladies?"

"My mistress," answered he, "is at the Episcopalian Church, with all the best society of the city. Miss Susan is at the Presbyterian Church."

"With her brother, of course?"

"No, Massa, with young Mr. Rose. Massa Henry is at the Baptist Church."

"Very well," said I, drawing a sigh; "and you, Sambo, are, doubtless going to join Martha?"

"No, no, Massa," exclaimed he; "Miss Martha is a Tunkeress; I am a Methodist. We, poor negroes, whom the whites reject from their churches, are all of the same religion."

"I understand; you have a black church and a colored Christianity. Go, my friend, pray to Christ in your own way. Among these hostile sects which rend the Gospel into shreds, the Lord will recognize his own."

While Sambo departed with long strides, I walked on slowly, my head cast down. The discovery which I had just made overwhelmed me. My house, my refuge in all my troubles, was only a Babel, the den of all heresies. The husband Catholic, the wife Episcopalian, the daughter Presbyterian, the son Baptist, the maid-servant

Quakeress, the man-servant Methodist; each one having a different faith and contrary hopes! What confusion! What anarchy! It was hell in my dwelling! Yet, nevertheless, Jenny loved me passionately, the children were happy only by our side, the servants respected me, I saw around me none but happy and placid faces. Each read the Bible in his own manner, each had his particular symbol, yet no one quarrelled with another. Nowhere unity, everywhere love and concord. It was a contradiction to the ideas of my childhood, a mystery which confounded my reason.

"No," thought I, "I will not suffer this moral disorder. There is here a false peace; these flowers hide the precipice. If it continues I am lost. I mean that in my house every one shall think with me or be silent; I must have uniformity. Let me be an indifferent Christian, it matters little; I am a Catholic in soul and mind; in the Church, in the State, in the family, there should reign but a single law, but a single will. If need be, I will employ salutary rigor; I will terrify my wife, I will threaten my children, I will dismiss my servants, I will sacrifice everything to impose obedience or silence. I am a Frenchman, long live unity!"

In the midst of these sage reflections, time passed. It was striking ten when I entered Acacia Street. This was an immense avenue which, in majesty and length, scarcely yielded the palm to the rue de Rivoli, with this difference that, every hundred paces, some Grecian, Byzantine, or Gothic monument proudly raised its spire or cross to the sky. In a country where each one makes his own creed, it is natural to run against a church at every step.

To find my way in this labyrinth was not easy. I addressed a good woman who was walking by my side with prayer book in hand, and entreated her to point out to me the Congregationalist Church.

"Nothing is easier, my dear sir," answered the old lady, with an amiable smile. "It is a little way off, but with my directions you will have no difficuly in finding it. Pay no attention to the churches on the left, the Congregational Church is on the right. Count the steeples, and you cannot make a mistake. The first church," added she, with the volubility of a woman telling her beads, "the first church is St. Paul, the Catholic Chapel; the second, the Ursuline Convent; the third, the Episcopal Church; the fourth, the Capuchin Convent; the fifth belongs to the Baptists, the sixth to the Dutch Reformed, the seventh to the Lutherans, the eighth to the colored Methodists, the ninth is the Jewish Synagogue, and the tenth the Chinese temple. You see it yonder with its multiplied roof and little bells. Once there, you have only to go down the street; you will find the Mennonites; after the Mennonites, the Reformed Germans; after the Reformed Germans, the Friends or Quakers; after the Quakers, the Presbyterians; after the Presbyterians, the Moravians; after the Moravians, the white Methodists; after the white Methodists, the Unitarians; after the Unitarians, the Unionists; after the Unionists, the Tunkers. Then count four churches; that which calls itself preëminently the *Christian* Church, then the Free Church, then the Swedenborgian Church, and lastly the Universalist Church; this will give you in all twenty-three churches; the twenty-fourth, which is nearly at the middle of the street, is the Congregationalist."

Having recited this litany without stopping to take breath, the fairy made me a graceful courtesy and continued her way.

"Upon my word," thought I, "if the devil should lose his religion (I suppose that in hell one has some reason to believe in God), he would find it again in this street! In this country, the Ministry of Public Worship must be no sinecure. In France, where the State has scarcely four sects (I do not count Algeria), the administration has its moments of difficulty; but here, how does it set to work to apportion the church moneys and put an end to the quarrels among thirty churches, each pulling its own way, and which, doubtless, are jealous of and excommunicate each other Christianly? This is a problem which I do not take it upon myself to resolve. Long live Spain! There is a people faithful to tradition, and which has preserved the true principles. The country is a checker-board, where each thing has its compartment, and where the body and soul are equally and uniformly administered. Thanks to the union of the Church and State, everything is easy. One has a bishop as a prefect, a curate as a mayor; functionaries, temporal or spiritual, have their marked place in the same list, and walk in the same steps. Birth, baptism, education, communion, confession, conscription, taxation, the press, death, and burial, are all linked together. The church is the ruling power, the ruling power is the church. Deserters and journalists are excommunicated, heretics are sent to the galleys. The nation, that eternal child, is led by gentleness or force, and without its having any hand in the matter, to the end which has been chosen for it without consulting it. An admirable police, which made the happiness of Christianity before the abominable Luther unchained, at the same stroke, religious and civil liberty, a double pestilence of which the world will never more be cured! Since men have been left the care of their souls and lives, there is no longer either religion or government."

On reaching the Ursuline Convent, I entered it. To meet with the worship of my country was to draw near to the France from which a jealous fate held me aloof. The Church is another country; from this at least exile does not expel you.

The chapel was small, but richly decorated. At the end of the sanctuary, under a canopy of red cloth embroidered with gold, a marble Madonna held the infant Jesus in her arms, and gazed on him with the ineffable tenderness of a Virgin who has just given birth to the Saviour. Rare plants, new flowers, and clusters of white lilacs surrounded the altar, blazing with light. The organ rolled its harmonious waves, the incense rose in clouds, pierced by a sunbeam, while behind a grating, covered by a curtain, nuns and young girls chanted, in a soft, slow voice, *Inviolata, integra et casta es, Maria.* In an instant, and as in a dream, I again beheld my vanished youth, my long-lost friends. I fell on my knees and wept. No; a religion which reaches the heart through the senses is not idolatry: why should not our body as well as our soul serve the Lord?

Having quitted the convent, I entered the Episcopal Church, a few paces off. Here was the Catholic mass, not so well said, and not so well chanted. At sermon time, the clergyman ascended into a long gallery, carrying a thick book under his arm, which he placed before him and slowly turned over. It was a MS. collection of sermons for every Sunday and fast day in the year. When he had found the discourse which he sought, he put on his spectacles and, in a monotonous tone, commenced his reading, amidst the profound attention of the assembly. The subject which he had chosen was the eternal generation and consubstantiation of the Word—one of those mysteries which defy the human intellect, and before which the faithful can only bow their head. But nothing dismays the audacity of a theologian; with a text, a definition, and a couple of syllogisms, he will trace them back to Saint Paul, and render faith superfluous.

Judging by the silence that reigned, the audience was edified. Jenny kept her eyes fixed on the speaker, and did not lose a word. One would have said that she understood everything, to the Latin, Greek, and even Hebrew quotations with which the dissertation was crammed. I did not think that scholastics had so many charms. For my part, I left after the first head: I abhor these sterile discussions. To seek to demonstrate to me what is undemonstrable would render me sceptical. I accept mystery; it surrounds me on every side. In nature as in my soul, I feel the Infinite which overflows me; but reason tells me that I can feel it but not understand it—I, who am but an atom lost in the immensity. The hand which sustains me, and which also sustains the worlds, I do not see; I abandon myself to it, and adore it! To give himself to us, God does not bid us comprehend him, he asks us to love him.

On passing the Methodist Church, I thought of Sambo, and entered through curiosity. The assembly was numerous and greatly animated. The negresses, covered with gold and jewels, displayed the immense breadth of their crinoline. The negroes, singing in a true and plaintive voice, praised God with all the ardor of loving hearts. The minister, a negro of great stature and venerable appearance, addressed the assembly in a sermon which pleased and touched me. Where this negro had received his theological education I know not. He was a former slave, whom the goodness of God, he said, had ransomed from a servitude less harsh and shameful than that of sin. But this slave had suffered and reflected; he was a man! Life had taught him what is not taught in the schools: his energetic and familiar language went straight to the heart. It was evident from the emotions of the audience.

In the beginning, he eulogized Methodism—a religion blessed of the Lord, he said, judging by the conquests which it made daily. He enumerated at length the number of its believers, and the wealth of its churches. Four million communicants, twelve thousand ministers, sixteen thousand churches, and fifteen million dollars' worth of property—such were the fruits of a zeal that never slumbered. To Old Europe, which subjects the church to the state, and holds it in a perpetual minority, he opposed Young America, which leaves to Christians the care of their worship as of their conscience.

"Liberty," said he, "when sanctified by religion, works miracles which the Old World, buried in its prejudices, will never witness. England, so proud of its opulence, corrupts its bishops by surrounding them with pagan luxury, and degrades its vicars by condemning them to wretchedness without dignity; while in the live churches of the United States, the generous piety of the members surrounds with comfort and respect a minister who owes nothing except to his flock. A prince believes himself a new Constantine, when by chance he erects and endows a chapel; the Methodists alone of the North built four hundred and fifty churches in 1860. The poor negroes of Acacia Street treat their chaplain better than the kings of the East.

"But, continued he, with a mingling of shrewdness and naïveté, "this minister, so well paid, must pay to the negroes who have chosen him a debt which the almoners of princes do not always acquit. This debt is truth! Hear, therefore," he exclaimed, "what truth compels me to tell you. The negro has a yielding heart, and a liberal hand; this is good—it is Christian; but sometimes he carries generosity so far as to endanger his soul. 'We have never heard of such a thing,' you say. 'We are told again and again that the Christian endangers his soul when he yields to avarice, when he abandons himself to covetousness; but who has ever taught that a man loses his soul through too much generosity?' My brethren, I will tell you what this perfidious liberality is: it is what you practise in church, as you listen to the sermon.

"If I should condemn anger or coquetry, drunkenness or license, would each one of you take the lesson to himself? Would he profit by it? 'Good,' says a man who lives on brandy, 'I know this portrait of a drinker; the minister means my cousin Samuel.' Stop, drunkard, take it all to thyself. 'Good,' says a beautiful Midianite, who, to gain a new dress, urges on her husband to lie and deceive; 'the minister does right to unmask the faults of my neighbors; you are caught, Miss Deborah; you are caught, Miss Ichabod; it is all for you, coquettes, nothing for me.' Thus, brethren, out of my words you reserve nothing for yourselves. The first third you give to your neighbor; the second, to your friends; the last, to your husband or wife. This is the way that the teaching of the Lord is barren, this is the way that you lose your souls through too much generosity. Christ is generous, but in a different manner; he is a miser who takes everything to himself—our sins, our miseries, our weaknesses, our sufferings. We see him on the cross—his head cast down, and panting like a man overburdened with sorrow. When, brethren, will we take back from him our share of the burden? When will we relieve Christ, our Redeemer and friend, who died for the slave and the sinner?"

At this appeal, the assembly threw themselves on their knees, and in the midst of tears a formidable *hallelujah!* arose to the sky. The impulse was worthy of admiration; it saddened me. I am neither an aristocrat nor a planter; I believe that a negro is not an ape, because he has hands and can speak; but, after what I had just heard, I began to suspect that the black was a man like myself, and perhaps a better Christian; this thought appalled me. Sambo my brother! Jesus Christ died for these woolly heads! It was more than my pride could suffer!

"If this be true," thought I on quitting the church, "then what a crime is slavery! This civil war, which is laying waste the South—is it not the chastisement inflicted by God upon Cain?"

CHAPTER XVIII.

A CHINESE.

It was half-past eleven; Truth was to preach at twelve. I hastened my steps in order to arrive early at the Congregationalist assembly. But I could not resist the desire to visit the Chinese temple. In a country where reigns religious anarchy, the parent of all others, I was curious to see how the children of Confucius had adapted Christianity. A secret voice told me that an old worn-out people would have more sense and wisdom than the generality of Protestants.

On entering, I uttered a cry of disgust. I was in a Buddhist pagoda. Opposite me, on a platform, in a carved and twisted niche, was a horrible, grotesque figure, of painted and gilded wood, seated, its legs crossed, on a lotus flower. It was Buddha, with his enormous belly, bald head, humpy forehead, large ears, and great eyes. Indeed, I am liberal, and I pride myself upon it. For the last thirty years I have been a subscriber to the *Constitutionnel*, and I have changed no more than my journal. Like it, and without knowing why, I hate the Jesuits, which is the mark of strong minds; but to make use of liberty to enthrone idolatry —this is too much! I accept Lutheranism, Calvinism, Judaism, and even Mahometanism, provided it does not come from Algeria; but to go further is no longer liberalism, but paganism. As well return to the worship of Mithra.

There was no one in the pagoda except two children, two horrible little Chinese, placed on either side the platform. Each was turning a horizontal cylinder, stuck or rather larded with numberless bits of paper, as if roasting coffee. It was a form of worship wholly new to me.

At the sound of my footsteps a species of monk emerged from a neighboring cell. His brown, patched gown, naked feet, shaven head, little, oblique eyes, and yellow, wrinkled skin gave him the air of an old woman disguised as a Capuchin; it was a bonze. He approached me, and without speaking, held out a wooden cup; I threw an alms in it to rid myself of the mendicant.

"Thanks, brother," said he in excellent English. "May the divine Fo recompense your charity. May you never appear again in another life, under the form of a woman or a jackal!"

And leaving me astounded by this singular benediction, the bonze ascended to the altar, took from a little cupboard some bits of silvered and gilded paper, and burned them under the nose of the idol.

"What are you doing there?" I asked.

"Brother," he answered, "I have just changed your ten cent piece into ingots of gold and silver, and offered them to the Master of the Truth."

"Your ingots are paper and are not worth two farthings."

"What does that matter?" said the monk. "Fo cares for the intention, not for the metal."

"Ah, that our Ministers of the Finances were Chinese!" I was on the point of exclaiming; but I kept this rash reflection to myself, and asked the bonze what those children were doing, whose arms were indefatigable.

"They are praying for the whole world," replied he. "Upon each of these papers is inscribed the sacred syllable;" saying this, he prostrated himself, crying, "OM! OM! OM! Each of the cylinders bears a thousand of these sacred devices, and makes fifty revolutions a minute, three thousand an hour, seventy-two thousand from one sunset to another. A hundred and forty-four million prayers, therefore, arise every Sunday from this temple alone. During the week there are more; I have my cylinders turned by steam; but on Sunday, in this country of infidelity, the very machines observe the Sabbath, and I am reduced to the handiwork of these children."

The foolish credulity of this idolater inspired me with horror.

"How is it that you are suffered in a Christian land?" exclaimed I. "If there were still faith in Israel, you would have been long since exterminated, prophets of Baal."

"Why should we not be suffered?" replied the bonze in a calm voice; "liberty is like the sun, it shines for all. The Americans send missionaries to China, why should not the Chinese send missionaries to America? It is said that France has made war on the Children of Heaven for nothing but to avenge the death of a few monks legally assassinated by our mandarins; it is added that the Catholic Church, long since closed, has been reëstablished in Pekin; I execrate the shedding of blood on both sides, my religion abhors murder, and knows no other weapons than peace and gentleness; but I bless the conquered liberty, and demand that it shall profit the Chinese as well as the French."

"A pagoda in the Champs-Elysées!" replied I. "Official idols! My good man, you are mad; we have no occasion for Chinese at Paris. We have enough of them—in porcelain."

"It seems to me," continued the monk with absurd gravity, "that rights are reciprocal. If it is glorious, if it is just to open a chapel at Pekin, why would it be unjust to open a pagoda at Paris, and preach the truth freely therein?"

"Stupid bonze," exclaimed I, carried away with holy zeal, "dare you speak of the truth? Do you not feel that your doctrine is falsehood and your worship idolatry? If you see this, you are a charlatan and should be punished; if you do not see it, the first duty of the State is to shut your mouth that, in your ignorance, you may not pervert its subjects. The liberty of error is the liberty of poison, the torch, and the dagger; truth alone has a right to speak."

"I thought," said the Chinese, "that in France and England there were several Christian churches, and even Jewish synagogues."

"Doubtless, and even in France the State supports all recognized religions; for, learn, my good man, that France is at the head of civilization, in religious liberty as all other liberties."

"The State," continued the bonze, "recognizes therefore, three or four religious truths which mutually combat and destroy each other? To the Christians, for instance, Jesus is a God, what is he to the Jews?"

"My friend," said I to the barbarian, "I pity your ignorance. If you could comprehend the nature of official truth, you would see that it lives by contradictions. It is the dream of Hegel realized. Thesis and antithesis mingle and are confounded there in an admirable synthesis."

The bonze opened his little eyes and raised his head towards heaven. It was evident that the great conceptions of civilized Europe could not enter this narrow brain. I would have thought that there was less distance between a German philosopher and a Chinese. I resumed my demonstration under another form; that is, I changed the words without troubling myself about the things—the true way to carry on a discussion.

"The truth which the State protects," said I to the infidel, "has nothing in common with vulgar truth. It is a broad and comprehensive truth which embraces all the communions based on the Bible, our sacred book. Judaism, Christianity, and even Mahometanism are branches of this primitive religion, as ancient as the world, and which has on its side numbers, morals, and civilization. Outside these churches, which share the universe, there is naught but idolatry and barbarism. To convert you by cannon balls is our right and our duty. Truth germinates in the bloody furrows opened by war, the God of Christians is the God of armies, *Dominus Sabaoth!*"

"You are not a Yankee," exclaimed the fanatic, his eyes sparkling suddenly with a strange lustre. "I have been observing you ever since you came. In the face of the Saxon there is the bull and the wolf; in yours, there is the ape and the dog. You are afraid of liberty, you speak of what you know nothing, and in set phrases. You are a Frenchman."

Seeing me mute with surprise—"Dare you," said he, "make numbers the proof of truth? The numbers are on our side. How many are there of you Catholics? One hundred and thirty million. Of Christians? Three hundred million at most. There are five hundred million of us, Buddhists. Our faith extends from Kamschatka to the White Sea. It softened the savage tribes, it charmed the Chinese and Japanese; that is to say, the civilized peoples, at a time when Europe was a forest and America a desert. Do you talk of antiquity? Do you reflect that in the days of Alexander, Buddhism already held its councils, and that the inscriptions of King Acoka, engraven on the rocks of India, preached to the universe alms and sacrifice? Do you not know that Buddhism is a reform of the religion perverted by the Brahmins; and that the Vedas, the holy works of our ancestors, date back to the earliest days of the world? Leave aside numbers and duration; these are, perhaps, but happy accidents. What religion was the first to preach voluntary poverty, devotion, and charity? Are you ignorant that Fo has had five hundred and fifty existences, and that he has offered himself up as a sacrifice in each of these incarnations? He has become a sheep for the tiger, a dove for the hawk, a hare for the famished hunter. Have you not read the holy story of Vesavantara, who, through charity, delivered up his wife and children? Are we not the only communion which, through abhorrence of murder, abstains from the flesh and blood of animals. Do I not filter the water I drink in order to spare the life of some invisible flesh worm? You Christians, your religious history is nothing, they say, but a succession of quarrels, wars, and massacres. To-day the victims, to-morrow you are the executioners. Among us Buddhists, there are only martyrs. During two thousand four hundred years, our blood has more than once been spilled, we have been driven from India, but our hands are pure. We have nothing to efface from our annals, what religion can say as much?

"Your Gospel announces an admirable doctrine; I know it, and do not judge the faith of Christians by their conduct. The words and sufferings of Christ have moved me to the heart. But I have been reared in other ideas: I devoted myself twenty years ago to a life of poverty, which sustains and consoles me. Like you Christians, I have kept the faith of my fathers; like you, I can neither accuse my ancestors of falsehood nor of error. Which of us is mistaken? Which has truth on his side? I know not, and ask only to be enlightened. Let us have done with the reign of violence; let us have done with ignorance and disdain; let us give full scope to all beliefs; let us leave reason to do the work which God has confided to us. In broad daylight, all shadows disappear. Abandoned to itself, the religion which is of men will melt away like snow; that which is of heaven will rise like an oak, and cover the earth with its branches. Open the world to speech: I have faith in liberty because I have faith in truth."

"You are nothing but a Chinese," said I; and departing with a majestic step, I left the wretch confounded by my superiority.

CHAPTER XIX.

A CONGREGATIONALIST SERMON.

When I arrived at the meeting, the service was not commenced. Nothing is more dreary than a Protestant church. Oaken pews, large wainscots darkening the walls; no pictures, no flowers, no lights; a dull and gloomy air, which freezes the senses. One would call it a worship made for the blind. I am mistaken; there was an ornament—a large placard, on which was written, in enormous figures, the number 129.

The church was crowded, but it was a mute crowd. Motionless in his place, and absorbed in his black book, each believer was praying, as if alone in the world with God. No noise, no moving of chairs; nothing of that charming exchange of looks and bows among beautiful ladies, delighted to display their piety and dress; nothing of that pleasing confusion which makes our churches resemble a fashionable drawing-room—it was the silence of a forest.

At last the minister entered. Directly, from all the pews arose a harmony softer than the sigh of the wind upon the wave. Men, women, and children—each sung with his whole soul, with infinite ardor and spirit. For the first time, I felt that song was the natural form of prayer. Astonished at my silence, a neighbor pointed to the mysterious figure and offered me his psalm-book in which the music was written. They were singing the 129th Psalm, or rather a Christian imitation of that sublime prayer which the Catholic Church has adopted for the office of the dead. To call it by its name, it was the *De profundis*, a cry of hope and love, whose beauty is hidden to us through habit:

"Out of the deeps of long distress,*
The borders of despair,
I sent my cries to seek thy grace,
My groans to reach thine ear.

"Great God! should thy severer eye,
And thine impartial hand,
Mark and revenge iniquity,
No mortal flesh could stand.

"But there are pardons with my God,
For crimes of high degree;
Thy Son hath bought them with his blood,
To draw us near to thee.

"I wait for thy salvation, Lord,
With strong desires I wait;
My soul, invited by thy word,
Stands watching at thy gate.

"Just as the guards that keep the night,
Long for the morning skies,
Watch the first beams of breaking light,
And meet them with their eyes,

"So waits my soul to seek thy grace;
And more intent than they,
Meets the first openings of thy face,
And finds a brighter day.

* Watts' version of Ps. cxxix.

"Then in the Lord let Israel trust,
Let Israel seek his face;
The Lord is good as well as just
And plenteous is his grace.

"There's full redemption at his throne
For sinners long enslaved;
The great Redeemer is his Son,
And Israel shall be saved."

The song ended, Truth addressed the assembly. De Maistre was right in defining a Protestant minister—*A man in black clothes, who says plain things.* Never had a man a less sacerdotal appearance than my poor friend. With no costume to distinguish him from his flock, no high pulpit from which to overlook the assembly, he spoke, standing on the floor, with brotherly familiarity. One would have said that he sedulously refused himself the resources of rhetoric. The voice thundering, then softening its tones, the arm calling down vengeance or invoking forgiveness, the clasped hands raised towards heaven, the eye seeking God and beaming on perceiving him—all these beauties of Christian art Truth ignored. Scarcely did he move his hand, scarcely raise his voice, yet there was in this simple speech an indescribable harmony, which thrilled every fibre of the heart. Never was the veil of language, which always hides the idea, lighter and more diaphanous. It was not an orator that was heard, it was a man and Christian. To use a hackneyed phrase, Truth spoke like every one else; that is, as every one would like to speak, and as no one does. To express great thoughts familiarly belongs to great souls. Art, which is only an imitation, cannot go so far.

The following is nearly the substance of his discourse. But who can render the quivering of this voice, full of emotion? The words freeze on the paper; they are faded flowers, which have lost their color and perfume. I will endeavor, nevertheless, to give an idea of this teaching, which made a profound impression on me, although in the free manner of treating the Gospel there was a boldness and novelty which surprised and dismayed me.

JOHN, xviii., 37, 38.

"*Pilate therefore said unto him, Art thou a king, then? Jesus answered, Thou sayest that I am a king. To this end was I born, and for this cause came I into the world, that I should bear witness unto the truth. Every one that is of the truth heareth my voice. Pilate saith unto him, What is truth? And when he had said this, he went out.*"

"MY CHRISTIAN BRETHREN:

"Among the names assumed by Christ while on earth, there is none which occurs oftener than that of *Truth.* Before Pilate, in his last hours, Christ declares himself king, but of a kingdom which is not of this world, the kingdom of truth. The night before his death, in his last supper with his disciples, he leaves them, as a farewell token, this great saying—'*I am the way, and the truth, and the life; no man cometh unto the Father but by me.*'* In other words, if we would translate into our modern terms this Hebraic form of speech, *I am the living truth, which leads to God.*

"*The living truth!* Do you comprehend the meaning and scope of these words? Are there not many among you to whom truth is nothing but the relation of things to each other—an equation, a figure, an abstraction? Are there not those also to whom it is only a word devoid of sense, a synonym of the public

* I John, xiv., 6.

opinion, which changes again and again without cessation? How many wise men would willingly say with Pilate, '*What is truth?* The paradox of yesterday, the error of to-morrow? There is nothing true but the interests of the present moment.' To please Cæsar, to enjoy the present, and to give no thought to the morrow, is the highest philosophy of men who hope to die entire.

"Let us not suffer this return to pagan scepticism. It would be to condemn our mind to servitude, and our heart to every species of corruption and cowardice. As in the early ages of the Gospel, '*Ye shall know the truth, and the truth shall make you free.*'*

"When the locomotive traverses our streets, dragging after it a long train, why do you step aside at the sound of the whistle which announces its coming? Because you have been taught that the mass which is advancing will crush you with all the force of its weight multiplied by its velocity. Here is a scientific truth which is no longer an abstraction to you. It has become transformed into a strong conviction, which protects and saves your body. This conviction is now a part of yourself, it is living like you.

"In this city, which glories in its civilization, there are thousands of men who brutalize and kill themselves by means of alcohol. Why do not you, my brethren, abandon yourselves to this passion, more terrible, though not more guilty, than so many other vices which do not call forth a blush? Because you know that alcohol is a poison which knows no mercy. Science stands you instead of virtue. Here is another truth, physical and moral together, which, once entered into your soul, becomes identified with you.

"Is this all? Do you not know noble hearts, to whom debauchery, ambition, and avarice are as hideous as drunkenness? Ask the father, whose daughter has been robbed of her honor; ask the mother, whose son has perished on some distant shore;

* I John, viii., 32.

ask the man, who disputes with the usurer the life of his wife and children! These poor victims hate by experience the vice from which they have suffered. Others are happier; they owe to education all their science. The piety of a mother, the devotion of a teacher, have inspired them with the instinct which saves them. Here is again a living truth—a truth which we confess by our remorse, even when we refuse to listen to it.

"In our republic there are patriots who resist the caprices of the crowd. Is this pride? Is it calculation? No. Provided that it can rule, pride adapts itself to every species of baseness; interest finds it to its advantage to bend to the wind. But a pure soul, an enlightened mind, sees higher and further. Man or people, whoever names a despot, names a master whose passions are unchained, and who cannot escape the low appetites of those who surround and deceive him. Criminal wars, foolish expenses, corruption in high places, misery and ignorance among the masses, such are the fruits of all power without control, the scourge of all force which nothing moderates. He who knows this will never descend to the trade of flatterer. Truth stands aloof, and consoles in their solitude minds that cannot debase themselves.

"These are old maxims, you say, which are deduced everywhere. For more than twenty centuries, they have been taught in the schools; the world goes on none the better. Why? Because in the books, where it is left, truth is dead; give it your heart, espouse it, and it will live. It will become your conscience, your honor, your salvation. The mind is like the body; it draws no nourishment from words, it must have the substance of things. To fling liberty to an enslaved people is to entrust children with a weapon which will explode in their hands. Why? Because respect for one's self and others, the feeling of right, the love of justice—these essential conditions of liberty are not articles of the law, they are not decreed; they are virtues which the citizen acquires by dint of patience and practice. So long as liberty does not live in the soul, it is but *a sounding brass and a tinkling cymbal;* when once it has entered into our very essence, all the artifice and fury of tyrants will not wrest it from us.

"There are living truths, therefore, which are at once in things and in us. These put us in communion with Nature and with our fellows. By revealing to us the laws of the moral and physical world, they subject us to it; in every man that thinks like us they reveal to us a friend and brother. But this light which guides us here on earth does not warm our heart. It charms our mind, tempers our passions, enlightens and mitigates our selfishness, it does not give happiness. Man has a thirst for the infinite, an impatience of earth, a need of loving which science cannot satisfy. To procure for ourselves the good after which our soul sighs, a new truth is necessary, which shall put us in communion with God, which is in us and in him. This truth, which can be naught but God himself, it is necessary for us to know and love.

"To love God, and in return to be loved by him is what ancient wisdom was never able to comprehend; modern philosophy perishes through the same powerlessness. In vain the conscience seeks God, in vain it calls on him with the earnestness of the shipwrecked man about to sink; cold reason stands ready to repeat to us that between God and man, between the Infinite and the creature of a day, there is an abyss which nothing can cross. An inflexible nature, a Supreme Being, the slave of his own laws—this is all that the greatest efforts of the greatest minds can offer us. The love of God is an illusion; prayer, the cry of the soul, is a vain murmur dying in a mute sky. Be silent, mortal; stifle thy heart, shut thyself up in a despairing resignation; thou art only an atom, crushed by the wheel of inexorable fatality.

"Well, my brethren, nineteen centuries ago, a man came upon earth to bring *the glad tidings*, to reconcile God and humanity. This prophet called himself the Son of God and the Son of Man, or (which is perhaps but another name of the same mystery) the light and the truth. '*I am*,' said he, '*the way, the truth, and the life; no man cometh unto the Father but by me.*' The world listened, the world believed. On the day that the Word was made flesh, that the divine truth put on a body, faith, hope, and love appeared here on earth and entered the heart of man. This problem, which reason declares improbable, in which it sees nothing but contradictory data, Christ has resolved. A living truth, an incarnate truth, which God can love as a son, and which man can love as a Saviour—behold the bond of union which has united heaven and earth, which has given a father to humanity and children to God! Herein is the mystery of his revelation, herein is the proof of his divinity. Never would the mind of man have arisen of itself to this conception which confounds our intellect, and which nevertheless, illumines it with infinite splendor. Yes, if God loves men, it can be only in loving himself, in the contemplation of his eternal truth; yes, if man can render to God a worship which is not an insult, it is when he adores a ray of this highest light which does not disdain to descend even unto him.

"To love Christ is to love truth; to love truth is to love Christ. This is the great secret of the Gospel. He who does not comprehend it is a Christian only in name.

"Now, my brethren, commune with your own hearts and reflect when you love Christ, what is it that you love? Perchance, is it not the martyr who has given his life for his own? Is it not the crucified victim, whose wounds are still bleeding? Beware! this is a human love; all parties, all religions have their martyrs. Christ exacts more, Christ is something else than a worshipped corpse, whose wounds we kiss; Christ is truth; it is by this title that he demands your love. Is it thus that you love him?

"You have faith, doubtless; you believe the Gospel. But is not this a hereditary prejudice, a symbol which you dare not look in the face for fear of finding yourselves infidels. Do you reason on your belief; do you take away from it all Jewish or heathen alloy which lessens its purity? Do you make your faith the rule of your actions? Do you break with the world and yourselves? Do you say with the prophet and apostle, '*I believe, therefore have I spoken?*' If this be so, you love Christ as he wishes to be loved; you love truth.

"But if religion is to you only a form; if you seek in it only a refuge from the voice of the truth which pursues you; if your faith dies on your lips and is not translated into your actions; if, wholly devoted to your fortune or repose, you fear error less than scandal; if, in your cowardly prudence, you leave to God himself the care of defending his word; if your charity employs itself only in alleviating the miseries of the body, and does not combat ignorance and vice; if you do not feel that your first duty is to snatch immortal souls from the servitude of sin; if you have not the holy madness which braves and treads under foot the wisdom of the age; if, finally, you do not yourselves the works which Christ did here on earth, my brethren, do not delude yourselves—you are, I grant, able, prudent, wise, and feeling, you are not Christians, you do not love truth.

"'I have doubts,' you say; 'if I believed I should love Christ.' And I tell you, love him, you will then believe in him. Love him as the living truth which leads to God. These ceremonies displease you, leave them alone; these dogmas appal you, cast them aside; perhaps they are human inventions, perhaps you will understand them later. Christ has established neither dogma nor ceremony. Simplify your faith, and, in the words of the most believing and boldest of the apostles: '*Quench not the Spirit, prove all things, hold fast that which is good.*'* There are passages in the New Testament which trouble you, put them aside. What matters it if the evangelists differ among themselves, so that the Gospel is always in harmony with itself, so that the words of Christ always glow with the flame of the eternal truth?

"Is Christ an object of scandal to you? Do you not yet comprehend that it was necessary that the truth should become incarnate, that it should be living, and that you could love it,

*1 Thess. v. 19, 21.

Ah, well! Christ himself has pity on your weakness and restores to you your liberty. '*Whosoever shall speak a word against the Son of Man it shall be forgiven him; but unto him that blasphemeth against the Holy Ghost*, (or, under another name, *the Spirit of Truth*),* *it shall not be forgiven.*† Seek therefore after truth *for itself*, but seek in good faith: after a long circuit, truth will lead you back to Christ.

"'I seek the truth,' you say, 'but do not find it.' No, my brother, you do not seek it. The pride of your mind, the passions of the flesh, hold you back. Science escapes you, perhaps; but moral truth, religious truth, you know where to find. At your fireside, mute, veiled, like Alcestus escaped from the kingdom of the dead, there Truth awaits you.

"You well know that when you return, wearied of life and of yourselves, it gazes at you there from under its veil, and this gaze judges you. At night, when, in darkness and alone, you dream of the ambitions and, perhaps, crimes of the morrow, it is there, still there. Its eye follows you in the obscurity; its silence chills you. You despise men; you set yourselves up as judges over laws, but you tremble before this spectre, which you can neither corrupt nor slay.

"This guard, which keeps watch over your soul, you will never flee. The hour will come when the hand of death will weigh heavily on your forehead; when you will no longer see, but in a mist, all that you love—your money, your honors, your wife, your children. But, in the midst of despair and tears, it will still be there—that veiled figure ready to receive you and bear you away into the invisible world. Guilty or innocent, you will not escape it: it will be your remorse or your hope.

"Follow it then here on earth; follow it in the midst of your troubles and uncertainties; follow it despite your incredulity. Cling to truth and it will save you. Yes, when you have crossed the threshold of the tomb, the figure will cast aside its veil, and Christ, visible at last in all the splendor of his divine

* John, xiv. 17. † Luke, xii. 10.

smile—Christ will say to you, 'My son, know me, I am the truth.'"

The moment the sermon was ended, I left the assembly and hastened into an adjoining room. I caught Truth in my arms, panting and exhausted. I took his hand: it was burning.

"Unhappy man," said I, "you are killing yourself!"

"My friend," murmured he, laying his head on my shoulder, "let us do our duty: the rest is vanity."

CHAPTER XX.

A MINISTER'S LUNCHEON.

Amidst a crowd congratulating the new apostle, I brought Truth back to his house. He was in great need of repose, and I urged him to throw himself for a moment on the bed. Unfortunately he was forced to remain standing, and to expose his health still further. Mrs. Truth had prepared a formidable luncheon for her husband's friends, and she had the kindness to number me among the guests.

Jenny and Susan were there, delighted with the sermon which they had heard, and, perhaps, had not understood. The empire which speech exerts over women is something incredible. More than once, when in my chamber, alone and with double-bolted doors, I have asked myself in a whisper whether woman is not naturally superior to man. She has less violent passions, and a greater aptness for education. While Adam slumbered in his innocence, Eve was curious for knowledge. It seems to me that since then, if we have inherited the good-natured simplicity of our first father, the daughters of Eve have not degenerated from their ancestress. I believe with Molière that it is prudent not to instruct too much this malicious and restless sex. By holding woman in honest ignorance, we give her all the vices, but also all the weaknesses of the slave; our reign is secured. But should we elevate these ardent and ingenious souls—should we inflame them with the love of truth, who knows whether they would not ere long blush at the folly and brutality of their masters? Let us keep knowledge for ourselves alone; this it is which renders us divine:

> "Our empire is destroyed, if man be recognized."

We sat down to table. I confess that I was not sorry. In my religious ardor I had forgotten to breakfast, and the wolf began already to gnaw at my stomach. The mistress of the house did me the honor to seat me at her left hand, and served me, with the tea, two or three slices of Cincinnati ham, which I had great difficulty to devour decently. Susan stared at me, to reproach me for my voracity. This seemed quite natural in my daughter. In the United States, as in France, in every well managed household, the children give lessons to their parents.

When my terrible hunger was somewhat appeased, I entered into conversation with my neighbor, a good and amiable person, who adored her husband. It is the custom in America. The health of Truth gave me fears; it was certain to me that the pulpit would wear him out still faster than the newspaper, and I endeavored adroitly to insinuate this to his wife. Not to render her uneasy, I said to her, in a general way, that speaking was a hard profession, and that, to certain nervous and delicate temperaments, absolute repose was sometimes necessary. Lost labor! Mrs. Truth talked to me of nothing but the greatness of her new condition. She was intoxicated with pride.

"To be a minister's wife," said she, "is the dream of every young girl. If you knew what sorrow I felt when my dear Joel renounced his first calling to become an editor! The ministry alone crowns the wishes of a woman; in this only she becomes, in the full force of the term, the companion of her husband, his veritable half, with the same pains, the same pleasures, and the same duties."

"Perhaps you preach?" I asked.

"Not in the church," she replied; "the Apostle Paul forbids it. But is it only in the church that the ministry is exercised, and the word of God proclaimed? To instruct young girls, to counsel young wives, to visit women in child-bed, to weep with widows, to watch with the sick, to read the Gospel to them, and, if need be, to smooth their dying pillow—these are works in which I can aid my husband, and sometimes even take his place. Joel," added she, raising her voice, "is it not true that I am your vicar, and that you have confidence in me?"

To this singular speech, which, strange to say, surprised no one but me, Truth replied by a wave of his hand and gentle smile. The wife of the pastor, a pastor herself and assistant minister! Such an absurdity had never crossed my mind. It is true, that I had always lived in a reasonable country. The ball, and the pot on the fire—these are to a Frenchwoman the two poles of existence. To depart from them is contrary to rule, and, which is still worse, ridiculous.

"Nevertheless," continued Mrs. Truth, "there is something still more glorious than the ministry—the mission."

"Have you female missionaries?" I exclaimed, terrified.

"No," she replied, "the Catholics alone have this privilege, which I envy them. We have no Sisters of

Charity; we have simply wives of missionaries. It is a character which I regret. To partake the labors of one's husband is sweet; to partake his dangers is great in the sight of God. Do not be astonished at my ambition. I am a minister's daughter, and my two sisters have married missionaries. One is at the Cape, and the other in China; both bless the Lord, who has given them a glorious lot."

"Your married missionaries," said I, "have not so hard a life. To carry with them their wives, children, and firesides, is scarcely to change their country. Join to this a commodious and fixed installation, accompanied with a good salary, and in such conditions it does not need a very great virtue to preach the Gospel."

"Do you think so?" returned my neighbor, astonished at my irony. "I know not whether it is better to journey over the world, scattering on the way the Word of Christ and remitting the germ to the grace of God, or to shut one's self up in a narrow field, to plant, water, and cultivate this precious seed to the harvest; but I do know that the happiness of having those he loves near him takes away nothing from the charity of the missionary, and adds perhaps another merit to his devotion. Peter was married; was he therefore the less chosen as the prince of the apostles? At the Cape, where my sister has established a school and work-room for the young negresses, and makes use of civilization to prepare souls to receive the Gospel, the Boors have burned down the mission three times; my brother-in-law, who is a physician, like the greater part of our missionaries, has lost his hand in extracting a poisoned arrow from a poor Caffre. In China, the Tai-Pings have driven my sister from province to province. She is now near Shanghai, ruined and sick, but always full of faith. Her house is a hospital for the wounded, an asylum for the widows and orphans. In the midst of fever and in perpetual anxiety, she aids her husband to preach the Gospel. More deeply tried than Abraham, God has already twice demanded again from her the life of her children. Happy is she, notwithstanding, to have been chosen for such a sacrifice, and to serve the Lord, even at the price of the purest of her blood."

I answered nothing. In the history of Abraham, there are things which move me more than the episode of Isaac. Virtue or fanaticism, such obedience is beyond my strength; I do not comprehend it.

To put away reflections which troubled me, I turned to my neighbor on the left. He was of the true Saxon type—broad shoulders, full chest, a long neck surmounted by a long head, rugged features, a bald forehead, with shaggy eyebrows, under which glittered blazing eyes—strength and will united. Noah Brown—so my new friend was called—was the pastor to whom Truth succeeded. I seized this occasion to instruct myself, and asked the nature of this Congregationalist church, the name of which perplexed me.

"What!" said Brown, surprised at my ignorance, "do you not know that it is our old Puritan church—that which our Pilgrim Fathers, exiled by intolerance, brought with them in their first ship, the Mayflower? In breaking with the abominations and idolatries of the Anglican Babylon, our ancestors wished to root out the heresy of hierarchy. After the example of the early Christians, they made of each gathering of believers a church, or independent congregation, a perfect republic, governed by the elders and administered by the pastor. From this nucleus of independence and equality arose our parish. Herein is the secret of our political life and greatness. America is only a confederation of sovereign churches and parishes; it is the blossoming-out of Puritanism. Here, as everywhere, religion has made the man and the citizen in its image; a free church has given birth to a free society."

This paradox, delivered with all the Puritan arrogance, shocked me. To believe these fanatics, their catechism rules the world. Let them look at France, that country of enlightenment and philosophy; they will soon know to what is reduced the influence of religion on the State and society. One is very Catholic at church, and whatever he likes elsewhere. This I attempted to demonstrate to my preacher, but he was as obstinate as a Saxon lined with a Yankee. The more I heaped up proofs which ought to have overwhelmed him, the more he struggled.

"See the English," exclaimed he. "Whoever knows their church knows their history. Spiritual lords, assemblies, rulers of the faith, an immutable charter in thirty-nine articles, a prayer-book established by the authority of the bishops and sovereign, privileged schools and universities, enormous estates, an important patronage—what can all these produce if not an aristocratic society? Had it not been for the dissenters, who are the salt of the earth, England would have long since been fossilized like ancient Egypt."

"And the French?" asked I, to embarrass him.

"The Frenchman," replied he, "is a Catholic, monarchist, and soldier, while the American is a Protestant, republican, and citizen. All these are linked together like the fingers of the hand. It would be as impossible to make France a republic as it would be to make the United States a monarchy. The difference of the churches creates the difference of the societies."

'May I know to which of these societies you attribute the superiority?"

"Judge for yourself," he answered. "The one is a society of children, the other a society of men."

"I see with pleasure that we are of the same opinion."

"I am delighted to hear it," returned he; and he tranquilly began to sip his cup of tea.

"It is certain," added I, leaning towards him, "that the Americans are less a people than a swarm of emigrants scattered in the desert. At the present moment, perhaps, liberty has few inconveniences; but in proportion as America grows older it will feel the necessity of forming a veritable society, and will rally under the flag of authority."

"Sir," said he, abruptly setting down his cup on the table, "you do not understand me. I think just the opposite of what you say."

"What!" I exclaimed, "do you perchance take the French for a people of children?"

"In politics," said he, "there is no doubt of it. From what epoch do they date their liberty? and what liberty? From 1789. Ours dates from 1620; we are therefore their elders by one hundred and seventy years. We have three times their experience and twenty times their wisdom."

"Then," returned I, in a trembling voice, "it is to America that you decree the palm of civilization?"

"Let us avoid confusion of terms," replied he, coldly. "Civilization is a complex word. It comprises so many different elements, that every people, in its turn, might pretend to the first rank. What is it that constitutes civilization? Is it religion, politics, manners, industry, science, literature, art? Is it a single one of these things? Is it all these things combined? See how complicated is the problem. Art, for instance, which the Gentiles call the flower of civilization, blossoms too often only on a decayed stalk. Among us moderns, who live in imitation of the ancients, I willingly grant that the oldest people is the most artistic. In France the taste is more refined than in England; but an Italian has naturally more ingenuity than a Frenchman. In industry, all free nations are equal. Science has no country. As to literature, each people recognizes in its own the expression of its thought. I leave to critics the puerile pleasure of assigning ranks to Dante, Molière, or Shakspeare; but religion, politics, and manners form an inseparable fasces. Therein is the pith of a country, therein is its future. In this point, I boldly give the first place to my church and my people. I believe in liberty: I am an American and a Puritan."

"Mohican," thought I, "one perceives beside. You do not even know how to prevaricate to be polite."

I was about to confound this insupportable preacher when, happily for him, we rose from the table, Leaving this narrow and uncivilized mind, I approached a young minister, whose engaging manner pleased me. Truth had introduced Mr. Naaman Walford to me as one of the pillars of the new Zion. Desirous of seeing that phœnix styled a reasonable theologian, I wished to make myself welcome to Mr. Naaman, and commenced, therefore, by congratulating him on the admirable acquisition which his church had made in the person of my friend, Truth.

"Pardon me," said he, "I am a Persbyterian."

"A Presbyterian!" I exclaimed, "and you come to compliment a rival? This is noble-minded; for, between ourselves, this man, this minister whose hand you take, is a heretic whom you damn."

"I," said he, greatly surprised, "I damn no one, it is unchristian."

"I explain myself badly, my dear Mr. Naaman; I simply meant to say that, after the example of the divine shepherd who gathered up the strayed sheep of Israel, you do not fear to live familiarly with men whose errors you detest."

"Mr. Truth has edified me this morning," replied he, "and I do not believe him in error."

It was my turn to be astonished; I feared that I had misunderstood him.

"Sir," said I to the young minister, "do you believe that your Church teaches the truth?"

"Doubtless, otherwise I should not remain in it."

"Then," rejoined I, "there are two truths as there are two Churches; a Presbyterian truth and a Congregationalist truth? Perhaps there is also a Baptist, a Methodist, a Lutheran, and even a Catholic truth. I supposed, excuse my ignorance, that truth was a unit, and that the mark of error was that it could be divided to infinity."

"Doctor," said Naaman, somewhat moved by my French vivacity, "when you are at sea, and wish to know the time, what do you do?"

"I consult the sun and it gives it to me. Do you pretend to answer me by an apologue? At my age, my dear sir, one has little taste for examples, he accepts nothing but reasons."

"I am young, doctor, and venture to count on your indulgence," answered Naaman, with an amiable smile. "The sun gives you the time. When it is noon at Paris, can you tell me what time it is at Berlin?"

"No; all that I know is that a telegram sent from Berlin at eleven o'clock is received at Paris about half past ten; that is, it apparently arrives thirty minutes before it is sent. Besides, it matters not; I grant to you that when it is noon at Paris, it is one o'clock at Berlin, two at St. Petersburgh, and if you like, nine in the morning at the Azores, and seven at Quebec. All depends on the meridian."

"Thus," said Naaman, "there is everywhere the same sun, and nowhere the same time; how does this happen?"

"Really," returned I, "you are an astrologer, and wish to make me an adept. I answer you, Mr. Professor, that it is the same sun, seen from different points."

"One more question, doctor, and I will ask your pardon for my indiscretion. Among all these times, which is the true one?"

"A strange question! the time is true to each one, since to each one the sun rises or appears to rise at a different point. Is the professor satisfied with his grey-bearded pupil?"

"Yes, doctor, I see that we agree in theology as in astronomy."

"Mr. Naaman," said I, "I begin to comprehend you. The truth to you is the sun, which each of us sees according to the horizon which surrounds him. It is noon, doubtless, in the Presbyterian Church, while the hour has passed to the Baptists, and has not yet come to the Methodists. Who knows indeed if the Catholics are not placed at the antipodes? It is an ingenious method of reconciling one's pride and charity."

"Sir," said Naaman, blushing, "you wrong me. You have seized my thought; you misconstrue my words. Yes, to every Church, I dare say to every Christian, there is a different horizon. Birth and education give us the starting point; it is for us now to proceed towards the truth which calls us, for us to draw nearer to it without ceasing by dint of study and virtue. That there may be Churches better illumined by the divine light I feel, but I no more doubt that in the most obscure Church may be found the best Christian. It is a great advantage to be placed near the sun, it is not always a reason for seeing it the most clearly. This, sir, is why I love my Presbyterian Church, and why, notwithstanding, I damn no one."

All this was said with charming ingenuousness. What a beautiful thing is virtue in a youthful soul; it is the smile of the dawn in the opening days of May!

"My young friend," said I to Naaman, "your illusions have something seductive; the sentiment from which they are born is worthy of respect, but the first breath of reason dissipates them. If every Christian sees the truth in his own manner, there is no truth. Behold us returned to the scepticism of Montaigne! You will not find a dogma that is not attacked, not a belief that is not shaken. Your theory, however Christian in appearance, condemns us to unconquerable doubt; it ends in universal incredulity."

"Doctor," replied the young man, with an air of modesty which touched me, "it seems to me that you arraign the human mind; that is, the work of God.

From the diversity and weakness of our eyes, it might also be concluded that we see nothing. It would be the same logic, and the same sophistry. In natural studies, each of us takes only the part which he can appropriate to himself; do we see that this diversity of opinion destroys science? In physics, is there a single theory which escapes discussion? Will you deny, notwithstanding, that a physical exists?"

"The comparison is a bad one, my dear Naaman. Of the physics of thirty years ago, what now remains? The truth of yesterday has become the error of to-day."

"No, doctor; the error has fallen like dead leaves; the truth has not changed; for it is, under another name, only the knowledge of nature, and nature knows no change."

"I concede you this, young man; but religious truth is of a different order from natural truth."

"Doctor," returned Naaman, "even though I should grant you this contestable hypothesis, we should be no further advanced. Whatever may be the number and variety of the bodies which fill the world, we have only our eyes to see them; what we do not see does not exist to us. Whatever may be the character of a truth, we have only our mind to comprehend it. Is our soul double? To discover natural truths, God has given to each one of us an inquiring, restless, laborious faculty, called reason. Is there in us another power which, without individual effort, receives religious truths in the same manner that a mirror reflects the object presented it? If this faculty does not exist, diversity of religious opinions is unavoidable; it belongs to the age, to education, to the country, to the natural energy of our mind, or to its activity. If, on the contrary, this faculty exists, we ought all to think alike, as we all breathe alike, by a law of nature. We are not in this condition, I bless God. He has left to each one of us the liberty to mistake him, in order to give to each one of us the right to love him. This liberty, which appals you, is our fairest appanage; this it is which makes of religion a love, and of faith a virtue."

"Naaman," exclaimed I, "you are the prophet of anarchy! You dissipate the most beautiful dream of humanity. *One faith, one law, one king*, was the device of the Middle Ages—a device which every man wears in the depths of his heart. What do you offer us in exchange? Confusion. What is a church in which each one speaks a different language, and does not understand that of his neighbor?"

"Sir," returned the young man, "I love unity as much as you. Christ has told us that the day will come when there will be no longer but *a single flock and a single shepherd;* I believe the words of Christ. But unity is not uniformity. Contemplate nature; what an admirable whole! Yet there is not a tree, a plant, a flower—what do I say?—not a leaf that is like another. From infinite variety God draws living and perfect unity. Why should not the law of nature be also that of humanity? Why should not the voice of each created being have its place in the concert of praise which the earth offers to the Lord? By the side of this fruitful harmony, what is the sterile monotony of a single note? My unity is the universal church—that church which embraces all faithful souls. Whoever loves Christ is my brother; I look at his love, and not at its symbol. Augustine, Chrysostom, Gerson, Melancthon, Jeremy Taylor, Bunyan, Fénelon, Law, Channing—all are soldiers of this holy army. What matters to me their regiment? Their banner is mine; it is that of truth."

"Bravo, Naaman!" said Truth, resting his hand on the shoulder of the young minister. "Convert this heathen for me."

"Heathen, yourself," exclaimed I. "I believe that I am the only Christian here, or, if you like better, Catholic, in the true sense of the word. While you tear religion in pieces and abandon it to every caprice, I alone, faithful to ancient and solid prejudices, wish a single symbol, which shall be the law of minds; and to maintain this law of truth, I summon to my assistance the secular arm."

"Just as I told you, my dear Naaman," returned Truth, laughing. "He is a heathen of the Decline, one of those worshippers of force, who imagine that we can decree truth as we scribble laws."

"I am not so absurd," replied I, a little touched. "I, too, love truth; but I am not blind, like Utopists. To them, liberty is a universal panacea which everywhere cures evil and error; experience has rendered me less confiding. The world is not an academy of philosophers, peacefully discussing the rashest theories; the people, that many-headed hydra, is an assemblage of feeble, ignorant, perverse, foolish, and criminal beings; to contain and direct them, we must have a curb; this curb is religion, imposed and maintained by external authority. If the ruling power does not take in hand the cause of the church, Christianity is at an end, society is delivered up to atheism, anarchy, and revolution. This is why, gentlemen, I believe in the necessity—what do I say?—the sanctity of force, placed in the service of truth. Am I, then, a heathen, when, after the example of St. Augustine, Bossuet, and so many other excellent Christians, to say nothing of your Calvin, I demand that society shall lend its sword to the church—in other terms, that the state shall have a religion?"

"A religion of state?" said Brown, suddenly stretching out his bull-dog head; "What kind of a monster is that? Has the state a soul, that it must have a religion?"

"Sir," replied I, drily, "you doubtless insist on an impious state and atheistic laws."

"Sir," returned my testy preacher, "I do not bandy words. What is a state? In a monarchy, it is the prince. Thirty million Christians will therefore have the religion of Achab, when by chance Achab has a religion. Among us, where the power alternates, the faith will change every four years. This is what I call atheism of the first water. To believe by order, is to believe nothing."

"When I speak of the state," interrupted I, "I mean the political society."

"Well," resumed he, "the majority will decide on the symbol and faith, after discussion and amendments. We shall have a parliamentary religion. The Incarnation or the Trinity will be put to vote and voted. What a farce! Strange to say! since the world existed, there is not a natural truth that has not been discovered by a single man. Long trials, sometimes even the martyrdom of the inventor, have been needed for this truth to collect a few believers: a century has not been too much for it to win the majority. But in religion it is a different thing: the majority is never mistaken. Pleasant infallibility! Restore us the Pope. I accept a miracle; I reject an absurdity."

"Mr. Brown," said I, raising my voice, "you do not answer my objection. If the state has no religion, the law will be Atheistic."

"Still words, sir," returned the intractable preacher. "The state is an abstraction. It is a fashion of designating the sum total of the public powers. But society is a living thing; it is the reunion of all the citizens inhabiting the same country. If these men are Christians, if their code of morals is Christian, how will the sanction which such men will give to public morals; in other words, how will the law be Atheistic? A good tree cannot bring forth evil fruit."

"Imprudent man!" exclaimed I, "how can you imagine that, if the state permits every species of belief, the Gospel will not suffer it?"

"You have little faith, sir," said Brown, darting on me a terrible glance. "You forget that Paul has said, *We do not fight with carnal weapons.* Christianity has never been more glorious or stronger than in having the whole world against it. Look around you, sir; you see that nowhere is religion more blended with life than in America, yet, notwithstanding, the state does not recognize it. Do not imprison souls, do not keep them in darkness which corrupts them: leave them free, and they will go to God."

"But, lastly, my dear Mr. Brown; it is impossible for the state to support all communions, and make itself the treasury of the first fanatic who may open a church."

"I wish it to support none," cried the savage Puritan. "By what right would it interfere? Has it any other money than ours? What! shall the Jew support the Christians for them to call him a deicide? Shall I support the Unitarians, who dispute to me the divinity of Christ? What injustice! what an outrage on my faith! See, moreover, what a rôle you give the state. When the legislator declares that religion is not under his jurisdiction, he proclaims respect for conscience; he is a Christian by his very abstention. Suppose now that he protects ten different communions, ten inimical beliefs, what will this insolent tutelage signify, if not that the state sees in religion a political instrument, and has for all religions only equal indifference and like contempt? This fine system, which you have not invented, sir, is the police of Paganism."

"Very well," returned I, "leave to each believer the support of his worship; you will see how many churches you will have. Men will turn Atheists through economy."

"You are mistaken, my dear doctor," said Truth, in a friendly tone. "The thing has been proved and decided against you. We have forty-eight thousand churches, all built by private individuals, the value of which is estimated at more than a hundred million dollars. We erect twelve hundred new churches a year. The average salary of our pastors is about five hundred dollars, which makes a total expenditure for public worship of twenty-four million dollars. Look at the countries where the worship is supported by the state. I am sure that you will not find one which expends half as much.* The reason is simple: it is the duty of the state to be sparing of the money which it takes from the community, while

* In France, the expenditure for religious worship for 1862 is fixed at 49,869,936 francs, yet our population is one-fourth greater than that of the United States.

the individual takes delight in enriching his church, and does not recoil from any sacrifices. Nothing is so lavish as faith and liberty."

"Very well," said I; "but the question of money is not everything. The political question remains. To give to the first comer the right to establish a church is to recognize all associations, to open a full scope to religious ambition and fanaticism; that is, to what is most ardent and perfidious in the world. Suppose that one of these churches gains the ascendancy, that it takes possession of souls; here is a state within a state. You will then feel, but too late, the mistake which you have made in abdicating a protection more necessary to the government than to the church—a protection which at the bottom is only the safeguard of the sovereign power.

"This is what I expected from you!" cried the Puritan, rushing again into the combat in the fashion of a wild boar. "I know you, Messrs. politicians; Spinoza, the prince of Atheists, and Hobbes, the materialist, and Hume, the sceptic, long since betrayed to me your secret. It is to rid yourselves of religion that you must have an official church. Political influence is not what troubles you, it is of no account in a free country. What you dread is moral influence. Christianity is by its nature restless, aggressive, and conquering. It must have the man entire—society, government, it wishes to invade all, and to penetrate all with its spirit. This is what animates us and terrifies you. Bishops slumbering in their seignorial purple; poor vicars, whose zeal is moderated and directed; a religion, a species of hackneyed and sterile morality, which preaches obedience to the people, speaking always of their duties, and never of their rights;

such is the ideal which charms you and inspires us with horror. You reject liberty for the very reason which makes us desire it. We believe in the Gospel, you are afraid of it."

"I am afraid of associations," said I, "not of the Gospel."

"Yes, because association is the only possible form of liberty. You must have a State whose omnipotence nothing disturbs, and which has naught opposed to it but isolated individuals and mute consciences. This is Roman despotism in all its deformity. We Christians, between the State and the individual, between force and selfishness, place association; that is, love and charity, the true bond of hearts, the true cement of societies. To spread the Bible, to propagate the divine word, to enlighten souls, to succor the wretched, to console the suffering, to raise up the fallen, we need hundreds of associations and thousands of reunions. We wish a Christian people to do good by the free coöperation of all its members, and to remit to no one a duty which it alone can fulfill. But all these companies can exist but on one condition; namely, that the Church, the first and most important of all, shall be absolute ruler in its sphere. It is the Church which, through its liberty, shelters and guaranties all associations; it is through this that religion, far from being dangerous to the State, is the very life of society. This, sir, this is why we need religious liberty; we need it because Christ has given it to us, we need it because it is the parent of all liberties. He who does not know this is neither a Christian nor a citizen."

In reply to this fanatic I was about to silence him, when a little hand took mine; I recognized Susan, and smiled.

"Dear papa," whispered she, "it is almost ten o'clock; we must go."

"Yes, it is time to go to the forest. Is the carriage here?"

"Papa, it is the Lord's day, when we do not ride in carriages. It is to the Sunday School that I wish to take you."

"You are right," thought I. "A Parisian astray in this glorious country of liberty, stands in great need of going to school. He must learn everything, and forget everything."

Once in the street, far from this theological atmosphere, I breathed freely.

"Ouf!" said I, yawning, "how heavy these people are! They are like oxen yoked in the riding-school, and going round constantly in the same ring. An hour of religion and politics!—it is too much for a Frenchman, it is enough to disgust him with the Gospel and liberty. Who will talk to me of something reasonable and amusing; of painting, the opera, music, or war? Paris, Paris, I need thy ambrosia to wash myself clean!"

I know not what folly I was about to say to Susan, when I perceived the handsome Naaman walking near us with the step of a shepherd following his sheep. I had forgotten that I was in America, and that my daughter was for the moment a Presbyterian!

CHAPTER XXI.

THE SUNDAY SCHOOL.

Who can tell me whence comes the weakness of a father for his daughter? Is it the illusion that he recognizes himself in her as the mother fancies that she recognizes herself in her son? To us, grey-beards, visages wrinkled by life, is it the pleasure of seeing ourselves born anew under a graceful and smiling form? Is it the charm of a pure love which asks only to sacrifice itself? I know not; but the inevitable Alfred was not there, and I jealously relished the happiness of talking and laughing with Susan. I was mirroring myself in her limpid eyes, when suddenly a red hand, with a long arm for its handle, seized me in passing, while a sepulchral voice cried: "*This night thy soul will be required of thee.*" At the same moment, a paper was thrust into the pocket of my coat. I turned round, another hand seized me, another voice cried: "*Think on thy salvation,*" and a paper was thrust into my other pocket. At the sound, three black men rushed forward, raising their hands as in the oath of the Horatii, and each of them, howling anew, plunged into my breast, not a sword, but a little book. Then the vision disappeared.

"What does this mean?" asked I of Susan, who was laughing at my fright.

"Papa," said she, "it is the Religious Tract Society, which is laboring for your conversion."

"Many thanks!" I exclaimed, putting in my pocket *the Mark of the Beast*, *the Rose of Sharon*, and *the Trumpet of Jericho;* "here you are enriched, as elsewhere you are robbed. What am I expected to do with these treasures of edification?"

"Be easy, papa," returned Susan, "in a moment they will serve to make others happy."

"Acknowledge," said I to Naaman, "that you abuse type. To distribute the Bible may pass, since it is your hobby, but of what use can this puerile theology be which you scatter in the streets?"

"You are too severe," replied the young minister; "reflect that all our religion is in the Bible. It is from the Scriptures that each one of us is to draw the rule of his faith and life by the free effort of his reason. A Protestant that does not read is a Christian that does not practise. What is more simple than a proselytism which brings us back unceasingly to the Bible? To awaken the conscience, to force the vilest of men to read and reflect, to repeat to him that he alone is charged with the care of his salvation—such is the object of all these publications. *Think of thy soul, thou only art responsible for it*, is the uniform conclusion of these little books. If you call this theology, all our literature is theological; the most insignificant novel is imbued with the same spirit. The Bible recurs in it on every page. What charms us, is not the picture of the storms which devastate the heart and crush the will, but that of a young soul which, placed between temptation and duty, repulses Satan and calls on God. Our very fictions are treatises on education."

"Yes," said I, smiling, "it is morality in action."

"It is better than that," returned he; "it is religion

in action; it is faith entered into the soul, and inspiring the whole life. We comprehend nothing of this false distinction between morality and religion. There are not two consciences. The natural man expired with the last Pagan: we know now only the Christian. Whoever is a Christian, is a Christian everywhere; at church, in the family, in the district, in the state."

I think that the pious Naaman was seizing with pleasure this occasion to preach anew some old sermon, when, happily, we arrived at the Presbyterian meeting-house. It was the sixth church that I had visited during the day—a too-just expiation of my past lukewarmness.

We entered the lecture-room—an immense apartment adjoining the church. Upon circular benches were seated a thousand children and youth, divided into groups. At regular intervals were seen standing the shepherds and shepherdesses of this graceful flock; or, as they were styled, *monitors*. At the sight of Naaman, the whole assembly rose; the organ played a warlike march; then all the young voices sang in chorus, with a flourishing accompaniment:

"The children are gath'ring from near and from far,
The trumpet is sounding the call for the war,
The conflict is raging, 'twill be fearful and long,
We'll gird on our armor and be marching along.
    Marching along, we are marching along,
    Gird on the armor and be marching along,
    The conflict is raging, 'twill be fearful and long,
    Then gird on the armor and be marching along.

"The foe is before us in battle array,
But let us not waver nor turn from the way,
The Lord is our strength, be this ever our song,
With courage and strength we are marching along." [*Chorus*

Is there a secret charm in the voice of childhood? In rendering us disinterested with respect to ourselves, do years render us more tender towards these young souls who are entering life without knowing its dangers? I know not; but I was moved by the song of these little soldiers, who enrolled themselves so valiantly under the banner of the Gospel.

"In twenty years," thought I, "how many will be left around this flag? No matter; a youth which has courage and faith is a glorious spectacle. God preserve us from those old men of eighteen who believe in nothing but their selfishness; gangrened souls which infect all that they touch, and leave after them only corruption and death."

Susan stood near me. My daughter was a monitor. She had much to do, for she had a double class, and the school was in revolution.

"Where is Dinah?" cried a mutinous voice. "Dinah is my little teacher; I do not know you."

Susan took the little rebel in her arms, who struggled, in tears, and whispered in her ear. Directly the smile returned, like sunshine after a shower.

"Do you promise?" murmured she.

"To-morrow," replied Susan. The child threw her arms about the neck of her young teacher, and kissed her on both cheeks. Peace made, the lesson began.

It turned on the history of Israel in the time of the Kings. For the first time, I confess to my shame, I became intimately acquainted with the prophet Elisha. He was a worthy man, when he was not in a passion. Despite the beauty of the moral, I was a little displeased with him for causing forty-four little children to be eaten by bears for mocking at his bald head. At such a price, I would not be a prophet, even in my own country.

Two episodes had the greatest success with the children; these naïve souls have so lively a sentiment of good and evil. These were: first, the story of Naaman, the general of the King of Syria, imploring Elisha to be delivered from his leprosy. Naaman returned healed and converted, but converted with politic reservations, which prove once more that there is nothing new under the sun.

> "And Naaman said, . . . thy servant will henceforth offer neither burnt offering nor sacrifice unto other gods, but unto the Lord.
>
> "In this thing, the Lord pardon thy servant, that when my master goeth into the house of Rimmon to worship there, and he leaneth on my hand, and I bow myself in the house of Rimmon: when I bow myself in the house of Rimmon, the Lord pardon thy servant in this thing.
>
> "And he said unto him, Go in peace."

The tolerance of the prophet, I must say, scandalized the children. Naaman was hooted unanimously, as a coward who compounded between his conscience and his interest. Bravo! youth, keep this holy anger. A day will come when Rimmon, Mammon or Baal will extend to you a hand full of silver or honors on condition that you fall down and worship him; happy he who does not bow before the idol, but keeps for God alone the sacrifice of his heart!

Next came the story of Gehazi, the servant of Elisha; a shrewd knave who took pay for the miracles of his master and trafficked in the virtue of others. What fury in the young audience, and what joy when Susan, swelling her voice in imitation of the prophet, uttered the terrible anathema:

> "Is it a time to receive money, and to receive garments, and oliveyards and vineyards, and sheep and oxen, and men servants and maid servants?
>
> "The leprosy, therefore, of Naaman shall cleave unto thee, and unto thy seed for ever. And he went out from his presence a leper as white as snow."

It still exists—this honest posterity of Gehazi, although a little changed by time. Outside it remains as white as snow, but the leprosy has struck in; it no longer gnaws upon the body, but the soul.

This education given to children by youth charmed me; I congratulated the minister upon it.

"But," added I, "I suppose that you reserve the Catechism to yourselves. The doctrine runs a risk of being changed in passing through the mouth of these novices."

"No," said he, "the doctrine, like all the rest, we entrust to the monitors—under our surveillance, of course. At eighteen, one is not heretical; if there is anything to fear, it is too much attachment to the letter."

"Yes; but if these young brains become perplexed?"

"Well," said the pastor, "we are here to open to them the way. Our motto is that of Paul: '*Where the Spirit of the Lord is, there is liberty.*' We have no taste for the faith of the boor—that credulous ignorance which would sanctify alike a Christian, a Mohammedan or a Buddhist. There is in youth a crisis of the mind as of the body. The hour comes when it is necessary to struggle with the truth, like Jacob with the angel; he alone is *convinced* who has been *conquered* by the Gospel. We wish a faith reasoned upon."

"And reasoning," added I; "for each of these monitors must go out from here with the taste and mania for preaching."

"So much the better," said Naaman; "to us, every man is a priest, every woman a priestess. Why should there be less ardor and faith in religious than in political society? Is the title of Christian less glorious and does it impose less duties than that of citizen?"

I was silent; this fashion of considering religion as the common patrimony of believers contradicted all my ideas. I had been taught that the Church was a monarchy, not a republic. Like a wise man, I had always left the care of my conscience and faith to the church which had reared me. It was not I, but my director, who was charged with the care of my salvation. Why then assume a useless fatigue, and take upon myself a dangerous responsibility?

The lesson ended, Susan rid me of all my little books, to the great joy of the children A beautiful farewell song was sung, and the festival ended by a distribution of gifts and shakes of the hand. Rank, fortune, age, dress—for two hours all had been forgotten. One felt as if again in the early ages of Christianity, when the host of believers had but a single heart and soul. And to say that one day in seven, the Lord's day, all the American youth come into these fraternal gatherings to give or receive a lesson of love and equality! In moral effect, what teaching, were it that of a Bossuet, would be worth this mutual education?

We departed. Alfred was at hand to take Susan's arm from me. I did not envy his happiness; my ideas took another course: more than ever I felt in my heart a paternal weakness. I said to myself that it was time for Susan to exercise her great capacities as monitor in a household. I saw already in the future a whole army of grand-children, more religious, more energetic, and happier than their grandfather. And, gazing at my lovers, who walked before me with a light step, I reached home still dreaming.

The rest of the day was passed in talking over all that had been seen and heard in the morning; and God knows how many things are seen and heard on Sunday in America! What are our plays by the side of these festivals of the heart and mind? Never had I passed a more serious day, never had the time appeared to me at once more rapid and better filled.

The evening ended, as usual, with the reading of the Bible. Martha brought me the great black book. It was already a friend to me. Every day I found in it an answer to some secret demand of my soul—a strange chance, which confounded my philosophy.

We left off at the seventh chapter of Daniel. The vision of the four apocalyptic beasts, which were typical of the four great monarchies of antiquity, scarcely interested me. I have too little imagination to take delight in these gigantic dreams. It was not so with Martha, who sighed at every word. The horn, "which *had eyes like the eyes of a man, and a mouth speaking great things*," drew from her a cry of admiration. She was filled with emotion when the prophet spoke of the "*Ancient of days, whose garment was white as snow, and the hair of his head like the pure wool, seated on a throne of flames, and ministered to by thousand thousands of angels, while ten thousand times ten thousand stood in silence before him.*" What to me was but an allegory was to her truth, the only manner, perhaps, in which the divine idea can enter a simple soul which is in need of images to feel the infinite.

After these great pictures came the two verses in which the prophet announces the Messiah:

> "I saw in the night visions, and behold, one like the Son of man came with the clouds of heaven, and came to the Ancient of days, and they brought him near before him.
>
> "And there was given him dominion, and glory, and a kingdom, that all people, nations, and languages should serve him: his dominion is an everlasting dominion, which shall not pass away, and his kingdom that which shall not be destroyed."

On listening to this passage, I felt like Daniel: "my cogitations much troubled me, and my countenance changed in me: but I kept the matter in my heart." Had I not just witnessed on that very morning the spectacle of this royalty which nothing has arrested for nineteen hundred centuries? Christianity, whose funeral knell is sounding in Europe, I saw in America, younger, stronger, more triumphant than ever. Thirty million men living by the Gospel—what an enigma to a Parisian who had read Diderot, and who, one winter evening, imagined that he comprehended Hegel:

Retired to my chamber, I paced the floor a long time, agitated by a host of opposing thoughts. The memories of childhood, the studies of youth, the reflections of mature age, new ideas, revolved in my brain and filled it with chaos. It seemed to me that a mysterious voice was hovering in the air.

"Bravo, Daniel!" murmured this ironical voice, "you are turning monk. Here you are, mystical, fanatical, and ridiculous into the bargain. You will ere long snuffle like Mr. Brown, and speak the dialect of Canaan better than he. Oh, Frenchmen, everlasting chameleons! Chinese at Canton, Bedouins in Algeria, Puritans in Massachusetts, comedians everywhere, when will you be men? Return to Paris, Daniel: you will leave at the barrier this insipid cant, and this great black book which men of taste respect without touching. A philosopher politely takes off his hat to Christianity; it is unnecessary to be on bad terms with any one; to go further is the weakness of a small mind. The God of the nineteenth century is ancient Pan, too long eclipsed by the suffering figure of Christ. Plunge into the infinite, Daniel; adore your Father, the unfathomable; it is the fashionable mode of worship, the only one that can be acknowledged by the infallible reason of to-day."

"No," exclaimed I, "my eyes are opened; I have shaken off the painful dream which enervates our soul. These children have taught me this morning what a sacred bond unites in a common embrace liberty and the Gospel! If for us all ends with the body, we have neither rights nor duties: we are a mischievous flock, who are to be fed and chastised till death sends it to rot in an eternal grave. He only is a person whom immortality brings into communion with God. He only is a man and a citizen who can hold fast to a living justice, to a truth which knows no death. The poor, the sick, the enslaved, the wretched, the criminal became sacred only on the day that Christ ransomed them with his blood and covered them with his divinity. Adieu, Hegel and Spinoza! Adieu, words put in the place of things! Adieu, divinized matter! I have seen whither these doctrines lead people and men. I desire neither the base enjoyments of the crowd nor the stoical resignation of wits. I must have something else than drunkenness or despair. I must live! To live is to believe and act. Returned from the illusions of youth and the ambitious schemes of mature age, oh, Christ! my reason calls thee, my experience brings me back to thy feet. After so many deceptions, restore me hope; after so many betrayals, restore me love; and may the happy day dawn ere long when, Old Europe imitating Young America, a single cry will arise from earth to heaven—a saving cry—God and Liberty!

CHAPTER XXII.

THE TRIALS OF AN AMERICAN FUNCTIONARY.

After a well-spent day and a tranquil night, to rise early, refreshed in body and mind, wrap one's self in an ample dressing-gown, cradle himself in a rocking chair, and, smoking a Maryland pipe, give himself, as the Germans say, *a feast of thought*, is a true pleasure—when one is no longer thirty years old.

Seated at the window, I amused myself by seeing the city awakening from its sleep. Milkmen, coalmen, butchers and grocers were hastening through the streets and, descending to the subterranean story by the staircase outside, serving each house, without disturbing the inhabitants. It seemed as if all was calculated that nothing might trouble the sanctuary where the master of the habitation reposed. The dwelling of a Frenchman is like an apartment in an inn, all enter who will; the home of a Saxon is a fortress, defended with jealous care against the importunate and curious. It is a fireside, in the sacred and mysterious sense of this ancient word, borrowed from the east.

While I was admiring the street, already swept and watered by my laborers, a gig, drawn by a fast horse, came noisily on my side. I have always loved horses; I followed with my eyes the proud bearing of the American trotter, when suddenly the horse stumbled. From the back of the gig, an immense hat, hurled at full steam, darted like an arrow over the head of the animal, and, after the hat, a little man enveloped in a long coat. It was friend Seth, pursued doubtless by the manes of the dog whom he had assassinated.

"Martha!" cried I, putting my head out of the window, "Martha! water, vinegar; run, I am coming."

When I reached the street, the man had already risen from the ground and shaken himself; he passed his hands along his body to assure himself that he had broken nothing, swallowed a glass of water, and set to work to unharness and raise the horse without saying a word; Martha was by his side, trembling throughout her frame.

"Come in," said I to Seth; "a little rest will do you good. If you need any assistance, I am here."

"Doctor Daniel," replied he, drily, "I have no occasion for thy services. We will meet again."

And taking the horse by the bridle, he led him, with a limping step, towards the house of Fox, the attorney. Seth had doubtless come to the city on account of a lawsuit, and would not have been a Quaker if a sprained limb or a bruised head had made him forget his interest.

Ascending again to my observatory, I filled another pipe. Without passions or cares, I enjoyed my repose; I took a childish pleasure in watching the sunbeams descend slowly into the street from the roofs of the houses. Three knocks at the door aroused me from my revery. It was my neighbor Fox, a portfolio under his arm. His visit surprised me. I knew that he was greatly provoked at his electoral defeat, and he was not a man to forget his rancor and envy in a day.

"Good morning, Mr. Inspector of the Streets and Roads," said he on entering my chamber.

The manner in which he emphasized each of these

words was disagreeable to me; I am patience personified, but I do not like to be laughed at.

"Good morning, Mr. Attorney," replied I in a curt tone. "May I know what procures me the honor of this visit?"

"Well, my dear doctor," resumed he in a derisive voice, "you are an important personage! Here you are on the road to greatness! Your very adversaries bow before your talent and fortune. What do your rivals say now?"

"I know nothing about it, Fox; what do you say?"

"I," replied he, winking his eye, "I say nothing, except that the Tarpeian rock is close by the capitol."

With this hackneyed maxim he threw himself into an easy chair, opened his snuff-box, slowly inhaled a pinch of snuff, and leisurely shook off a few grains which had fallen on his waistcoat. Then, crossing his legs, he raised his pointed paw towards me, and gazed at me in silence, with the air of a weasel watching a rabbit.

Perplexed at this conduct, I rose.

"Have the goodness," said I, "to speak clearly. What brings you to my house?"

"A trifle," said he, stretching himself in his chair, and twirling his thumbs, "a mere trifle. A small demand for five hundred dollars."

"I owe you nothing that I know of," returned I, greatly astonished at this claim.

"Doubtless, my dear doctor, you owe me nothing; but my client, that is another thing."

Upon which, opening his portfolio, he took from it the following paper:

Bill of Costs and Indemnities due to SETH DOOLITTLE *from* DOCTOR DANIEL SMITH, *Inspector of the Streets and Roads, and civilly responsible for the bad condition of the aforesaid Streets and Roads.*

1. To breaking a shaft, and dislocating the wheels of a new carriage.................. $50.00
2. To wounding a horse in the shoulder, and depreciation of the said animal, at the lowest price.................................. 100.00
3. To indemnity to the said Mr. Doolittle, for a barked knee, bent hat, torn pantaloons, scratched face, etc., calculated at the lowest rate, through respect for the doctor........ 200.00
4. To anxieties, concussion of the brain, loss of time, etc., etc........................... 100.00
5. To divers cares, results of the wound and fall, consultation with physician, advice of lawyer, etc.............................. *See bill.*

"Sir," said I to Fox, flinging into his face this apothecary's bill, "hoaxes are not to my taste. I am astonished at your playing a part in this ridiculous farce."

"Very well," said Fox, "you prefer a suit. As a neighbor, I would have liked to spare you; but, never mind. Here is the summons."

"A suit!" exclaimed I, shrugging my shoulders; "a suit brought by a citizen against the inspector of the streets and roads! a functionary! a public man! a representative of the authority! What a farce! And article 75 of the constitution of Year VIII."

Strange to say, and which surprised me myself, I uttered this last sentence in French. These Saxons are so rude, so ignorant in administration, that their language is powerless to supply these splendid words, which make the glory and greatness of the Latin races.

"The summons is for to-day," said Fox, with a *sang froid* which baffled me. "I hope that you will attend to it, so as not needlessly to detain my client in town. In a quarter of an hour, our new justice of the peace, your friend, Mr. Humbug, will conclude this affair, which, to tell the truth, is an easy matter."

"What! Do you persist in pretending that I am responsible for accidents in the street?"

"Who is, then, if not you?" returned the attorney. "Did you not solicit and accept the functions of inspector? Are you not the agent and servant of the people, who elected you? If there is negligence, who is to blame, and who ought to suffer for it?"

"This is not the question," replied I, with just spirit. "I am not a pavier—a laborer, at the mercy of his employer—I am an officer of state, a member of the ruling authority, a delegate of the sovereign power."

"You are the overseer of the paviers," said Fox; "an overseer elected by the citizens, and responsible to those who elected you. Do you know of a country on the globe where functions exist for the benefit of the administrators, instead of those under their jurisdiction? For my part, I know of none but China, with its mandarins."

"Ignoramus!" I exclaimed, "read the law."

"Read it yourself," answered Fox; "it is at the head of the summons."

I read the article, and cast down my head. Fox was right; I was taken in the snare of my foolish ambition. This pretended honor, which flattered my wife, my daughter, and myself, was only a charge full of cares and dangers. In this abominable country, it is the people that command and the functionary that obeys. If I had known it!

A reflection restored my courage. "However behindhand these Yankees may be," thought I, "they are not wholly barbarous. In France, the centre of civilization, we have a thousand laws which contradict each other; the ruling power, do what it may, always ends by finding one which decides in its favor; who knows whether in the United States there is not also a *Bulletin des Lois?* I will consult a lawyer."

"Let us go," said I to the attorney. "The court is doubtless open; Humbug will judge us. If I lose my suit, I shall know at least how much to rely on this American liberty which is dinned into my ears. Fine liberty indeed, that of a people where the authority; that is the nation incarnated, bows before the decision of a justice of the peace

On reaching the street, I found the Quaker still impassible. On a sign from Fox, he followed us in silence, Martha approached me, sighing.

"Master," said she, "it is the same pavement where thy daughter and I fell the other day."

Power of a word! This simple speech overturned my ideas. Susan, my Susan, it was thou that disturbed my conscience! Indeed I have a political faith which is proof against modern follies; with my head on the scaffold, I would maintain towards and against all that the authority is never wrong; that if it suffers itself to be discussed it is lost. Let a horse, and even a Christian break his neck on a badly kept pavement; it is a misfortune; but what matters it? Horses pass away, principles remain. The general interest is above these calamities of private interest. This is the conservative dogma which has been taught me; I profess it; yet, four days before, the sight of my daughter wounded had made me forget my symbol. I, too, in my mad anger, would have gladly found in my way, a responsible functionary, and if I had had him, would have acted like this wretched Quaker, with the exception of the bill of five hundred dollars. How weak is our heart, and how we are all infected more than we think with the republican poison!

Humbug was in his office; we entered; Martha had not quitted her beloved. Was this a new enemy conjured up against me?

"Good morning, doctor," cried Humbug, the instant he saw me. "It is kind of you to honor my humble courtroom with your presence. We cannot teach men too much to respect justice, the sister of religion. *Discite justitiam moniti et non temnere Divos.*"

"Mr. Magistrate," said I, "it is not a friend but a litigant that appears before you."

"A suit," said he, bending his shaggy eyebrows. "Have you forgotten the wise lesson of our fathers? To carry on or defend a suit, needs six things: *primo*, a good cause; *secundo*, a good lawyer; *tertio*, good counsel; *quarto*, good proof; *quinto*, a good judge, and *sexto*, a good chance. To unite all these conditions is so great a risk that I advise every one to abide by the Gospel, '*If any man will sue thee at law, and take away thy coat let him have thy cloak also.*' You will gain repose of mind, and the costs of law in the bargain."

While Humbug was signing some papers, I perceived Seth and Martha in a corner in eager discussion. A few words caught at random did not permit me to follow the conversation. Seth spoke of an *insult*, a *good oppor-*

tunity, going to housekeeping. Martha, sighing and gesticulating, talked of *honesty, the Bible, marriage.* It was evident that the two turtle doves were having a quarrel on my account. Honest Martha; she at least took in earnest the Bible which she read daily. Her domestic fidelity prevailed over her love. Perhaps too she was not sorry to assure herself before marriage who would be master in the house.

"It is taking or leaving," said she, drawing away from the Quaker with a gesture of impatience.

"That is to say," answered Seth, "that it is escaping a great danger."

Upon which, with a tranquil step, he went to find Fox, who had no trouble in demonstrating to him that to a wise man it was clear gain to lose a wife and win a suit.

The clerk announced that the time for the hearing had come.

"Let us go in," said Humbug. "Doctor, I give you the first turn. Lawsuits are like decayed teeth, to be gotten rid of as soon as possible; once gone, they are forgotten."

"How does it happen," said I, "that there are so few people in the court room; I thought that in a free country justice was the business of all the citizens."

"My dear doctor," returned the justice of the peace, "do you see those three phonographic reporters preparing their pen and paper? I tell you with Lord Mansfield, 'The country is there.' Be tranquil, before two hours are over, all Paris will be occupied with your suit. The publicity of justice is the publicity of the newspapers. Suppress the report and you will be judged in secret and strangled with closed doors, were there three hundred persons within this enclosure. Our forum—a people of thirty million souls—is the newspaper. Thanks to it, the most insignificant litigant, the most obscure criminal, has the whole country for judge, witness, and counsel. The press, my good friend, believe an old journalist, is the only guaranty of justice and liberty."

In these words of Humbug, I saw but one thing—that diabolical placard which was about to be hoisted in the street, to amuse all Paris with my misadventure. To escape this annoyance, I made a bold resolve, "I will lose my suit," thought I, "but I will have the laugh on my side."

I was about to speak, but Fox had already read his points and commenced his plea.

"There are," said he, waving his hand towards me, "there are certain men who, without genius, without talent, without capacity, but afflicted with a ridiculous ambition, or rather morbid itching for publicity, beg the popular suffrage, and imagine that public functions are made for the satisfaction of their puerile vanity."

This exordium sufficed me; I was not anxious to see more of it in print.

"Permit me," said I ——

"Do not interrupt me," cried he in his shrillest tone, bristling up his plumes like an enraged cock, "do not interrupt me."

"Excuse me, honorable attorney," rejoined I, "before pleading, there must be a suit; there is none here.

"Mr. Judge," continued I, "elected inspector four days since, I might excuse myself on the ground of the newness of my functions, and throw back upon my predecessor a negligence for which I am not culpable; but God forbid that a public officer, a proxy of the people, should permit himself such caviling. Functions impose duties; I wish to be the first to set the example of respect to the law. I acknowledge myself responsible for an accident which I regret; it is useless, therefore, to attack a man who does not dream of defending himself."

"Very well," exclaimed the Quaker, incapable of containing himself. "Friend Daniel, thee is a functionary after God's own heart—a Boaz, a Samuel; give me the five hundred dollars or sufficient security; I declare myself satisfied."

"A little patience," replied I; "I am ready to pay on the spot all lawful indemnity; this indemnity I will not even discuss. Put my opponent on his oath; this holy man, the Quaker, shall himself fix the amount of damage which I have caused him."

"I refuse it," cried Seth, angry and troubled. "I had rather prosecute; my lawyer promises me full success. Can a Quaker take oaths? Daniel, does thee not read the Gospel? Christ says, '*Swear not at all, neither by the sky, for it is God's throne; nor by the earth, for it is his footstool; nor by Jerusalem*'"——

"Enough," said Humbug, "leave this useless cant. You are only asked to say in the presence of God, and as Christ counsels you, *this is* or *is not so*. Commune with your conscience, think of your salvation. I ask you for the truth, the whole truth, and nothing but the truth. Upon which, may God be your aid."

The Quaker scratched his head and gazed at his lawyer with a piteous air. Fox remained mute. Seth turned round, and seeing Martha standing near him, grew pale and began to stammer. His conscience, interest and love were waging a terrible battle; and, it must be said to the honor of the Quaker, interest did not gain the victory.

"Here is the bill," said he; "the facts are exact, but naturally, some deduction may be made on the price. The shaft was not a new one; nevertheless, it must be mended. Five dollars is not too much, is it, Martha?"

The tall woman gave a nod, like the statue of the Commander in the opera of Don Juan.

"We will say five dollars," resumed the Quaker, in a lamentable tone. "The horse was galled already, but the wound is freshly chafed; this is well worth five dollars, is it not, Martha?

"For myself," continued he, "I ask nothing; but my pantaloons are torn, and I have lost my day. I will say ten dollars, shall I, Martha?"

"And the lawyer," cried Fox; "are you going to forget him?"

"The lawyer," rejoined the Quaker, happy to turn the rage of his avarice on some one, "the lawyer is a fool, who has given me nothing but bad advice. Five dollars to pay for ten useless words is even too much, is it not, Martha?"

And Seth's eyes sparkled on seeing his beloved laugh heartily at the discomfiture of Master Fox.

"Here are the twenty-five dollars," said I, in my turn, happy to be released so cheaply.

"Ah, Martha," cried the Quaker, "what a ruinous thing is conscience! I am sure that those who make large fortunes have little, or make no use of it."

"Silence, son of Belial!" said Martha; "bless Heaven that placed me near thee."

"Bravo, doctor!" said Fox, bowing respectfully, "you are a cunning dog. It is lucky for us that you are not a lawyer."

"You are mistaken, brother," answered I, laughing; "I belong to the trade."

"How is this?" said Humbug.

"I wrote a paper on legal jurisprudence, a few years since, with respect to women who soften the disposition of their husbands indefinitely, by means of laudanum, discreetly administered. This procured me a diploma from the University of Kharkoff; I am barrister and doctor of laws among the Cossacks."

"Brother," said Humbug, in a solemn tone, "do me the honor to take a seat beside me. And you, Messrs. Phonographers, do not forget this wonderful fact. A physician, doctor of laws of the University of Kharkoff, is seen only in America; I am sure that throughout old Europe would not be found the parallel of this phœnix which we possess at Paris—in Massachusetts. Kharkoff, gentlemen, do not forget it; Kharkoff!"

CHAPTER XXIII.

THE JUSTICES' COURT.

I TOOK a seat near Humbug, taking care to remain respectfully in the background; and while unimportant civil cases were called, I looked about at the court-room and its actors.

There was no platform to elevate the magistrate above those amenable to his jurisdiction; a simple wooden railing separated the court from the spectators. Humbug was seated behind a large desk; at one of the lower sides, the clerk was writing. Facing the judge was a sort of latticed stall, destined for the defendant; a little in front of this was a table for the plaintiff and witnesses. Nothing more. What added to the simplicity of the spectacle was that no one wore costume. Humbug sat in a black coat, his hat on his head; the lawyers had no particular dress. No gowns, no bands, no wigs. This primitive people has so naïve a faith in justice that it believes in it without ceremonies. One feels everywhere the Puritan coarseness. Let me add that there was a seat of honor for the phonographic reporters. They represent the people, watch over the magistrates and judge justice. Oh, democracy, this is thy work! Yet, notwithstanding, there is no country where respect for the law and confidence in the magistrate are carried further. This is one of the whimsicalities which prove beyond dispute that the Saxon was created for liberty, as the Frenchman for war, and the German for sourkrout and philosophy. To suppose that this strong nourishment suited all stomachs was the folly of our fathers. In their ignorance, these good people did not divine that there were individualistic races and centralistic races, (two fine words!) the one made to hover solitary in space, like the kite; the others to live in flocks and be shorn like sheep. Politics, religion, philosophy, liberty—these are questions of natural history, varieties which distinguish the *homo civilizatius* from all the other bipeds and quadrupeds. Admirable discovery! Eternal honor to the brilliant geniuses of our time!

When the list of civil suits was exhausted, a prisoner was brought into the stall. He was a pale young man, with long locks and an effeminate but impudent air. In reply to the interrogation of Humbug, he gave his name and residence, adding that he was a tailor, and that he pleaded *not guilty*. He then seated himself, passed his fingers through his curls, and gazed at his accusers with a smile of disdain.

"Your honor," said a policeman, "this is one of the most adroit pickpockets of the city; in the crowd where we arrested him, six pockets had been cut out in a quarter of an hour. We took this rascal who is well known to us; he had these large scissors in the lining of his coat; nothing else was found on him."

"Is there no other witness or proof?" asked the judge.

"No, your honor."

"Then release this gentleman, and try the next time to be more adroit.'

The thief bowed to Humbug, and withdrew with a tranquil step, like a man who had never doubted his acquittal.

"What!" said I to Humbug, "do you let this knave go?"

"Doubtless; there is no offence proven."

"But the bad reputation of the wretch, the cut pockets, the scissors are proofs."

"No," returned Humbug, "these are mere presumptions. It is most probable that the man entered the crowd to steal; but the law punishes the crime, not the intention. It leaves room for hesitation, fear and remorse. If people were condemned for intention, what good man would not be subject to hanging, ten times in his life? And besides, if you give the judge a right to read the soul of the accused, what is human justice but hypocritical despotism? It is no longer the guilty act which makes the offence, but the caprice or prejudice of the magistrate."

"Happy country," exclaimed I, "where the law protects the thief!"

"It still better protects the innocent," rejoined Humbug. "With your inquisitorial system, who would escape private hatred or political vengeance? With your right of interpretation, what judge would not be exposed to error and repentance? Themis is blind, my good friend; she does not see, she feels. If you wish her to act, throw into the balance an actual offence, something material, heavy, which will weigh down the scale; but presumptions, intentions, vexatious memories, all these have no weight, '*Sunt verba et voces prœtereaque nihil.*'"

At this moment, a sort of Hercules, clad as a policeman, entered the audience, carrying in his outstretched hand a little man, gesticulating like a devil in a font of holy water—I do not answer for the exactness of the comparison. The giant threw the dwarf with all his force into the prisoners' box; then, readjusting his coat, the collar of which was wrenched off, and wiping his scratched face:

"Here is a man that has broken the public peace, your honor," said he.

"Excuse me," said I to Humbug, "but you are not going to judge on the spot an act just committed outside the court?"

"Why not?" asked the judge, surprised at my question.

"The forms of law!" said I; "begin by putting the man in prison; let the police enter upon an inquiry; then lodge a complaint, proceed from this complaint to a cool and calm private examination, then investigate this examination itself to leave room neither for error nor passion. Take a fortnight, take a month, take three months, if need be; time is nothing; but observe the forms of law, they are the guaranties of liberty."

"Be calm, doctor; we are about to make an examination in court, in public, with the country for witness. Such light dissipates all error and passion.

"'Adsum solem quis dicere falsam
Audeat.'

"All the guaranties you demand, the accused will have, except the preliminary imprisonment, which I do not suppose that he insists on as much as you."

"Well," said the policeman, "I came in from the country yesterday; as I was making my first round this morning, this man ran towards me scared, out of breath, and as red as a beet. 'Policeman,' cried he, 'I have found you at last. Quick! quick! help, you are needed.' 'What is the matter?' said I. 'The matter!' said he, panting, 'the matter is that a horrible murder will be committed if you do not put a stop to it. See that crowd yonder; there is a man beating his wife with a great stick. Listen! they are crying assassin. Run quick, prevent a murder!' 'Which is the man?' asked I. 'He is a little man,' said he, 'but he is savage.' 'Well,' said I, 'I have seen worse than he.'"

"Be short," said Humbug.

"I have almost done, your honor. I ran, I shoved aside the crowd which did not stir, and there was the man beating his wife on the head."

"Did you arrest him?"

"No, your honor," said Hercules, scratching his ear and lowering his voice, "it was—it was Punch."

"Go on," said Humbug, biting his lips, while the spectators and prisoner himself roared with laughter.

"Well, your honor, I went back to my post a little vexed, naturally. And then came all the blackguards of the city, with this fellow at their head, all howling, 'Policeman, you are wanted! Murder! murder! Punch is killing Judy!' I said to myself, 'They have played a trick on me, the law does not forbid it, I have been caught; no matter, one must pay for his apprenticeship.' I walked on at my usual pace as if nothing were the matter, but this fellow, who seems as if he were paid to amuse the city, planted himself in front of me, with his arms folded, and shouted, 'I know you; you are a thief and assassin!' 'I?' I cried. 'Yes, you. Citizens, I take you all for witnesses and judges; say if he has not killed an ourang outang to steal its face?'"

"'Very well, sir,' said I; 'each one has his turn; this is an insult; I have the law on my side. Come with me to the court.' He tried to run away, I caught him by the arm; he answered me by a blow in the face with his fist; upon which I picked him up and brought him here without stopping. And here he is."

The prisoner rose abashed, declared that he did not dispute the facts, and excused his resistance by saying that he did not think that he was committing a crime by playing a joke in the fashion of Punch.

"You are mistaken, sir," replied Humbug, in a mocking tone. "If you were better acquainted with your worthy model, you would know that after each of his exploits he is imprisoned in a tightly-closed box. I shall be less severe towards you; it will cost you only ten dollars' fine, and ten dollars to repair the damage caused to this honest policeman. Thank him for his goodness; had he shut his hand you would be dead."

The little man drew some bank notes from a greasy pocket-book, which he handed with an ill grace to the clerk and went out sighing, saluted by the hootings of the crowd outside, who applauded the policeman. Goliath this time had beaten David; it is true that he had the law on his side.

After the knight of Mrs. Punch, the frequenters of the police court defiled before us—beggars, vagrants, drunkards, debauchees, fighters, swindlers, gamblers, and other thieves—every species of misery and vice. On seeing the rapid manner in which Humbug examined and judged each case, on seeing especially how the criminals accepted without complaint an anticipated punishment, I became reconciled to the American mode of proceeding. The publicity of criminal examination might be indeed one of those modern discoveries which suppress time. By seizing the words of all the parties in their first warmth, instead of congealing them on a document which preserves neither the sound nor sense; by bringing face to face accused, accusers, witnesses, and lawyers, the American judge condenses into a few moments the truth, which among us too often evaporates in a thousand channels, or grows cold to us. To do fair and prompt justice without encroaching on liberty—such is the problem which these Yankees have resolved. Science has deceived us, chance has served them.

Upon one point, nevertheless, some scruples remained to me. I asked Humbug if he were not dismayed at his power. To have in his hands the fortune, honor, and liberty of so many accused, to dispose of them alone was a terrible responsibility; would he not rather divide it?

"No," replied Humbug, "the interest of justice is opposed to it. To form a tribunal of three or four persons is not to multiply the responsibility, but to divide it; the accused thereby loses his best guaranty. Alone, and under the public eye, it seems to me that God is watching me; I feel all the sanctity of the duty which I fulfill. The more comrades I have the less I believe myself pledged. What is a third, a fifth, a tenth of responsibility? And if the judgment be iniquitous or cruel, who is public opinion to blame for it?"

"Nevertheless," said I, "see the jury."

"That is the example which I was about to quote to you," said he. "In this country the majority rules; numbers in all things, make the law. Justice alone is exempt from this condition. The agreement of eleven jurors cannot take away either the life or honor of the accused; the abstention of a single man suffices to hinder their verdict. Whence comes this? Because there is a moral question involved here and not an arithmetical problem; the voice which absolves has perhaps more weight than the eleven voices which condemn. Then too, what the legislator demands is not majority, but unanimity. What he expects is not one responsibility divided into twelve parts, but twelve responsibilities. You see that there is not here even the appearance of an exception; it is the same rule, but strengthened—the unity of the judge, full and entire responsibility."

This reasoning surprised me. I had always believed that the unanimity of the jury was one of those old remnants of feudal barbarism which amuse us at the expense of England, and make us better feel our superiority. Humbug disturbed the serenity of my faith. In vain I recalled the wise words of Montaigne, "Oh, what a sweet and soft pillow, and healthy one too, have ignorance and incuriosity to repose a well-balanced head on!" Doubt is like the rain, no traveller escapes it. Frenchmen! would you keep that legitimate pride, that just satisfaction in yourselves which makes your strength and glory, never lose sight of your weathercock!

A movement among the audience, followed by a prolonged murmur, announced the arrival of an important personage. A corpulent man advanced majestically, his head erect and eyes half closed, panting at every step, and looking at no one. On reaching the plaintiff's table, he greeted Humbug with a familiar gesture and patronizing smile. It was the banker Little, bearing on his puffy cheeks the insolence of his twenty millions.

Behind him, two policemen brought a man of large stature, emaciated, with hollow cheeks and glittering eyes, looking like a gamester who has staked his life on a card and lost. He let himself fall on the prisoners' seat, and buried his face in his hands.

"Sir," said the banker, "this morning this draft for two thousand dollars, which I lay on your desk, was presented at my bank. My cashier, an intelligent lad—you know him, Humbug—not finding the payment noted on the bills-payable book, took it in his head to bring me the draft, despite the insignificance of the sum. The name of the drawer, the endorsements, my name, all are forged. Three similar drafts have been already presented this morning, but the holders took care not to leave them. It is a plot concocted among a band of swindlers. It was calculated that I would be chosen mayor; that I would be absent to-day, and that my cashier would not dare refuse drafts bearing my signature. I have seized this fellow; it is for the law to discover his accomplices."

"Prisoner," said Humbug, "have you anything to answer? Remember that all your words will be noted down and used against you. Reflect before you speak."

"I have nothing to say at present," murmured the prisoner.

"I am obliged, therefore, to transfer you to the criminal court for the crime of forgery," said Humbug, in a pitying tone. "Can you furnish two securities for five thousand dollars each? Otherwise, I shall be forced to remand you to prison."

"I will try to find bail," replied the accused.

"Very well. Go in a carriage with two policemen and see your friends. On your return, we will go with you to visit your books, and, if necessary, take other precautions."

"Do you think of leaving this forger at liberty?" said I to Humbug. "He has accomplices; he will warn them, and besides will make his escape."

"The law," replied the judge, "exacts imprisonment before trial only for crimes entailing capital punishment. In all others it is entrusted to the discretion of the magistrate. Why would you have me take away from this man the means of defending himself, in order that he may appear in the criminal court as a victim, and that interest may be attached, not to the robbed but the robber? Verifications, reports, inquiries will be necessary. Can all these be made blindly, in the absence of the prisoner? Has not the accused a right to discuss and criticise all the charges accumulated against him? Criminal examination is not a penalty, it is a search for truth."

"With your false humanity," exclaimed I, "you disarm society. I do not understand justice in this manner."

"How do you understand it then?" asked Humbug.

"Permit me a comparison," replied I. "In society, as in a forest, there are birds of prey, and ravenous beasts—enemies to which the police and justice give continual chase. The police tracks them, justice secures them. The magistrate, a skillful hunter, fells and destroys the execrable brood. Take bail for the wolf, offer a safe conduct to the fox; you will see what will become of the lambs and chickens. To protect honest men is the first duty of justice. To evil doers it owes nothing but punishment and extermination."

"My dear friend," said Humbug, "your jests are cruel.

"'Quænam ista jocandi
Sævitia.'

"If there are wolves among human beings, which I am far from denying, at least they have the same skin as the lambs. Before killing the brigand it is necessary to recognize him. This is a work which demands a more delicate hand than that of the hunter. Justice is, under another name, only society, the mother of all the citizens.

Until condemnation, she believes in the innocence of her children. This maternal confidence is not an idle word; it is an active tenderness, which protects and sustains the prisoner, without abandoning him for a moment. You believe, perhaps, that it is the jury that punishes the crime—undeceive yourself. The examination is conducted among us in so broad, so full, so generous a manner that, to speak truly, it is the culprit who condemns himself and accepts the expiation. Observe our criminal courts; you will see that what disarms the accused is the gentleness of our proceedings. Attacked, a man rebels; insulted, he rails back. Pride and anger sustain the villain quite as much as the honest man; but to justify himself where facts alone accuse him, to set forth his conduct simply, to render an account of his action, is the privilege of innocence. Nothing dismays a criminal like feeling himself alone, face to face with himself, having for witnesses and judges the judge who protects him and the jury who listen to him. He oftenest ends by confessing his fault, or by shutting himself up in a silence which is an acknowledgment. What you call the weakness of our laws is what makes their virtue and beauties."

"I comprehend nothing of your chimerical philanthropy," I answered; "it is not in this manner that justice is understood and practised"——

"At Kharkoff, among the Cossacks," interrupted Humbug, laughing; "I believe it; these people are not Christians."

"They are Christians like myself," replied I; "but"——

"Good morning, your honor," cried a purple-faced man, whom two policemen were shutting in the box, with eyes starting from his head like those of a crawfish, and a hoarse and asthmatic voice; "it is Paddy; don't you know me?"

"Twice in four days; this is too much," said Humbug.

"Forgive me, your honor," said the prisoner, pointing to the policemen; "it is these fellows' fault. They have no pity for the poor world. Yesterday, Sunday, I went out to take a quiet walk, with a bottle of gin in my fist, like a good Christian, who didn't want to go mad for lack of something to drink on Sunday. I met this great devil of a fellow yonder, and politely asked him the way to the hospital. 'You have it in your hand,' says he. 'This!' said I, holding up my bottle; 'it is the comfort of my life.' 'It is your enemy,' says he. 'Well, well, policeman, we must love our enemies,' said I. Upon which I drank my own health, and ran against Patrick O'Shea, a son of green Erin, who hates all the Saxons. If you meet a friend on Sunday you must fight a little with him—this is a funny story, isn't it, your honor? We hadn't begun to draw blood when the policeman put his hand on my shoulder. 'Have you three dollars?' said he. 'No,' says I, 'there is a hole in my pocket, and my wife hasn't mended it yet.' 'If you have no money to pay the fine, why do you fight?' says he. 'Policeman, you are right,' says I; 'every one must amuse himself according to his means.' So I went away, arm in arm with Patrick, in a friendly way. But Patrick began to bully me about the election—he is a Democrat. 'Your judge isn't worth a fig,' says he (meaning you, your honor); 'as for the doctor, they say he's a conjurer!' Naturally, I shut his mouth with a blow of my fist; he answered in the same way; I put out my leg and threw him down. 'I will choke you,' says I, 'if you do not own it.' And I made him own it."

"What?" asked Humbug.

"That you are worth a fig, and that the doctor isn't a conjurer."

"Paddy," resumed Humbug, with a serious air, "we are obliged to you for your good opinion of us; but your getting tipsy and fighting in the street will cost you ten dollars."

"Ten dollars!" exclaimed the drunkard. "Where do you expect me to get it?"

"If you do not find it between now and to-morrow, five days' imprisonment will do as well."

"And my wife and children?" murmured Paddy.

"You should have thought of them yesterday," answered the judge; "to-day, it is too late."

"Pharisees!" exclaimed I, "at last I have you. You have two weights and measures. Thanks to his money, the rich man can indulge in all the vices; while the poor man expiates in prison the only crime which you do not pardon—poverty. Is this equity? For the same offence I admit only the same penalty; shut up all the culprits, or shut up none. Justice is but another name for equality."

"Happy logicians," said Humbug, "admirable leaders of the people! it matters little to you if you kill liberty, provided you conduct it straight to perdition. When the Russian executioners put to death nobles and women under the knout, I suspect, sublime doctor of Kharkoff, that your heart leaped for joy, and you exclaimed, 'Glorious victory of equality!'"

"No, no," said I, in my turn, "I abhor despotism; I desire the equality which elevates, not that which degrades; I demand that the serfs shall be treated like nobles, not the nobles like serfs."

"Very well, my good friend," rejoined the judge,

but it is here that the difficulty begins. There is always a point beyond which, unless you imitate Procrustes, the most skillful of logicians, you will never attain equality.

"Our old Saxon laws, which you find harsh, and which I find just and gentle, always take care to treat liberty with circumspection. With the exception of atrocious crimes, they attack the purse and not the person of the culprit. If the true means of arresting the man drawn on by passion be to put before his eyes the responsibility which awaits him, nothing equals pecuniary penalties—believe it from experience. There are countries where adultery is a pretty trick; breach of faith, a lawful amusement; duelling, an exploit which does honor even to the villain. Among us, men do not seduce their neighbors' wives or daughters, or kill men to repair the injury which they have done them. Why? For the very prosaic reason that they must pay fifteen or twenty thousand dollars for each of these amiable follies. No one cares to ruin himself to be the talk of the city, and to have the laugh against him in the bargain.

"Such is the law; the custom of a thousand years has consecrated its force and wisdom. But what is to be done when the accused has nothing? Are we to give to the poor the privilege of impunity? are we to sacrifice liberty through love of uniformity? Our ancestors decided, and we have kept their maxim: *Who cannot pay with his pocket, must pay with his skin; luat cum corio.* Among us, the fine is the rule, imprisonment the exception. Why? Because liberty is the principle; to speak truly, imprisonment is only a means of execution against an insolvent debtor. What do you see unjust in all this?"

"I do not see equality in it," replied I.

"Well, doctor, you are blind. There are two species of equality—the one, which is unsuited to human societies, is that material and brutal equality which takes into account neither age, nor rank, nor fortune. The same penalties in unequal conditions is absolute equality and supreme injustice. The other equality is that which proportions the punishment, not to the definition of the offence, which is only a word, but to the act itself and the person of the culprit. To the rich a heavy fine, to the poor a light fine, and in default of payment a few days' imprisonment—this is a law in which justice and veritable equality find their account no less than liberty."

"Paddy!" exclaimed I, calling the drunkard, who raised towards me his great, wonder-struck eyes, "take these ten dollars; pay your fine, my good man; go home and sin no more. This is my answer," said I, turning to Humbug; "it is a protest against the iniquity of your laws."

"It is the justification of their excellence," answered he. "If, through love of equality, we had established imprisonment as the penalty for drunkenness, what aid could you have given to this interesting victim? The fine, on the contrary, has this great merit, that tender souls can always correct the harshness of our judgments; and, whatever legists may say, that stony-hearted race, when there is a struggle between charity and justice, it is well that charity should have the last word."

"Thank you, doctor," cried Paddy, crushing my fingers in his hands, "I am going to drink your health. The first man who dares call you conjurer, by my faith, I will pummel him."

"Here is a reformed man!" said Humbug. "Now

if there is nothing more before us, we will adjourn the court."

I returned with him to his office. We found the judge of the criminal court there, in great agitation.

"I have been waiting for you," said he to Humbug; "behold me in the greatest embarrassment. The jury is assembled, and the attorney general is missing. He writes me that he is sick in bed, with such violent pain in the bowels that it is impossible to rise."

"Bowels—an attorney general! It is improbable," exclaimed Humbug.

"Do not laugh, my friend, but help me; give me some one to replace our public prosecutor."

"Take this precious Daniel," said Humbug, with difficulty restraining his laughter. "Here is the man you want. He is barrister and doctor in the university of Kharkoff; he is a prodigy of gravity, inflexibility, legality, and sentimentality. You have here, in a single person, Coke, Mansfield, Erskine, and all the rest."

"Come quickly, sir," said the judge, taking me by the arm; "you are my saviour."

"Excuse me," said I.

"No, no!" interrupted he, "I will listen to nothing. No false modesty; you are a doctor, that is enough."

At the same moment, Humbug seized me by the other arm; I was dragged into the hall, presented to the jury, and installed, without having been able to breathe a word. Humbug placed himself near me, and, smiling at my misadventure, showed me, on the defendant's bench, Fox, stupefied, gazing at me, and winking his eyes.

There was no retreat. Fate, which was mocking me, condemned me to play a new farce—*The Attorney in Spite of Himself.*

CHAPTER XXIV.

AN ATTORNEY GENERAL.

My dear reader, if ever a treacherous hand flung you into the water by surprise, without your knowing how to swim, you can form an idea of my deplorable situation. I did not feel in a condition to say two consecutive words; yet to withdraw would have been ridiculous. There would not have been hisses enough for me throughout the city. I resolved, therefore, to put a bold face on the matter, and to sustain my part to the end.

Taking out my memorandum book, I tore from it some leaves, on which I wrote from memory a few of those fine phrases which mean nothing, but produce the best effect, when opportunely thrown in a carefully prepared improvisation. Thus armed, I awaited the battle with the firmness of a soldier going to the fire, resolved to stand it.

The first prisoner brought in was an execrable villain, who had slowly poisoned his wife, after having dictated a will to her; the crime was flagrant, the proofs overwhelming, the wretch did not even attempt to defend himself.

"I plead guilty," murmured he, in a trembling voice, with pallid face and wandering eye; "let me die; I ask only to be delivered from life."

There was a profound silence throughout the assembly.

I rose majestically, put my quizzing glasses on my

nose, coughed three times, and, holding my cards in my left hand while waving my right arm in cadence, I commenced in a slow, deep voice:

"YOUR HONOR AND THE GENTLEMEN OF THE JURY:

"*Nemo auditur perire volens*—listen not to him who wishes to die—is one of the great and salutary maxims bequeathed to us by the profound wisdom of our venerable ancestors—a wisdom far superior to the insane science and proud reason of the generations of to-day. *Nemo auditur perire volens* is a maxim invented not only to protect the culprit against his own despair, but to secure to society the satisfaction of a legitimate vengeance.

"Yes, gentlemen, when an execrable crime has been committed—when our admirable city, wholly rejuvenated by the splendor of those glorious structures which do infinite honor to the prodigious genius of our able and wise edileship—when, I say, our city, modern Rome, a thousand times more beautiful and greater than the Rome of the Cæsars, awakens in the morning, terrified at the unexpected news of one of those horrible crimes which reveal unqualified depravity, the poisonous fruit of a system of civilization corrupted by revolutions and journalism—then, gentlemen, it is the duty of justice, which is ever on the watch, to accomplish a sacred mission—a mission as difficult as imposing. In default of ready speech, in default of that magisterial eloquence, the appanage of so many of my illustrious colleagues, whom I refrain from naming to spare their too great modesty, magistrates inspired at least by their conscience, bring within these walls their forcible conviction, their humble but firm devotion to the cause of order, the laws, and society.

"Here, gentlemen of the jury, here is offered a great and glorious spectacle; here begins, in all its details, a tragedy, painful doubtless to honest men, but necessary to the expiation of crime, and to the edification of the whole country. In this appalling drama, debauchery is the prologue; covetousness, ending in poison, forms the second act; public trial, by its marvelous adroitness, precipitates events, and we arrive, through it, to the fatal and speedy denouement. This avenging denouement, gentlemen of the jury, is in your hands; your verdict is not doubtful. Crushed beneath the weight of his fault, vanquished by justice, the culprit has confessed all; yonder he stands before you, weighed down, overwhelmed with remorse; his condemnation is written on his villainous forehead, as it is written in your noble hearts.

"Let him not believe that this forced confession can free him from the shame which he deserves. In vain he turns aside his guilty head, in vain he puts away from his impure lips the bitter cup which his execrable crime has prepared for him; the law, blind and mute, the law, justly inexorable, the law, divinely pitiless, decrees that he shall drink his heinous crime to the dregs. His torture is the punishment of the past and the lesson of the future."

"Enough, for God's sake, enough," said Humbug, pulling the skirt of my coat. "*Res sacra miser*, my good friend."

"Leave me alone," said I with a gesture of impatience. "The prosecution has nothing to do with humanity."

"On us," continued I, becoming animated, "on us, the minister of the public prosecution of crime; on us, the representative of outraged authority; on us devolves the painful but sacred duty of silencing the beatings of our human heart; to us it belongs to stir this mire and to surmount unconquerable disgust; to us"——

Imprudent man! in a magnificent gesture, I raised my arms and opened both hands, when lo! all my papers fell to the ground and my eloquence with them; I stooped to pick up the whole together, the prisoner profited by this unlucky chance, and rising abruptly.

"Your honor," said he, "how long will you suffer the attorney general to play with me like a cat with a mouse? The law says that you are the protector of the accused; why do you let me be insulted in my wretchedness? I expect my sentence, what is the need of prolonging my torture?"

"He is right," said an unmannerly juror; "we are here to do justice, not to hear a sermon."

I was about to speak; the judge stopped me with a gesture and, covering his head, he purely and simply pronounced the condemnation of the prisoner and the sentence of death. No summing up, no impressive words, no lesson given either to the prisoner, or the jury, or the public, nothing to add to the solemnity of this scene palpitating with interest. On the contrary, with a familiarity in bad taste, he began to negotiate with the culprit.

"Prisoner," said he, "henceforth you have nothing to expect from the mercy of man; it only remains for you to make your peace with God. How many days do you need to settle your affairs and become reconciled with your conscience?"

"Three days will be enough," replied he; "I am in haste to have it over."

"Well," resumed the judge, "in five days, reckoning from the present moment, you will appear before the only judge who can pardon you."

The condemned bowed respectfully to the judge, and went out, casting on me a glance which troubled me. Had I not done my duty? Is pity due even to assassins?"

The second prisoner was brought in. He was an impudent knave who, released from the State prison two days before, had rendered himself guilty of burglary, robbery, and attempted assassination. He had broken into a house at Montmorency, threatened an unfortunate servant maid who kept the house, and taken everything, even to the carriage and horses.

The face of this rogue was enough to condemn him. It was villainy personified. We beheld a man to whom society was only an enemy, and who had as much contempt for the law as hatred for the magistrate—in a word, one of those wild beasts which we must slay if we would not have them devour us.

"Prisoner," said the judge, "do you plead guilty or not guilty?"

"That is a pretty question," answered the burglar with audacious nonchalance. "Guilty or not guilty? Neither you nor I know until we have heard the witnesses."

"Gentlemen of the jury," exclaimed I, "what need is there of hearing further? Lay hold of this confession. Did an innocent man ever hesitate for an instant to proclaim his non culpability? None but a professional villain would have this effrontery. Look at the wretch; is not crime written on his impudent face?"

"I protest againt this theory," cried the counsel of the prisoner.

His squeaking voice made me start—once more mocking fortune opposed to me Fox, my eternal enemy.

"Yes," continued he, "I protest and I will always protest against a doctrine which has never been received in the courts of free America. You have no right to torture the words of a prisoner to turn them to his conviction. You have no right to interpret his mien, his gesture, the tone of his language in evidence of his guilt.

If it were permitted to invoke these deceitful signs which passion explains as it pleases, who would escape the eloquence of attorney generals? Is the accused silent? it is because remorse overwhelms him; silence is confession. Does the accused protest calmly? it is effrontery; effrontery is confession. Does he fly in a passion and rail? he is an insolent fellow who outrages justice; insolence is confession. Weakness, energy, humility, pride, tears, anger, all is confession to prejudiced minds who see only one side. Ah! gentlemen, begin by establishing the physical characteristics of virtue and crime. When science shall have realized the dreams of Lavater, you can condemn men by their countenance; until then leave to fortune-tellers this perfidious and dangerous art. Justice knows nothing but facts, discusses nothing but facts, decides on nothing but facts. Therein is its security and greatness. Let Mr. Attorney General keep his talent for a better occasion—we will proceed to hear the witnesses."

"Your honor," cried I, "it is through respect to the court that I have endured the impertinence of these words to the end; an attorney general does not need to receive lessons from the counsel; I require"——

"Be calm, sir," interrupted the magistrate; "everything is permitted the defence except abuse; the words of the honorable counsel have in no wise transcended the right of his function. As to his doctrine, it is what our precedents have sanctioned. You will find these principles, which I do myself the honor to profess, in all our authorities."

I fell on my seat like a thunderstruck Titan. The judge become the apostle of theories which sink the prosecution to the level of the defence! The judge a deserter from our ranks, and become the accomplice of the counsel! It was a last stroke! If this is what the Yankees call justice, I have no more knowledge of it. Travel throughout civilized Europe, you will see nothing like it.

"Very well," said the excellent Humbug to me, to restore me a little courage; "you speak like a senator, only with too much zeal. Moderate yourself, my good friend; you will produce more effect."

I was not at the end of my surprise. The witnesses were called. I expected that the judge alone would interrogate them in concert with myself. Vain hope! The judge was an impassive statue. Opposite him, the accused kept the same silence. When I attempted to question him, a general outcry taught me that, according to Yankee law, there was favor only for knaves. To see the magistrate and prisoner, both mute and motionless, one would have said that, strangers to what was passing in the court, they were the judges of the combat. The combatants, or rather victims, were the witnesses, given over to the mercy of the counsel, interrogated, contradicted, blamed, harassed, by a man without public character, and who had no other claim than that of defending the doubtful innocence of a knave grown old in crime. In this subversion of all received ideas, the accused might have been taken for a witness, the witnesses for the accused.

One of the questions asked by Fox appeared to me so impertinent, that I objected to the witness's replying to it.

"By what right?" exclaimed Fox, furious.

"You forget," said I, "that I have no account to render to you; I am the representative of the state."

"What new chimera is this?" returned he, with his

habitual insolence. "There is no state within these walls. There is no room here except for justice, admirably represented by the impartiality of the magistrate and the wisdom of the jury. You are a lawyer, like me; nothing more. I represent the defendant, you represent the plaintiff, to whom society gives you as support. You have no right which does not belong to me, I have no privilege which you may not claim. If it were otherwise, the balance of justice would be perverted—the prosecution would be stronger than the defence. What would become of the liberty of the citizen?"

"Your honor," said I, "is this also one of the theories sanctioned by your precedents?"

"Mr. Attorney General," replied he, in a grieved tone, "what you ask astonishes me. In a free country, can there be a question as to the equality of the prosecution and the defence?"

I had nothing to do but to be silent; I let Fox torture the witnesses at his ease. One thing alone consoled me. There is no abuse which, by the side of a thousand inconveniences, does not carry with itself some small advantage. Accustomed from childhood to the rude ordeals of public life, the witnesses did not suffer themselves to be intimidated by the harshness of the questions which were addressed them. In this duel of words, Fox had not always the best of it. It is true that his skin was tough; he rose each time with new fury. Never was the liberty of a man defended with more desperate energy. Among the witnesses figured Seth the Quaker, an important personage at Montmorency in his capacity of hotel-keeper. Seth bore a grudge against the lawyer, for his reverse of the morning, and answered him with a malice which made me smile in spite of my ill humor.

"Do you know the defendant?" asked Fox.

"Yes," said the Quaker, "I know him, to his misfortune and mine."

"Dare you affirm, under oath, that he is a dishonest man?"

"I have never said that he could be accused of being an honest man," replied friend Seth, with the greatest placidity.

"What interest had he in stealing a carriage and horses?"

"None, that I know of," said the Quaker. "He would have done better to have bought them and not paid for them, after the example of honorable gentlemen. Perhaps he had not as much credit as they."

After the hotel-keeper, it was the servant-maid's turn—a plump blonde, with a frank and merry air, but sharp as a needle, like every country girl.

"You pretend," said the lawyer, "that you recognize the defendant, and affirm that he has threatened you in a language more than improper?"

"Yes, sir," murmured she, blushing.

"Speak louder," said Fox; "the gentlemen of the jury cannot hear you."

"I cannot," said she, much agitated.

"You can; do like me; shout."

"You? That is a different thing; it is your trade. You were brought up to it from a child."

"You affirm," continued Fox, "that the defendant has made use of abominable words—so abominable, gentlemen of the jury, that modesty hinders me from repeating them in public."

"Yes, sir," said the poor girl, blushing more and more.

"Very well; repeat these words to the court and jury."

"Sir," said she, straightening herself up, "if your modesty does not permit you to repeat them, how can you imagine that mine permits me?"

"Very well," replied Fox, without being disconcerted, "the jury will take note. You say that the defendant spoke like an impudent fellow. Do you know how an impudent fellow speaks?"

"I think I do," said she, looking at the lawyer in such a way that the assembly burst out laughing, and Fox abandoned the witness.

The list of witnesses exhausted, I addressed the court. Indignation rendered me eloquent; I felt it, and abandoned myself to the pleasure of declaiming. In a speech which deserved to be phonographed, I gave the complete history of this robber. I seized him in the cradle, and did not let him go until he reached the court, where he was about to receive his just punishment. First, I painted him at three years old, as one of those detestable children which have never given their mother a moment's joy; then I accompanied him to school, and showed him idle, lying, quarrelsome, and preluding the gallows by stealing nuts and plums from the trees by the way. By unheard-of good fortune, I had found among the witnesses three honest comrades, who, twenty-five years before, had played the marauder with this future villain. From the school I passed to the workshop, and drew there a horrible portrait of this man, which must have resembled him. I uttered a tirade against drunkenness, that criminal poison, which carried away the audience. When I had gone through ten years of crime, the defendant was already destroyed in the opinion of the jury.

After my discourse, if there was any reason for astonishment, it was that at fifteen he had not killed his father. That this profligate had a soul capable of parricide, I did not doubt, as I said to the jury, but heaven had spared him the greatest of all crimes—the wretch had the happiness to be an orphan!

While the audience was suspended on my eloquent lips, I looked at the prisoner, who was writhing under the lash of my avenging words. Crushed by my reproaches, unable to resist his violently awakened remorse, he rose, and, interrupting me:

"Your honor," exclaimed he, in a husky voice, "if this is to last much longer, I have enough of it; I own myself guilty. I had rather serve my five years, than listen to this fellow."

"Stop!" cried Fox. "What are you thinking of? Take back these fatal words."

"No, no," said he; "this fellow drives me mad; I would give my head to shut his mouth."

"Prisoner," said the judge, "reflect before making a declaration which destroys you. Consider that, if you coolly repeat this avowal, I have nothing to do but to pronounce your conviction."

"Your honor," returned he, "I am obliged to you; you are a worthy magistrate; you do not trample on a poor worm of the earth in difficulty. How can it be helped? I have no chance; let me fall which way I will, I am sure to land on my head. After all, I have stolen; let justice take its course. But as to what I said to my mother, or what I did when I was an urchin at school, it is my opinion that it is none of this fellow's business."

My victory was complete, vanquished by my eloquence more than his remorse, the culprit confessed his crime. To crown my happiness, Fox, whose audacious language I dreaded, could no longer answer me. Force remained to justice and authority.

The session ended, one of the judges came and shook me by the hand. He was a celebrated orator, a mind full of resources, who had more than once in Congress beaten his adversaries when they were in the right. Such approbation added to my triumph; therefore, it was with ill dissembled joy that I received these glorious congratulations.

"I am charmed with your ingenious discovery," said my new friend. "On the first opportunity, I hope to imitate you, and to be no less happy than yourself. To take a man from birth, to seize vice, error and prejudice in the germ, and describe and interpret their long development, is admirable. I imagine that no one could come out intact from this historical review; with your method of proceeding, I would guarantee to demonstrate that Cato was a profligate and Socrates an atheist."

"I have invented nothing," said I, modestly; "you flatter me."

"No," said he; "never, in this country, has any one reasoned in this subtle manner. It is a new logic which does you the greatest honor. The Yankees are a rude people, who pursue the crime and not the man; while to you the material part is nothing, the man is everything. There is no sufficient proof of the crime of which he is accused—what matters it, so long as he is capable of committing it? the presumption is against him, and moreover it is probable he has been guilty of many others. This is what I call fair justice, justice which protects society and is anxious only for the public good. Are you American by birth?"

"This abrupt question astonishes you," continued he, without divining the cause of my surprise. "Excuse my indiscretion; my mother was French, and I owe to her certain ideas which never entered a Saxon brain. These ideas nearly approach yours, and inspire me with the most lively sympathy for the originality of your talent.

"To me, for instance, the state is everything; and despite the stupid prating of ignorant moralists, I maintain that the interest of a whole nation cannot be weighed in the balance with the pretended right of an obscure individual! I am a socialist in the best sense of the word—the state before the individual! The Yankees, on the contrary—contracted minds, narrow brains—have brought from England an egotistical and savage prejudice. Let a judge fail in respect towards an old gipsy, let an attorney general lose patience in prosecuting a pickpocket or brow-beating an assassin, directly a Saxon arises from the earth to proclaim above the house tops that the Magna Charta is violated and humanity outraged; and, lo! an imbecile crowd runs at the voice of the barker and howls after the magistrate, like dogs after a horse on full gallop. It might be called a nation of thieves, each one of which is afraid of appearing himself in court to-morrow, and defends the liberty of others through interest for his own liberty. Thanks to the solidity of my principles, I do not understand justice in this wise; I see with pleasure that in America, we are both of the same opinion. Saints do not appear before the jury, and I had rather send three innocent men to the gallows, than suffer twenty villains to escape. I am a clear-headed man; let us shake hands on it; together we will reform the education of this monotonous people which has but one word in its mouth—liberty!"

He took leave of me, shaking my hand in the most cordial manner; I did not return his warmth! Strange to say! his praises no longer pleased me; I was appalled at my success.

"What if I have gone too far!" thought I. "What if I have suffered myself to be carried away by the ardor of pursuit, like a hunter who listens only to his passion. I have not been in error, since the culprit has confessed his crime; but were the weapons which I used legitimate? Is everything lawful to the prosecution? Has the defendant no right to respect?"

Despite myself, these thoughts agitated me. The idea of public vengeance no longer sufficed me, I vaguely caught a glimpse of a purer doctrine, a doctrine which subjected human justice to the precepts of the Gospel. I said to myself that to Christians, all weakness is holy, all misery sacred, and that with the child, the woman, the poor, and even the guilty, the authority ought to distrust its power, and fear to be too much in the right.

CHAPTER XXV.

DINAH.

On quitting the court room, I found the Quaker, who congratulated me on my adroitness; this compliment gave me indifferent pleasure. Humbug, on the contrary, said nothing; I should have preferred his reproaches; I believe that, at this moment, his anger would have done me good.

Fox was awaiting me in the street; his contracted features and flashing eyes betrayed a passion which he could no longer contain.

"You ought to be satisfied," cried he, as soon as he perceived me. "This is a victory which does you honor. I hope not to be the last to render you justice. A journal will soon be found to glorify the eloquence and doctrine of the attorney general. A Jeffries in America is a monster never before seen, and that will never be seen again—we must make haste to admire him.

"Besides," added he, gnashing his teeth, furious at my silence, "this scarcely surprises me. None are so cruel as those who have domestic troubles; they are a race without pity."

"Domestic troubles!" said I, shrugging my shoulders. "You have lost your reason, Mr. Fox; you do not know to whom you are speaking."

"Indeed," answered he, sneering, "I thought that I was speaking to the happy father of the too amiable Susan."

The face of the man appalled me; his diabolical laughter chilled me to the heart.

"Be silent," said I; "I forbid you to utter a name which all should respect."

"Bah!" said he, with a disdainful smile; "this is ill-placed severity."

"Wretch!" exclaimed I, seizing him by the throat, "explain yourself, or I will crush you on the spot."

"Gentlemen," said the lawyer, struggling, "I call you to witness this violence. Mr. Humbug, you will do me justice!"

"Without any doubt," replied the magistrate. "Sue for damages for this rather hasty answer, and I will give you a dollar. But if the doctor claims three or four thousand dollars from you, in turn, I will not spare you a farthing. It will be a pleasure to me to punish slander."

"Slander!" cried Fox, foaming with rage. "Where does this precious damsel, whose name cannot be spoken, go every day? Is it my fault that I see her every morning, on my way to court, gliding mysteriously into one of the most disreputable houses of the city? Who can the honorable daughter of the honorable attorney general visit in the notorious Laurel street? I saw her go in there a few hours since; I suppose that she is still there, for usually she makes a long stay. Sue me for slander, doctor, it will be an amusing scandal; I shall be avenged!"

I fell into Humbug's arms. My daughter insulted, my Susan defamed!—the blow was too much for a father; I could not see, my whole frame trembled, I was suffocating with sorrow and anger. At last I wept; tears of rage and despair, which, without allaying my trouble, restored to me some dominion over my senses and permitted me to speak.

"Sir," said I to Fox, "Laurel street is two paces from here; you shall follow me there. Humbug, come with me. Mr. Seth, do not quit me. Above all, do not let that man escape. Justice must be done; it shall be done."

"Be easy, friend Daniel," replied the Quaker, "we will all three accompany thee." He dwelt on the last words, *all three*, eyed the lawyer from head to foot, and, rolling up his sleeves, began to cleave the air with a horsewhip which he held in his hand.

"Gentlemen," said Fox, with a sardonic laugh, "I am at your orders. Observe, I beg, that I have nothing to do with a movement which a certain person may regret. There is still time to pause; I am not cruel; but I warn you that, once in this house, whatever may be your prayers and tears, I shall only quit it with the firm resolution to tell all that I have seen there."

"Let us go, sir," said I, "I do not want your pity." I advanced like a drunken man, clinging to the arm of Humbug. Suspect thee, my Susan! I could not; I believed in thy purity as in that of the angels; but the assurance of this man troubled me. I feared an unforeseen stroke, an ambush, a snare. Alas! when one loves, he has courage only for himself.

"Here is the house," cried Fox; "and here is the landlord."

I raised my head; the house had a forbidding appearance. A dark and damp entry, grimy walls, window-panes broken or replaced by bits of paper, or rags stuffed into the windows—it was more than poverty, it was the squalor and filth of vice. Susan in this den! it was impossible.

On the door-step was a man, his coat unbuttoned and hands in his pockets, smoking a pipe and gazing at the passers with all the insolence of an idle vagabond. On seeing us, he took off his shapeless hat, and, flinging himself on me, seized both my hands with an affection which filled me with horror. It was Paddy, half drunk, smelling of rum and tobacco.

"Good morning, my saviour," said he; "you are very good to come to see a friend. Come in, gentlemen; if you are not afraid of a glass of gin, you will find some one to help you drink it."

"Paddy," said I, "does this house belong to you?"

"No, my saviour," answered he, laughing; "if this palace had been mine, I should have drunk it up long ago. It is my wife's—a fine business, isn't it?"

"Do you let furnished rooms?" said I, pointing to a bill.

"At your service, doctor."

"Whom do you lodge in this house?" asked Humbug, in a harsh tone. "Frequenters of my court?"

"Your honor," said the drunkard, yawning, "we are not rich enough to be nice; we take what we can get, and get virtue when we can."

"Who lives in the apartments on the first floor?" said the lawyer, with a cunning air.

"What is that to you, chatterbox?" replied the drunkard. "Do you pay for them?"

"Answer," said Humbug; "do not forget that you are before a magistrate."

"I have nothing to be afraid of," said the Irishman, excited. "You know, your honor, that none but honest people would live in apartments at three dollars a week, paid in advance. A lady lives on the first floor, a pretty lady," added he, lowering his voice, "gentle, polite, and not particular; the pearl of the house."

"What visitors does she have?" continued Humbug, who saw me turn pale.

"Excuse me, your honor, we are not in court. America is a free country, where every one sees whom he likes, so long as he pays for it. I never look at the people who come in the door; if I look at them, I do not see them."

"Don't pretend ignorance," said Fox. "Remember that I have put more than one better man than you in prison. An hour ago, I saw a young lady, with light hair and blue eyes, in a black silk dress and straw hat, come in here; where did she go?"

Paddy, intimidated, drew near me to implore my aid.

"My good fellow," said I, "oblige me by answering. Be sure that we have no bad intentions; I will reward you."

"My saviour," said he, "I have no secrets from you; you have helped me out of difficulty, and I am an Irishman—that says everything. I would go through the fire for you."

"In heaven's name, speak!" said I, giving him some money. "You are killing me!"

"Well, doctor," resumed he, "every day, at the same hour, this young lady with light hair comes to see the lady on the first floor. She is there now."

"I think that my presence is useless," said Fox, in an ironical tone; "the attorney general has no more occasion for my services."

"Sir," said I, with a threatening gesture, "I wish to confound your unworthy suspicions."

Alas! I spoke thus to deceive myself; I knew no longer what to say; I was desperate. Humbug took me by the hand. I entered the cavern like a man on his way to encounter death.

The door of the rooms stood open. There was an antechamber, a sort of kitchen, without curtains or furniture. I paused to regain breath; I heard the beatings of my heart. Seth assured himself that the lawyer had followed us, then closed the door noiselessly and put the key in his pocket. We had nothing more to fear from intruders.

I was unable to speak; I signed to my companions to remain where they were, and glided noiselessly to the entrance of the next room.

Opposite, her back towards me, a woman was half reclining in an old easy-chair; a little girl was seated on a rush-bottomed stool at her feet. By the side of the child, Susan, Bible in hand, was reading to her attentive listeners:

"They cast iniquity upon me, and in their wrath they hate me.

"My heart is sore pained within me, and the terrors of death are fallen upon me.

"Fearfulness and trembling are come upon me, and horror hath overwhelmed me.

"And I said, Oh, that I had wings like a dove! for then would I fly away, and be at rest.

"Lo, then would I wander far off, and remain in solitude.

"I would hasten my escape from the windy storm and tempest.

"Cast thy burden on the Lord, and he shall sustain thee."

"Oh, my Susan!" exclaimed the stranger, "next to God, you have saved my life. How much good these words do me! You, at least, have not forsaken me."

"And me—do you forget me, then?" asked the child.

"No, my dear little one," returned the young woman, "yet none but you missed me at Sunday school; and who remembers me in my family?"

The child threw herself on her teacher's neck, and the three embraced each other, weeping.

Is there contagion in tears? Was emotion too strong for me? I know not; but, whether from pain or pleasure, I could not restrain my sobs.

"My father!" exclaimed Susan, "you here! By what chance do you come?"

"My dear," said I, clasping her to my heart, and using my handkerchief furiously to hide my red eyes, "fathers are curious beings; they are not sorry, sometimes, to know where their children go."

"Curiosity is a bad fault," said Susan, holding up her finger threateningly. "A well brought up father would say to his daughter, 'My dear, will you permit me to accompany you?' and, without waiting to be urged, the lady would take her father's arm, as I do; she would bring him to a poor young woman in need of aid, and would say to him, with a graceful bow, 'Dr. Smith, I entreat your friendship for my dear Dinah.'"

"Sir," said the unknown, taking my hands, "bless her; she is my saving angel."

She rose as she spoke; the smile returned to her pale face, when suddenly she uttered a cry of terror, and fell back in her chair, hiding her face.

The Quaker stood before her, his arms folded, with an air of fury.

"Pardon, brother," murmured the unhappy woman; "have pity on me."

"Is it in this manner that thee keeps thy word?" said

Seth. "Thy mother believes thee on the way to California; she blessed thee when thee left; must she take back her blessing?"

"Seth," said the young woman, drowned in tears, "I set out; my courage failed me; I cannot leave my mother and those who love me."

"Say, rather, that thee cannot leave him, and must destroy thyself."

"No, no," cried she, "I am leading an honest life; he does not know that I am here; he will never know it. I have seen no one but my good Susan."

"And what does thee expect to do?" resumed the Quaker, with a harshness which pained me. "Thee knows that there is no more bread for thee at home."

"Seth," replied she, "do not crush me; I shall not be a burden on you. Susan has found me a place as schoolmistress in the suburbs, where no one will know me. I shall live by my labor. I ask nothing of you, but to go once a week to embrace my mother and see our house."

Nothing is more embarrassing in family scenes than the presence of a third person. I withdrew with Humbug, when, at the back of the antechamber, in a dark corner, I perceived Fox, in contemplation before a smoky engraving. It was a picture of *Monarch*, son of *Eclipse*, the winner of the Derby in 1812. To confound an evil doer, and enjoy his confusion, is a double pleasure; I had no scruples, therefore, in rallying the slanderer.

"I did not think that you had so great a passion for the turf," said I. "At fifty years' distance, that the laurels of Monarch should silence the most celebrated lawyer of Massachusetts is marvelous! It ought to be put in the newspapers."

"For pity's sake, doctor," said he, "let me go."

His face was so much changed, his voice so weak, that in truth it pained me. I had not believed him capable of so much remorse. "See," thought I, "how wrongly men are judged. It is imagined that lawyers feel only on others' account—what a mistake!"

I was about to re-enter the apartment to ask Seth for the key, which he had kept, when the Quaker suddenly appeared, dragging after him his sister, her hair dishevelled, then contemptuously casting her from him. Susan wept bitterly; Humbug endeavored to interpose some kind words; we were all moved; Fox alone had resumed his admiration for Monarch; motionless and mute, he seemed to wish to bury himself in the wall.

"Once more," cried the Quaker, endeavoring to force open the clenched hands which clung to his coat, "once more I repeat to thee thy mother's words, 'Thee shall never return home but in the arms of a husband.' Since this fine stranger has promised thee marriage, make him keep his word."

"Here is a suit in prospective," exclaimed I. "Come, happy avenger of innocence—come, master Fox—this is the moment to show yourself."

If a thunderbolt had fallen at my feet, it would have terrified me less than the outbreak which followed my impertinent pleasantry. Scarcely had Dinah raised her eyes to the lawyer, than she sprang up as if mad, laughing and weeping together.

"Gabriel!" cried she, "my Gabriel! Here he is, brother; here he is!"

I understood nothing of the storm which I had let loose; the Quaker was more intelligent. While Dinah threw herself on the neck of her Gabriel, Seth wound the lash of his horsewhip two or three times round his

wrist, and, approaching Fox, who turned pale at the sight:

"Friend," said he, in a tone far from reassuring, "collect and explain thyself; I am waiting."

Between the caresses of the sister and the threats of the brother, the lawyer presented a piteous appearance, which quite elated me. The natural man is a malicious animal; nothing less than the Gospel could make us love our enemies.

Humbug was a better Christian than I.

"Gentlemen," said he, in a grave but mild voice, "I think that my turn has come. In an affair as delicate as this, the last word belongs to the magistrate:

> "'Nec Deus intersit, nisi dignus vindice nodus
> Inciderit.'

"My dear Fox, I do not doubt your intentions. If any one should ask your advice in like circumstances, you would doubtless answer, that a suit for breach of promise would be followed by the most serious consequences to a lawyer, involving not only the loss of fortune, but the destruction of practice, and perhaps even the necessity of leaving the country. Is not this your opinion?"

"Yes," murmured Fox, sighing.

"Need I add," continued the excellent Humbug, throwing a rope to the drowning man, "need I add, that a man like you has no occasion to trouble himself about these considerations, however grave they may be? It suffices for him to have given his word to keep it; is it not so?"

"Yes," said the lawyer, sighing anew, "I have always loved Dinah; I was checked by difficulties."

"Which no longer exist," interrupted Humbug. "We are all agreed. The affair will end like all good plays—love, tears, and crosses in the first act, with marriage for the dénouement."

Fox embraced Dinah rather ungraciously, and gave his hand to the Quaker; Dinah, flushed with pleasure, ran to Susan.

"My dear friend," said she, "it is to you that I owe my happiness. And to you, too, my child," said she to the little one, who was pale with jealousy.

"All this is very well," said Seth, who never lost himself in the clouds; "but, since we are assembled, and have the justice of the peace here, there is nothing to hinder the marriage ceremony from being performed on the spot."

"Willingly," said Humbug. "Miss Susan, you shall be my clerk."

No sooner said than done. I thought that such unions were only fit for the theatre, where they are dissolved behind the scenes; I thought that the last village notary had long since passed away; but in America, men are always in such haste, that they maintain the old custom. The lovers once agreed, the relatives, and even the notary, are dispensed with. Two affirmatives before a justice of the peace, and you are married for eternity. The will is everything, the formality nothing. These people have no taste for ceremony.

With what pleasure I quitted this house, which I had entered with a troubled heart! Paddy reaped a harvest of dollars, sufficient to take away his senses for a whole week. Never had Laurel Street beheld so honest and joyous a company. I opened the procession with my

Susan, who gave her hand to her little protégé; Humbug and Seth formed the vanguard; between us walked the newly married couple, Dinah smiling like the dawn, Fox hanging his head:

> "Honteux comme un renard qu'une poule aurait pris."

But when one is happy, a little shame is soon swallowed. If the imprudent man had played too lightly with love, how had he been punished for his fault? By marrying a charming wife. At this price, I know innocent men who would become criminals.

It was necessary to prepare Dinah's mother for her daughter's return; it was also necessary for Fox to announce his marriage to his friends and arrange his household. Meanwhile, Susan kept Dinah with her. To me was reserved the part of father and guardian; the happy blunder that I had made gave me some right to it.

A remnant of liberty which he could no longer abuse was restored to Fox, and the whole company returned to my dwelling. There was a great festival in the house. Never had we dined more gaily. Martha opened a mouth as wide as an oven, and sighed like a volcano, while admiring and waiting on her sister-in-law; Susan and Alfred constantly had something to whisper to each other; Dinah alone was admitted as a third party to these mysteries, in which they laughed without ceasing. Seth devoured everything on the table with the satisfaction of a man who has done a good stroke of business, and is dining at another's table. Humbug, who, despite his enormous corpulence, ate little and drank nothing but water, made amends for his sobriety by quoting the most gleeful lines of Horace, that other drinker, who sang fasting the pleasures of intoxication:

> "Nunc est bibendum, nunc pede libero
> Pulsanda tellus."

For my part, with tranquil mind, I enjoyed the gaiety and happiness of the children. But nothing can express the joy and animation of my Jenny. She could not remain in her place; she went, she came; she changed all the plates with the roast beef, the potatoes, the ham, the pie, the cheese, the fruit, and the cake; she poured out the Scotch ale, Madeira, and Rhine wine, in profusion; she had a gracious word for every man, a caress for every woman. A marriage! It was to her the prize in a lottery. If there was a verse in the Bible which Jenny regarded as divinely inspired above all others, it was the great command which God addressed at creation to the first couple: *Be fruitful, and multiply, and replenish the earth, and subdue it.* The excellent woman was neither American nor Protestant by halves. In her eyes celibacy was a crime, or at least a disease, which could not be too soon cured. If she had had her own way, she would not have left a bachelor on earth; I fancy that she would have ended by marrying the Pope and Italy.

CHAPTER XXVI.

THE CHARITY HOSPITAL.

The next morning, at breakfast time, my heart was free from care. Dinah at my right and Susan at my left gave me the air of a patriarch amidst his children. Since I have begun to grow old, nothing pleases me more than to see about me these young faces, fresh as the dawning day, and smiling as hope. Alas! that we cannot put aside all thorns from their path. Alas! that we cannot lend them that experience which life sells to us so dearly, and which avails us nothing!

My wife did not do things by halves. If I had adopted Dinah, Fox was the protégé of Jenny—he was married! He had his knife and fork laid, therefore, by the side of his beloved. He entered without the least embarrassment, a bridal bouquet in his hand, and embraced his bride with a conquering air. When the sharp face of the lawyer was distorted by anger, he was not handsome; tender and gallant, he was hideous; he might have been styled an amorous serpent. This was not Dinah's opinion; in vain I said the most amiable things to her; she had eyes only for her other neighbor. Rachel had less admiration for Jacob, when he rolled away the stone in the desert to water the flocks of Laban. Women have in the highest degree the instinct of property; and, of all properties, that which is nearest their heart is a husband. But, while the Frenchwoman is a huntress nymph who, the game once caught, cares little for it, the American woman takes possession of her husband with the fierceness and jealousy of the French peasant who espouses the soil. He is her property, he is her thing; the unfortunate is no longer but a caged bird, a domestic slave; yet a bird that is caressed, a slave, all of whose desires are anticipated. The Americans abuse their independence to such a degree out of doors, that, on returning home, they have no longer a will of their own. The Yankee, who makes it his glory and pride to yield to no man, is nothing in his household but a compliant husband, who listens to his wife and takes delight in obeying her; gentle with the weak, intractable with the strong. This contrary minded people does nothing like us.

Fox wished to carry away Dinah to make her wedding purchases; Susan opposed it.

"Sir," said she, "I am sorry; but Dinah belongs to me. We have found her an engagement for six months as schoolmistress; this is the day that she is to enter on her duties, and she cannot break her word. In a little time, it will be easy for me to replace her, and leave her to you for a whole week; to-day, it is impossible. Papa," added she, "we count on you for our inauguration."

"My dear child," said I, "you forget that I also enter to-day on my duties in the Providence Hospital; I am already very late. That suit of yesterday"——

"It makes no difference," said Susan; go directly to see your little patients; our school is in Federal street, close by Walnut street; we shall expect you at noon."

On reaching the hospital, I inquired for the directress—it was a woman, Susan's teacher, the celebrated Mrs. Hope, doctor in medicine and professor of hygiene; another of those contradictions which are met only in the United States. She was, however, a respectable matron, who welcomed me as a comrade, and directly commenced the rounds with me. The hospital was a model; in no country have I seen so perfect an installation. Vast halls with a small number of beds, placed far apart, no curtains, plenty of air, a judicious light, silence, exquisite neatness, with nothing of that stale and nauseous odor which makes an hospital an object of repugnance, and often a poisonous abode. For the first time, I found united all the conditions demanded by hygiene no less than charity.

At the call of Mrs. Hope, a flying squadron of young ladies rushed toward us. A black dress, bib apron, and white cap gave them the air of counterfeit sisters of charity. They were the resident students of the hospital, the future doctors in petticoats of free America. They followed my clinic with the greatest attention; I was struck with the clearness of their explanations in giving me the condition of the patient, and the care with which they noted down all my words and prescriptions; but I had too much good sense to take this chimerical essay in earnest, and asked good Mrs. Hope what she expected from this singular education.

"I think," said she, "that we are about to effect a great reform. These young pupils have already been two years in the Maternity Hospital, next year they will go to the Clinic for Women; we shall make them true physicians."

"Bravo!" exclaimed I, "it will be charming for us grey beards to be attended by Hippocrates of eighteen, in crinoline and laces."

"No," said she, "we have nothing to do with you gentlemen. But accouchement, the care of infants, the diseases and maladies of women—these belong to us; we understand them better than you. We shall leave you surgery and extraordinary cases, but all that a mother or wife confides to you only with regret, we shall take ourselves; you will be driven from a domain which you have usurped. We shall introduce modesty into medicine; prejudice will cry out as usual, but we shall have the women, fathers and husbands on our side; we shall win, do you not think so?"

What could I reply to a fanatic, especially when this fanatic was a woman; that is, a being weak by nature and afflicted with organic obstinacy? I broke off the discussion, and continued my visit. The diseases were not serious, and the little patients were so tenderly and prudently cared for that little was left me to prescribe. I had to perform but a single operation and that of little importance. I opened an abscess of bad character and inconveniently situated in the neck of a child. Lightness of hand, and grace and elegance of dressing are the glory of our Parisian school; I achieved great success, therefore, with my young pupils; my bandage, with its ingenious folds, was directly sketched, and the drawing placed as a model in the operating hall. Indeed, on seeing so much intelligence, good will, and attention, there were moments when I would have admitted that women are good for something else than to give pap to infants. "*All this is not over uncomely*," Montaigne would have said, "*but what! they do not wear breeches.*"

I made this wise reflection in time and, I say it to my honor, remained faithful to the ancient religion of the Faculty. Novelties in politics may pass, there they are innocent; but elsewhere, long live prejudice! The proof that it is salutary is that it has the majority on its side, and that stones are cast at innovators. I found these young heretics charming, but their heresy was abominable, and I did not yield to it.

The visit finished, I repaired to the meeting of the board of managers; Mrs. Hope accompanied me, and took her seat among us without astonishing any one but me by her presence. Among the trustees or managers, I found faces that I knew; Rose, the apothecary, the gallant Colonel St. John, the amiable Humbug, and Noah Brown, the insupportable Puritan. The directress was the first to speak; she set forth, with documents in hand and in good language, the insufficiency of the house, and the necessity of purchasing an adjoining garden as a yard for the use of the convalescents. When she had ended, my opinion was asked.

"I fully approve this excellent idea," said I, "and I am convinced that by addressing a clear and well-written memorial to the administration, with proper recommendations, we shall obtain in eight or ten years this urgent improvement."

"Of what administration do you speak?" asked the colonel, who presided by right of seniority."

"I speak of the general administration of hospitals."

"What sort of a monster is that?" said Humbug, laughing." "Brown, is it a new name for Leviathan?"

"A truce to jests," said I to Humbug. "I suppose that this hospital, like all others, is dependent on a great protective and central administration. Does the State, the city, or a corporation, regulate, watch over, and organize charity?—it matters little, it is evident that it still depends on some one or something?"

"That is an evidence," said the rude Brown, "which is the opposite of the truth. Thank God! we depend on no one. We unite together to relieve misery; we put our good will, time, and money in common; we submit our statutes to the State, which makes us a corporation; after this, who can have a right to meddle with our affairs? Is charity a crime? Is it a political or municipal charge? I am a Christian, I succor the poor in my own way; who can impede me in the first of all duties? Is Heaven won by proxy?"

"Pardon me," said I, "no one hinders you from giving your money; no tyranny has ever pushed cruelty thus far. But the right to found a hospital is another thing; if we leave to the first comer the right to open one of these asylums, what disorder will not come of it? You will ere long have homeopathic hospitals, and I know not what besides!"

"Homeopathic hospitals," said Rose; "there are three in the city, and a fourth is about to be established. What harm does it do?"

"Rose, my dear friend, exclaimed I, "do you, an orthodox apothecary, utter such monstrosities?"

"My dear doctor," answered Rose, "we do not recognize, even in religion, an official orthodoxy. We leave to each one a right to seek God according to his own conscience. In good faith, we cannot be more rigorous towards the health of the body than that of the soul. Besides, my good friend, we are both augurs; we know how much to rely on official medicine and orthodox pills."

"So be it," replied I; "proclaim the freedom of quackery and poisoning. Nothing longer astonishes me in this republic, which should put on its federal flag the device of the Abbey of Thélème, *Do what thou wilt;* but I will address you in the name of utility and good sense.

With your let-alone system, how many hospitals have you?"

"A hundred, at most," said Mrs. Hope.

The number astonished me; I had not imagined such a fecundity of anarchical charity; but I was not at the end of reasoning.

"A hundred hospitals!" exclaimed I; "gentlemen, retrench this formidable number. If it does honor to the Christians of Paris, in Massachusetts, ask yourselves, as practical men, what this multiplicity, this rivalry must inevitably produce—duplicate offices, loss of money; here, superabundance; there, complete absence of aid; waste and poverty. Suppose, on the contrary, a vast administration uniting these dispersed threads, concentrating these stray forces; place at the apex of the pyramid a vigilant, active and economical man—directly order reigns, and with order all the blessings of unity. Hierarchy of physicians, regular clinics, disciplined instruction, central pharmacy, central bakery, meat shop, fish market, laundry, in a word, a veritable empire—the empire of charity, with its ruler, his ministers and subjects. This is not a dream; this ideal is a truth in the countries which are at the head of civilization. Thanks to the marvellous power of centralization, I affirm, that with a small number of large hospitals and an energetic organization, it would be easy for me to double the number of your beds without costing you a dollar more."

"I am convinced of it," said Humbug. "With his talisman, the doctor is capable of making the world anew and expelling from it all the disorders of liberty. I demand that by a unanimous vote it shall be put into his hands—mills, foundries, lumber-yards, manufactories, and so on. With central works and a hierarchy of engineers, I do not doubt that he will double the production while diminishing the expense."

"You are unbearable," said I; "do you take me for a communist? Do I not know that in industry this unity is chimerical?"

"Why so?" resumed the everlasting scoffer. "In industry, does not centralization necessarily bring about economy of force, regularity of production, hierarchy and discipline of labor?"

"Doubtless," answered I; "but this is a narrow side of the question. This mechanical uniformity destroys the moral law of production. What is this factitious regularity if it destroys the watchfulness of the master, if it annihilates individual effort, private interest, free competition? A drop of water in the ocean. What I propose to you, on the contrary"——

"Is exactly the same thing," interrupted Humbug, with vivacity. "Private interest, individual effort, free competition, all these motive powers which you appreciate so truly, are also the motive powers of charity, and it must be added, of patriotism which lives only by liberty. If the state or parish takes it upon itself to succor the poor in my stead and place, if this enormous mechanism rids me of the first of all virtues, I shall grumblingly pay a meagre tax, and there will be an end of it. But leave to my charge the care of wretchedness and the sweets of alms, and I shall bring you my last farthing. I care little for the other hospitals of the city, I am not acquainted with them; but this one belongs to me, these children are mine, I love them as if God had given them to me alone. When I have ended my day's labors, when I am sad and weary, I come here; in the midst of my little protégés, I forget my cares. Ask these gentlemen what their voluntary charity costs them. I estimate that, at the lowest figure, it swallows up one-tenth of their income; I defy the state to take a twentieth part for its official hospitals. Every one would cry out against the tyranny. That money may be wasted and strength lost, I grant; but it is the result which we are to look at; and I affirm, documents in hand, that individual charity is three or four times as fruitful as organized charity. Your system, my dear doctor, unceasingly casts an obstacle between the will and the deed, which freezes everything. We are not paralytics, let us act; see what a people gains by liberty. In a political point of view, it is wholly to the interest of the state to leave us the practice of the most amiable and sociable of the virtues; in an economical point of view, it is a good business; it multiplies assistance and studies; it serves, at the same time, science and humanity."

"Gentlemen," said the colonel, "it seems to me that we are digressing greatly from the question. We are asked for twenty thousand dollars to increase and improve our hospital; we have but one thing to do—to subscribe, and send the subscription list to our associates. I have no children, and have adopted these little ones; I will set the example, and subscribe a thousand dollars."

The list passed from hand to hand; when it came to me, I did like Rose, and subscribed fifty dollars.

"Permit me a last reflection," said I to the Board. "I see that we pay ten thousand dollars for a small garden; is not this too dear?"

"It is twice the real value," replied Mrs. Hope; "but the owner will not part with it for less."

"A fine thing!" cried I. "A landowner sets his convenience and selfishness above the interest of the poor!

Well, gentlemen, we must take forcible possession of it; do not encourage an odious speculation, by your weakness!"

"Dr. Smith," said Brown, frowning, "this is communism of the first water."

"Nonsense!" returned I, shrugging my shoulders; "ought not private interest to yield to public interest?"

"Doubtless," replied the Puritan; "but nothing is so dangerous as hackneyed maxims. High-sounding words are always used to kill liberty! Property is not an interest, it is a right. General interest is an elastic and vague word, which may cover the most unjust as well as the most legitimate pretensions. Before invoking, begin by defining it."

"Our laws have decided the question," said Humbug. "There are for us but four causes of forcible dispossession—a highway, a street, a railroad, and a canal. But, although we may be preëminently a municipal people, and the city be sovereign in what regards it, nevertheless, property is a thing so sacred that, before touching it, the legislature of the state must interfere. This it is which approves the route and authorizes the dispossession in consideration of preliminary indemnity. For everything else—schools, hospitals, town-houses, churches, the law places private right above an interest which, after all, is only that of a district. Doctor, where would your system lead? I would be despoiled of the inheritance of my fathers, my memories would be wrested from me, my affections would be mocked, the most sacred of possessions would be disturbed, and for what? To build a theatre or public house? This cannot be."

"What!" exclaimed I, "in a republic where the people rule, dare you defend these old feudal maxims?"

"Sir," said Brown, "you understand nothing of liberty. The more democratic a country is, the more necessary is it that the individual should be powerful and his country respected. We are a people of sovereigns; all that weakens the individual leads us to demagogism—that is, to disorder and ruin; all that strengthens the individual leads us to democracy—the reign of reason and the Gospel. A free nation is a nation where every citizen is absolute master of his conscience, person, and property. On the day that, instead of being told of our individual rights, we shall be told of the general interest, it will be all over with the work of Washington; we shall be a mob, and have a master."

"Gentlemen," said the colonel, who was indifferently interested in our debate, "there is nothing more before us; the meeting is adjourned. I ask pardon for leaving you," added he. "It is said that there is bad news from the seat of war; I am in haste to know the truth."

I was not sorry to have done with the Puritan and his harsh language; but, unhappily for me, I had pleased him; or, rather, I suppose that he had formed the glorious project of converting me to his fanaticism.

"Doctor," said he, "I have a favor to ask of you. We are just establishing a mechanics' institute in this ward. There will be a library, a museum of models, two halls of design, public lectures, a reading room—in a word, everything which will be useful to a club of this kind. The mechanics themselves will defray the cost of its support; far from us be the thought of interfering as benefactors, or in anywise disturbing the work of liberty. Never to weaken either the dignity or the responsibility of those whom we oblige is the first rule of charity. But the first expenses are considerable, and the purses of our mechanics would hardly suffice for them. At least ten thousand dollars are needed; to obtain this sum, we give public lectures, with an admission fee. The classic Everett has promised us his co-operation, as well as the eloquent Sumner. We shall have, I hope, the philosopher Emerson and the poet Longfellow. For my part, I shall give a lecture, in which I shall show that, by rehabilitating labor and upraising the laborer, the Gospel has created at once wealth and moral liberty. You will not refuse to join us. Two lectures on the hygiene of new-born infants, by the learned physician of the Providence hospital, will give us all the mothers, and be worth to us at least four hundred dollars."

"Have you the authorization of the government?" asked I.

"Really, doctor, you will go straight to Paradise," answered the crabbed preacher. "By caring for children, you have become like these little ones; you can no longer walk without leading-strings. What authorization is necessary to enlighten men and do them good?"

"What!" cried I. "Can you give courses of public lectures, and talk politics to the workingmen, without the interference of the government?"

"Assuredly," said he; "if we forget our duties, the law is at hand, and the writs with it; this suffices."

"No, it does not suffice; the state cannot abandon to the first comer the right of speech-making to the citizens. This science of parade, this semi-instruction, inspires the people with a disastrous ambition; you endanger the country, and religion itself."

"Twilight is better than darkness, the reign of the appetites and passions," said Brown; "and moreover, what means is there of finding light, if not seeking it?

It is necessary that we should address the people and be unceasingly in connection with them. To us democrats and Christians, there is here a question of life and death. What kills republics is ignorance; enlighten the people, if you fear despotism. What kills religion is an unreasoning faith; enlighten the people, if you fear infidelity. We must have light in everything and everywhere. If Christianity be a fable, let it fall; if it be truth, let it rule. Do you believe that we pastors are charlatans, who live by error and credulity?"

"Calm yourself," answered I, "and do not view the question from so high a standpoint. You will grant that, in giving the mechanics a place of meeting, you establish a club where they will be the masters."

"Of course, since they will be at home."

"Do you not see, then, that, on the first quarrel with their employers, this club will be the nucleus of a coalition?"

"If the mechanics wish to form a coalition," said the fanatic, coldly, "who can hinder them from doing so? Those who sell their labor have as many rights as those who buy it. It is a free bargain."

"But, sir," exclaimed I, indignant at this stupidity, "you are preaching anarchy."

"Sir," said he, with his usual rudeness, "you speak a language which is not that of America. Anarchy is the invasion of the liberty of others; it is not the defence of one's own liberty.

"Believe me," added he, raising his inspired eyes to heaven, "the cultivation of the soul is the salvation of Christian democracies; they live only through education. Let the workingmen read, instruct themselves and argue; elevate them, according to the admirable sense of the word, elevate them to yourself, elevate yourself with them, and you have to fear neither coalitions nor communism, nor any of those follies which terrify the old continent. These are maladies engendered by ignorance; it belongs to us, doctor, to cure them. *Sursum corda*, behold my motto!"

"I accept it heartily," answered I, carried away by the impetuosity of the inspired preacher, "count on me."

Left alone with Humbug, I asked him whether he would come with me to Dinah's inauguration.

"I shall take care not to miss it, Dr. Paradox," said he, with a wicked smile, "you are too amusing with your magnificent theories. The more I hear you, the better I appreciate the greatness of our institutions."

"Thanks for the compliment," answered I. "It appears that my praises of centralization have the effect on you of a demonstration of liberty *per absurdum;* you should be more charitable, my good friend, and remember that there are other countries in the world beside America."

"I see what you are aiming at," said he, "fanatic of Latin unity, pious worshipper of France. I, too, love the French, the grandchildren of Lafayette are to me brethren; but, I ask pardon of this ingenious people, for seventy years they have been pursuing an insoluble problem. To put liberty in a charter and despotism in the administration is to attempt to walk with the arms and legs tied; all the wit in the world would never succeed in it."

"Indeed," resumed I, smiling at this vanity. "Come, practical man, tell us then what Frenchmen lack to elevate themselves to the civilization of the Yankees."

"A single thing," said he in great earnest. "In all

their systems, they have forgotten the essential article. Their politicians are like absent-minded Sam."

"Who is absent-minded Sam?"

"He was our village carrier," said Humbug, laughingly; "a fellow full of wit and shrewdness, daring to temerity, economical to avarice, exact to minuteness, the pride and honor of Connecticut. He had but one failing, the lack of memory. One day, when he had more than fifty packages to distribute along the way he appeared constantly restless and agitated. 'I have forgotten something,' said he, 'what can it be?' On reaching home, his children ran to meet him, crying 'Papa! papa! where is mamma?' 'Heavens!' cried Sam, striking his forehead, 'that is what I missed; I have forgotten my wife.'

"So it is with Frenchmen; take at random one of those constitutions which have been manufactured for them by dozens; you will find in it the State and its rights, the individual and his rights, but there will be lacking"—

"What?" exclaimed I.

"Society," answered Humbug. "It has never occurred to a French legislator that society; that is, association under every form, the free action of individuals united, could have a place in the political life of the nation. We Americans give it the broadest domain—the district, the church, the hospital, the school, higher education, sciences, letters. Each association is to us a family enlarged, and all these associations rising from one degree to another, form so many strata ascending from the individual to the State. America is, to speak truly, only a union of families, transacting their own business. In France, is there anything which resembles this? But a single thing is seen there; the administration, a huge polypus, which stretches out its shoots everywhere, lays hold of everything, grasps everything, stifles everything:

"Monstrum horrendum, immane, ingens, cui lumen ademptum."

"The country is cut in twain; on one side the ruling power, with all the resources of a formidable centralization, on the other a crowd obeying more or less willingly. Thence all the revolutions which rend this beautiful country, thence their perpetual abortiveness. Now the authority is weakened and reduced to impotence, men think to increase liberty and arrive only at anarchy; then they rush into the opposite extreme and tighten all bonds, they think to serve order and arrive only at despotism. Deplorable spectacle of a noble people which raises itself from the abyss only to fall on the other side!"

"And the remedy, my dear friend? Who knows whether the national character be not the cause of this perpetual lack of success?"

"I do not believe," said Humbug, "that there are peoples born to serve; I do not even except the negroes. I do not see, moreover, that France has ever made a bad use of association. Thanks to the administration, which swims on the surface after every revolution and enriches itself by every shipwreck, Frenchmen have always been refused this peaceful liberty which moderates and subdues all the others. A vote which avails them little has ten times been given them, but the care of their own affairs they still await. Kings for an hour, they are refused on the morrow even the faculty of acting and speaking. In these conditions, the experiment is not made; sovereignty is not liberty. With the first, a people conquers often only a right to destroy itself; with the second, it lives, grows, and holds in its hands its fortune and honor. When Frenchmen shall have essayed to govern themselves, we shall be at liberty to condemn them; until then, no one has a right to accuse them. La Fayette, whose writings, neglected perhaps in France, we read, demanded half a century ago this free life, these free assemblies which make our greatness. If I had the honor to be his fellow-countryman, this is the inheritance which I would reclaim. He who shall teach Frenchmen that centralization enslaves them and that association alone can set them free, will pluck out forever the germ of revolution, and plant at last in a generous soil a tree which will never wither. He, far more surely than Archimedes, can cry '*Eureka!*' he will have discovered at the same stroke two treasures more precious than all the riches of the world—liberty and peace."

"Bravo, Humbug!" exclaimed I, "this is eloquence. But, my good friend, if you should relate these fables at Paris in France, you would be hissed as a dreamer, even if you should not be imprisoned as guilty of sedition, amidst the applause of modern Athens."

"This would little astonish me," said he; "the Athenians of former times had a philosopher, whom the Pythoness proclaimed the wisest of men; therefore they made haste to put him to death. The wits of Agora, the practical men accused Socrates of being a revolutionist and atheist. Where is to-day the memory of those great statesmen who repeated in every key that they had saved the country, and who naturally were recompensed for their services? A citizen is not checked by these miserable obstacles, he points out the rock, he struggles, he cries till the waves stifle him; he saves men sometimes in spite of themselves, and expects nothing but of posterity. Gratitude is the virtue of the future."

"Strange people!" murmured I. Among these shopkeepers, convictions are passions, while among us, a heroic and theatrical people, passions and interests are convictions which"——I kept the rest of the reflection to myself.

CHAPTER XXVII.

THE SCHOOL.

While talking, we reached Federal street. In front of us, on a hill which overlooked the city and country, proudly rose an edifice of imposing appearance, a square tower, flanked by two wings. Had I been in a civilized country, I should have called it the barracks of the gendarmery or the hall of the prefecture; among this people, without police or government, it was the palace of A B C—it was the school! A nation may be judged by its monuments.

"Well, doctor," said Humbug, "what do you think of our palace of youth?"

"Very handsome externally," replied I; "but very badly arranged. I see yonder great boys of fifteen and girls of the same age entering together at one door; this is improper. In every well organized school, the sexes are separated—a precaution of which you do not seem to have even an idea."

"Two entrances for children who study in the same room," said Humbug. "To what purpose?"

"In the same room!" exclaimed I; "what are you thinking of? It is the height of immorality."

"I see nothing immoral but your imagination," rejoined Humbug, laughing. "Our children, my dear doctor, are honest children; none are found amongst us but—

"'Virgines lectas puerosque castos.'

The school is a great family, where there are only brothers and sisters contending for the prizes of study. Where did you get these horrible affectations?"

"Then, my good friend, the Yankees are angels, males and females."

"The Yankees," returned the judge, "are men who take the trouble to reflect and reason."

"And is Europe," rejoined I, "with its twenty centuries of experience, but a dotard, knowing neither what it says nor does?"

"My dear doctor," said Humbug, "the English began by sneering at us; to-day, they imitate us. Before ten years have passed, there will be no longer a single school in England where the sexes are not together. As to the other peoples of Europe, their education has been so long clerical that more than a day will be needed to divest them of their prejudice. We rear neither monks nor soldiers, we prepare men for every-day life. Why not make the school, then, the image of the family and society?"

"You are imprudent men," I exclaimed; "you play with fire."

"We are fathers of families," returned Humbug; "we know by experience that to soften the heart, form the character and inspire generous ideas, nothing equals this first community of labor and study.

"'Emollit mores, nec sinit esse feros.'

"What is imprudent and insane is the pretended wisdom of old Europe. To separate boys and girls, to teach them from the earliest age that they are mysteriously dangerous to each other, to disturb and excite young imaginations, and then all at once, at the most critical moment, to fling upon the world ardent and rash men, restless, timid and defenceless women, is madness of the first order. I beg pardon of your gravity, my dear doctor. Your cloistral education is a dike which retains and swells all the passions; our common education accustoms our children to love each other like brothers and respect each other mutually."

"Is it possible," cried I, "that the dangers of your system do not stare you in the face?"

"Ask our teachers," replied he. "You will not find one that is not proud of our mixed schools. They are the invention and honor of America. As usual, we have had confidence in human nature and liberty; as usual, we have succeeded. Nowhere is the instruction stronger or morality greater than in our beloved institution. The emulation between the sexes is a spur that has no parallel. However much of a child he may be, the man is always ashamed to yield the first rank; the woman is patient, and has a more open intellect; in these first studies, in which there is nothing abstract, she almost always takes the lead. But this is only a narrow side of the question. The young girls gain as much in character and will as the young men gain in heart. They learn to know us; and, between ourselves, my good Daniel, we are dangerous only in proportion as we are not known. Respected, the young girls respect themselves; free, they take themselves the place which fits them—for instance, in recreations, a natural prudence separates them from their companions. As to the young men, they acquire in our schools that delicacy of feeling, that chivalrous politeness, which the society of women alone can give. What is rougher and more boisterous than the English schoolboy, abandoned to himself and the tyranny of his seniors?

Have you read Tom Brown? It is enough to make us blush for civilization. I had rather live among the red-skins than the schoolboys of Eton and Rugby. Among us, on the contrary, the youth of both sexes grow up together. At sixteen, at twenty, their relations are as simple and fraternal as when they were found on the same benches. More than one marriage is made among these former school-fellows; esteem and friendship bring love, and survive it. Has Europe, your idol, ever invented anything so Christian and so perfect?"

"It is a dream," said I.

"Enter, incredulous," rejoined Humbug, "and you will see that this dream is a reality."

"A word more," said I. "All these children are saints, that is a matter of course; but where do you find men capable of rearing these celestial phalanxes? Who is the master that can at once animate the timidity of your young girls, and quell the turbulence of your boys? Where find this phœnix who, in every district, is answerable for the honor and virtue of your children?"

"Enter," replied Humbug; "you will see at the work your protégé, Dinah, and perhaps your dear Susan."

"You are mad!" exclaimed I, striking the ground with my cane. "Is it to a woman of twenty that you entrust men with already a beard on their chin? A fine general for such an army! How she must be respected!"

"Again a prejudice of the Old World, my dear friend. To a young man who loves his mother and sister, nothing is more natural than to respect a woman, or less so than to obey a teacher who threatens and punishes him. Force has little hold on the heart of a child; the more generous he is, the more he resists; but he is without defence against gentleness and affection. On this point, again, experience gives the lie to ancient wisdom, which is only old error. It is the women of New England who, with missionary devotion, exile themselves among the corruption of the South and the solitudes of the West, to rear young souls, and give them to the truth and to God. We have masters who are second to none, but our best endowed instructors often fail where a Yankee girl does marvels. Childhood belongs to woman; it is a natural law, which we have had the merit to recognize and apply."

"Amen," replied I, shrugging my shoulders; "let us go then to admire these timid ewes and docile sheep, led by a shepherdess no less innocent than her flock."

I entered the schoolroom ill-humoredly; I cannot endure unreasonableness; but, I confess it to my shame, scarcely had I set foot in the sanctuary when I was fascinated.

I found myself in a vast apartment, well supplied with air and light from large windows; the walls were of exquisite neatness and hung at intervals with maps, pictures of natural history, and physical and geometrical figures. Each child had his desk, isolated by four passages intersecting each other about him. Seated before this varnished table, which shone like a mirror, alone and without a neighbor, the scholar was his own master; if he were abstracted, if he did not work, on him fell the whole responsibility. The teacher, placed on a platform, surveyed at a glance the long files of desks, ranged one behind another—a surveillance scarcely necessary among an ambitious people, where each one is anxious to instruct himself in order to arrive at fortune and power! The vices of the Americans serve them better than our virtues serve us.

Dinah was busy in an adjoining room. My Susan was the mistress of the large schoolroom. At this moment she was teaching geometry to seven or eight tall lads, who, to do them justice, listened like good children to their amiable teacher.

"Come, papa," said Susan, joyfully, "take this chalk, and demonstrate to us the properties of the square of the hypothenuse."

To make the demonstration would have been difficult for me; I had been too well brought up by the University of France to understand anything of geometry; all that I had retained on this point was reduced to an old song which perhaps is still hummed in the suburbs of the Polytechnic School to the air of *Calpigi.*

"Le carré de l'hypoténuse*
Est égal, si je ne m'abuse,
A la somme des deux carrés
Faits sur les deux autres côtés."

I left Susan therefore to draw on the blackboard the rectangled triangle A B C, erect on each side the square, etc., etc., and made my escape, that my daughter might not have to blush for the paternal ignorance.

In one of the class rooms, of which there were eight, Dinah was questioning children of eight or nine years, on the rivers of France and their tributaries. I was astonished at their memory and knowledge, I, a Frenchman

* The square of the hypothenuse
Is equal, if I mistake not,
To the sum of the two squares
Made on the two other sides.

who, questioned on America, could have offered nothing in exchange to these young erudite scholars but the Mississippi, the Hudson and the Potomac, the only water courses of which I had ever heard. It is true that America little concerns us, while France, the queen of letters and arts, must interest the Americans prodigiously. It is the admiration of barbarians for civilization!

After geography came reading aloud and declamation. A little fellow of nine rose, and without timidity as without effrontery, recited to us one of the most poetic passages of Longfellow's Hiawatha. Although the young prodigy spoke through his nose, a vice common in America, he gave us the extract with much precision of tone and true feeling; there are celebrated actors who have never attained thus far.

After the poetry, it was the turn of eloquence. A child, with flaming red locks, rose, set his feet square, and in an animated voice, intoned a hymn to the glory of America.

"Friends and Fellow-citizens:

"You are only in infancy, yet notwithstanding, you are already the first people on the globe. Who was the hero of the last century, the greatest man, and best, the friend of his country and liberty? The universe answers, George Washington; an American. Who was at that time the greatest natural philosopher? Franklin; an American. The greatest theologian? Jonathan Edwards; an American. Who is the greatest jurisconsult of the nineteenth century? Judge Story; an American. Who are the first orators of our age? Clay, Webster, Everett, Sumner; all Americans. Who are the first historians? Prescott, Bancroft, Lothrop Motley, Ticknor; Americans. Who is the first naturalist? James Audubon; an American. Who are the greatest moralists and truest sages of our times? Channing, Emerson, Parker; all Americans. Who are the first novelists of our age? Harriet Beecher Stowe;* an American. Who have been the greatest inventors? Whitney, who invented the cotton gin, Fulton, who created the steamboat, Morse, who discovered the electric telegraph, Maury, who traced infallible routes over the seas; all Americans.

"Courage then, sons of the Puritans! the future is yours. Before the close of the century you will be a hundred million men. What will enslaved and divided Europe be before you? Nature has given you the largest lakes, the largest rivers, the finest harbors. You have fertile lands, and in inexhaustible quantity. Your coal mines are as large as those of France. Industry has given you more railroads, more steamboats, more ships, than all your rivals together. Your men are the bravest, the most daring, the most ingenious in the universe; your women are the most beautiful in creation. Courage then, race blessed of heaven! the world is thine, for thou art at once the freest and the most Christian of peoples."

"My dear friend," said I to Humbug, "among the virtues which you teach your little saints, do you number modesty?"

"A little indulgence, my dear doctor," replied he, with an embarrassed air. "In bringing up children it is well to strain patriotism a little. It is the means of preventing selfishness later from taking the lead. I avow, moreover, that vanity is our weak side. Our prodigious growth turns our head, and makes us run into more than one fault. But let him who is without sin cast the first

* This was also the opinion of Alfred de Musset. One day when we found him bending over "Uncle Tom's Cabin," which he was devouring, his eyes filled with tears, he said, with the profoundest emotion, "This is the finest book of the time. Mrs. Stowe has found, in the *flow of her heart*, artistic effects such as none of us, who think ourselves artists, is capable of finding in his mind."

stone. John Bull is convinced that, by right of birth, he is king of the seas; and I am sure that in France it is repeated in every key to the youth that the French are the first people on the earth, and that the world has eyes only to admire them."

"What a difference!" exclaimed I. "France is France!"

"America is America!" answered he, laughing. "All Christians are imbued with the same madness. There is no folly into which a nation may not be drawn by crying with assurance, 'Englishmen, steal this province, you are English! Frenchmen, fight, right or wrong, you are French! Americans, be insolent to Europe, you are Americans!' The national pride is the red flag which is held out to the popular bull when it is wished to make him fall head-foremost into a snare. My dear friend, let us scatter education broadcast, let us carry enlightenment everywhere, if we would not have the people the eternal dupe of charlatans, who play with its noblest passions and best instincts."

At this moment the clock struck; it was the hour of recreation. I hastened to the yard, where I found the amiable Naaman become the captain of a new band. Three or four hundred children were ranged in columns, the girls on one side, the boys on the other. A glass door looking on the court was opened, a piano rolled to it, and Susan and Dinah struck up in concert Oberon's march. Directly the columns began to move: they skipped, they ran, they paused, in measure. The chain separated and linked itself together again with admirable precision. It was a mingling of dancing and gymnastics which charmed the eyes—something at once noble, bold, and graceful. Was it not thus that the Greeks exercised youth? For the first time I comprehended why Plato placed music and dancing among the duties of the citizen. I was delighted, and, despite my grey beard, and without a remnant of shame, would willingly have taken my place in this military ballet. Why should I not dance with children? the Spartans did so.

"My young friend," said I to Naaman, "this is charming, my heart is rejoiced at the spectacle; but solve one doubt for me—where am I? where have I been carried? This beautiful house, these elegant tables, these handsome books bound in sheep; all these, doubtless, belong to a private school, where only rich children are received. Who is the superintendent of this fine establishment?"

"Still jesting, doctor," said the handsome pastor. "You are in the primary school of the twelfth ward, third district. We have eighty houses of this kind in our good city of Paris, and this is not enough."

"Very well; but how can the son of the poor man defray the expenses of this costly education?"

"Where do you come from?" exclaimed Naaman. "Do you not know that education is gratuitous? Have you never looked at your share of the taxes? We are the sons of those Puritans who, scarcely landed on the arid rock of Plymouth, opened schools to combat Satan, whose true name is ignorance. The diabolical part of us is the animal; the divine part, the mind. Schools are our passion and weakness; therefore they are the great item in our expenditures, what war and the navy are among civilized people. Here, in our Massachusetts, the expense of schools is nearly one-fourth of our total expenses; in the little State of Maine it is one-third, which would be to France a total of over a million dollars."

"Great God!" thought I, "if these men are not fools, what are we? Tell me, Mr. Naaman, who votes these funds, and how are your schools administered?"

"The vote is general," said he; "all the inhabitants fix the amount of the tax; it is perhaps the only expense which continually increases with the approbation of those who pay it. On this point, there is no party in America; all communions, all opinions rival each other in making our schools the richest and best endowed institutions of the country."

"And naturally," said I, "each communion seeks to rule in them."

"No," returned he; "this will astonish you, perhaps, but no church influence enters within these walls. Every day commences with the Lord's Prayer and reading of the Bible, but accompanied by no comment. The instruction is Christian through the spirit of our teachers; it is neither Catholic nor Protestant. Here, we give our children the means of seeking truth; we arm them against ignorance; we prepare them to fight the good fight. As to dogmatic teaching, it is reserved for the church and the Sunday Schools. In this manner we avoid troubling these young consciences, and notwithstanding accustom our children to consider themselves all as brothers in Jesus Christ."

"Well; but who is answerable to you for the teachers?"

"The Board of Education," said Naaman—"a board freely elected by all the citizens of the same district, and which has over it the central board of the State. These boards number the leading men of the country. It is an honor to be called to watch over education; our best citizens, the Horace Manns and Barnards have refused a place in the federal senate to remain superintendents of our schools in Massachusetts and Connecticut."

"Is it possible?" I exclaimed.

"What is there astonishing?" rejoined the young minister. "Do you believe that in a country like ours, we have yet to ask what makes the prosperity and greatness of nations? In a republic, in a state where the people are sovereign, it is necessary to conquer ignorance or be slain by it; there is no medium. To rear a people that believes in truth and loves it, our politicians have found but one means—to enlighten it, to make the most obscure citizen a man learned enough not to be deceived, and wise enough to govern himself."

"And have you solved the problem?"

"Yes, the problem was solved on the day that we had schools so well kept and so completely gratuitous that a father could no longer be found who would dare refuse us his children. When the district furnishes everything, even to pen, ink, and paper, who would be mad or criminal enough not to profit by the national munificence, and to condemn his children to ignorance and wretchedness?"

"I hope," said I, "that the education is compulsory. After such sacrifices, the State has a right to force people to be instructed. It cannot suffer brutes in society."

"We have rejected all constraint," replied the young pastor. "Not that we doubt our right; but we fear to attach an odious idea to a benefit. Fines and imprisonment would make our schools hated; we leave these harsh measures to governments who care more for the obedience than the love of the citizens. To render education universal is the whole question; we have attained this excellent end without encroaching on liberty. Our schools, open to all children under sixteen, allure and attract the most rebellious. In New England, you will not find a citizen, born in the country, who has not received instruction from us."

"Bravo!" exclaimed I. "This is a work which does the greatest honor to the Christians of America."

"Politics finds its advantage in it, no less than religion," resumed he; "we have arrived at a result which may well surprise the moderns. By the perfection of our schools, we have reëstablished, without knowing it, the common education so dear to antiquity Our course of instruction is high enough to prepare the child of the rich man to enter college; it is simple enough not to appal the child of the poor man, and substantial enough to enable him to hold his place in society without ever having to blush at his ignorance. Here all the youth (mark well this sentence—all the youth) come to learn reading, writing, arithmetic, geometry, and drawing. We join to these a little geography, history, physics, and chemistry, and do not fear to speak to these children of ethics and politics. We explain to them the Constitution of their country—they are citizens. Thanks to the richness and solidity of our lessons, the son of the millionaire comes to study side by side with the son of the Irish laborer. I see yonder one of Green's daughters playing with the child of a poor apple-woman of Walnut Street. Here true equality reigns, equality from above, the equality which elevates; here patriotism and the love of liberty are maintained. To form a generation is to form a people. This is our motto, this is what makes our schools a place dear to all, and sacred for all."

"This is good," exclaimed I, "this is great; but forgive me a last scruple. When you have instructed the children of the people, do you not fear to have inspired them at the same time with a perverse ambition? Do you not cast on society men discontented with their lot? Have you not given them desires and needs above their condition?"

"This," said Naaman, "is an old objection, which has long since ceased to pass current in America. If we abandoned our youth on leaving these walls, your fears would be well founded; but reflect that our society and our government are schools which never close. On one hand, all our enlightened men make it an honor and a pleasure to instruct the citizens. See our walls, covered with placards; there is not an evening on which there is not some political, literary, or scientific lecture. We are inundated with enlightenment; we must be doubly blind to remain ignorant. By the side of this free teaching, place the church, always active, and the thousands of meetings where the rich and poor are constantly united for works of propagandism or charity. Join to these political life, which agitates all ideas and fructifies all souls. Lastly, and in the first rank, put the press; that is, the public speech, which is never hushed. There is not a church, not an association, not a body, not an individual, that has not its journal. The children, even, have theirs. The *Child's Paper*, established four years ago, has already three hundred thousand readers, the oldest of which is not fifteen. Who could resist this continually rising tide? Who would not be carried away by this wave of civilization, bearing humanity towards a better future?"

"Thus, you are a people of scholars?"

"No," said he, smiling; "erudition, like the arts, is

the luxury of old nations; we do not yet possess it. We are parvenus. A century, perhaps, will be needed for us to have the leisure which permits disinterested cultivation; but I venture to say that we are the least ignorant people that the sun has ever seen. Look around you; here are no peasants, but farmers; no laborers, but artizans. On leaving his forge, the smith puts on a black coat, and goes to hear a lecture on Washington, or on the new discoveries of Livingstone in Africa; his neighbor, the jeweller, goes to practise in a school of design, or to attend a chemical course. Despite their grimy hands, they are gentlemen; they love the pleasures of the mind quite as much as you can love them. Go to the West; enter a log house, buried in the forest; you will be received by the wife of the pioneer, and will see her knead bread and make butter. Wait till evening; this same woman will sit down at the piano, and will converse with you of politics, morals, and perhaps metaphysics. To read the *Perfect Cook* does not prevent her from appreciating Emerson and relishing Channing. We do not give to all material wealth, although competence may be easier to win in America than in any other country, but we offer to all that wealth which fears neither rust nor thieves. We place within the reach of the poorest those intellectual enjoyments which, at every age and in every condition, are strength and consolation. In doing this, we believe ourselves fulfilling the promise of the divine Master, and leading men to God, in cultivating their mind and heart."

I gazed at the young man with an emotion which I could no longer control; never had I seen human countenance beam with such enthusiasm and faith. To Naaman science and religion were a double name for truth; both clung to his heart with the same force; he loved them both with the same love.

"My friend," said I, "you have conquered. Behold me, like St. Paul on the way to Damascus, overpowered with light, and hearing a voice, crying, 'It is hard to kick against the pricks.' I surrender; my eyes are opened; I see, I admire the greatness of this country. What an intense life! The heart, the thought, all is action; no impediment; no barrier; man is master of his destiny; he has his happiness and virtue in his own hands. Here is no official falsehood, the truth rules; no prejudices, no fetters; everywhere resounds the cry of a people intoxicated with hope.—Forward! forward! to a world where wretchedness will be cured, where force will be overthrown, where mind will rule. I am proud to be a citizen of this glorious country. Long live liberty! Long live the United States! Long live the great republic!"

My voice was drowned by the roll of drums, followed by a flourish of trumpets. Two Zouaves entered the school-room; one ran to Susan, and tenderly took her hand—it was Alfred; the other threw himself on my neck—it was my son Henry.

"Father," said he, "the Southerners have crossed the Potomac; Washington is in danger; the militia is called out; volunteers are called for; we set out to-night. Come quickly; mother is waiting for you."

CHAPTER XXVIII.

THE DEPARTURE OF THE VOLUNTEERS.

Followed by my children, I quitted this peaceful retreat, where I had at last surprised the secret of American greatness. The city had changed aspect; the houses were decked with flags. At every window the Federal banner, agitated by the breeze, unrolled its red and blue stripes and thirty-four stars as a mute protest in favor of the Union. Here and there an immense placard announced the disaster to the Federal army, and called the citizens to the aid of the country in danger. Armed battalions were marching through the streets to the sound of drums and fifes. The churches were filled to overflowing with volunteers invoking the God of their fathers before marching to battle. Everywhere warlike songs mingled with religious hymns; fathers, mothers, and sisters accompanied the young soldiers, encouraging them, weeping, grasping their hands, embracing them, and raising their eyes to heaven. It was the fervor of a crusade!

I reached home greatly agitated. A Parisian, I had lived and grown up amidst riots and civil war, which had left me sorrowful memories; but here, in this departure to the frontiers, in this enthusiasm which impelled a whole people to arms, there was something so noble and great, that I felt myself exalted. The perils even which Henry and Alfred were to brave did not terrify me; a secret voice urged me to depart with them. Had I not also a fireside and family to defend? Was not America, where I possessed such cherished treasures, my country?

At my door I found a whole regiment of Zouaves, formed by the volunteers of the district. Old Colonel St. John was hoisted on a white horse; the brave veteran forgot his rheumatism and wounds to lead the youth to battle. By the side of the colonel marched Rose, in a captain's uniform, accompanied by his eight sons, and four handsome young men, the sons of Green. Fox, become lieutenant, was in the midst of a group, haranguing, gesticulating, and breathing nothing but blood and carnage. His false collar and snuff-box did not match very well with his uniform, and would have made me laugh on another occasion; but he spoke with so much fire that I detected in him a martial air. There was something else here than a soldier by profession—a citizen resolved to die for his country.

"Neighbor," said Rose to me, "we count on you; it is for the elders to set the example. We need a surgeon for our regiment of Zouaves; you have been chosen unanimously. Nothing is lacking but your consent."

"You have it," exclaimed I. "Yes, my good friends, I will go with you; I will be at hand to watch over these children, and if need be to shoulder arms with them. Hurrah for the Union! Hurrah for the country!"

The cry was reëchoed throughout the ranks, mingled with that of "Hurrah for Daniel! Hurrah for the major!" I felt elated to the heart by the acclamations of these brave youth. I entered my house with an erect head and sparkling eye. A new life awakened in my soul. I was happy!

Jenny, in tears, threw herself in my arms, but did not even attempt to shake my courage. It seemed natural to her that the father should accompany the son, and that the women alone should stay at home. Susan was no less resolute; one saw by her pallor that she was deeply agitated; her lips moved in prayer, her eyes were raised to heaven, but she did not say a word that could trouble Alfred, and appeared occupied solely in preparing for our departure. Dear women! they too comprehended duty and loved the country!

A few hours sufficed for me to procure a surgeon's uniform. Rose made me a present of an excellent case of instruments; I purchased a sword, a pair of revolvers, and a horse. In three hours I was ready; we were to set out the same evening.

Hitherto, I had not reflected; French impetuosity had carried me away. But at the moment of quitting the house where I had passed so many and well-filled hours, I experienced an indescribable sadness. It seemed to me that, once gone, I should never return. And if I returned, would I bring with me my Henry, and Alfred whom I was beginning to love as a son?

I was shaking off these sad thoughts which, continually repulsed, returned unceasingly to the attack, when the old colonel entered my house; the sight of him did me good. He was one of those brave soldiers, lavish of their own blood, and sparing of that of others; we could not have had a more honorable and surer leader.

"Colonel," said I, after receiving his congratulations, "here we are alone, I can speak to you plainly. Between ourselves, what value do you set on these raw recruits? Enthusiasm is a fine thing, but what is it by the side of exercise and discipline? Despite the courage of these good young men, their battalions will break at the first fire."

"Patience, major," answered the veteran. "I am less severe than you; nevertheless, I have been engaged in war all my life. Two months in the forts at Washington will transform these volunteers into soldiers. Discipline is of great value, doubtless, but it is a trade within the reach of the most ignorant. Heart, faith, the love of country—these are not given at will. Herein is the mainspring of action, whatever worthless fellows who carry a sword may say. To handle the bayonet needs an adroit and vigorous arm; but it is the soul that makes the strength of the arm. A few years of war and sufferings suffice to educate a people and bring both enemies to the same point. Moral energy then remains, this it is that wins in the end; and this is why the best armies are armies of citizens."

"Excuse me, colonel; I thought that nothing was equal to veterans."

"A mistake," said St. John. "In a review or parade, the thing is possible; for war, it is different. Good officers, young soldiers, and old generals—these are what we need. To march without complaining, to obey without murmuring, to brave danger with head erect, to march to death smiling, there is nothing like young men. The more intelligent, pious, and patriotic is youth, the more we can count on it. Old Europe has other ideas. There, prejudice and the adoration of brute force still rule. Here, civilization has enlightened us. Doubtless the victory will always belong to the general who, at the decisive moment, shall throw upon a given point the most numerous battalions; but, conditions being equal, a young and patriotic soldier is more valuable than a mercenary grown old in the trade. See the Crimean war: certainly, the Russian and English veterans fought well; but to whom belongs the crown, if not to the French conscripts—heroic children, a day from the plough—peasants yesterday, citizens to-morrow! These are our model; these are what we will make likewise of our young Americans."

"You have no generals," said I; "your country is a pacific land, which, until now, has brought forth more farmers and merchants than Cæsars."

"Be tranquil," answered the colonel; "you will have generals, and more than you want. War is like the chase—a very common occupation, in which some excel from the beginning. He who is to-day a blacksmith, mechanist, lawyer, doctor perhaps, to-morrow will awaken a general in the land. Open history: there are sterile epochs when letters, arts, industry, are dead; there are none which lack soldiers. Man has hunting and sanguinary instincts which peace represses, but never destroys; let war come, you will have heroes; Heaven grant that the people may esteem them at their just value, and not sacrifice liberty to them!"

"Really, colonel," said I, "you speak of war with little respect."

"It is because I have been engaged in it," said he sadly. "I know what this bloody game is worth. Let rhetoricians, quietly seated in their chimney corner, amuse themselves by celebrating battles and glory; I shrug my shoulders at these paradoxes; war is the greatest of scourges, the foe of labor and liberty, the destruction of civilization. Wo to those whose ambition lets loose on the earth this abominable pestilence, but thrice accursed be those who lift their parricidal hand against their country! With God's help, we will make them expiate their crime! War is also the chastisement of pride and folly—a cruel lesson, which is learned only when it is too late."

The sound of the clarionet announced the moment of farewell. I went down, holding Alfred and Henry by the hand. Jenny embraced all three of us, with the courage of a Christian wife and mother. Susan, silent and agitated, gave each of us a Bible, with which we were never more to part. Martha had prepared a prophetic sermon; but, at the first word, the poor girl broke into a terrible sob, and, taking Henry in her arms like a child, she inundated him with tears and kisses. I grasped her hand; she flung herself on my neck; I mounted my horse half strangled.

At the same instant Sambo ran up, with an absurd accoutrement—a red and blue sash, plumed hat, and sabre trailing on the pavement.

"Massa," cried he, "take me; I am brave. If my skin is black, my blood is red. If they do not kill me before victory, I will beat them all."

It was not without difficulty that I rid myself of the poor fellow. I reasoned with him most wisely to prove to him that his courage was ridiculous. When one has woolly hair, he is born, not to beat, but to be beaten. Vain words! Sambo had too acute a facial angle to grasp the great discoveries of our wits. The poor devil believed himself a man, a Christian, and a citizen—yet his skin was black! It was madness! We were obliged to employ threats to make him return to the house, whither he fled howling. It was time to end this sad comedy; the ranks were formed, the drums beat, we departed.

So long as I felt myself near home, I dared not turn back; tears were in my eyes, and I did not wish them to flow; but at the corner of the street I looked behind me; the three women were waving their handkerchiefs, and following us with a long look. My heart beat loudly. "Oh, God!" I cried, "I confide to thee all I love!" For the first time, I wept, I prayed, and felt comforted.

At four o'clock, we were ranged in battle array in the public square. Green passed us in review, and spoke to us of the country with an emotion which bordered on eloquence. His voice was drowned by our acclamations. Then all retired in silence, each meditating to himself. Alone, perhaps, of the regiment, I was agitated. Strange to say, I was in haste to encounter fire. In a moment of repose, I passed before my companions, laughing, talking, and gesticulating, having a word for every soldier; I rallied those who were moved, I encouraged those who tried to smile, I promised all my aid at the moment of danger; I was already feverish for battle.

Humbug, who had rejoined me on the square, gazed at me with an air of astonishment.

"What a man you are, doctor," said he, sighing. "I admire your good humor and gaiety. You were a timid citizen; here you are a bold soldier. Are you Irish? Have you in your veins the blood,

'Non paventis funera Galliæ?'

We Saxons, we go on the field of battle,

'Devota morti pectora liberæ;'

but we have neither this grace, nor elegance, nor bravery. In truth, to see you, the combat seems a festival and danger a pleasure. You would give the most fastidious a wish to die!"

The roll of the drums drowned my answer; Humbug

embraced me tenderly and styled me in Latin the half of his soul; an instant later, I had quitted my old friend forever.

The evening was beautiful; the moon, rising early, lighted the distant meadows, edged with poplars and intersected by willows; in the horizon, a river unrolled its silvery waves; there was a sort of charm in letting one's self be borne onward by his horse, and abandoning himself to reverie in the midst of this beautiful country. The soldier's happiness is the enjoyment of the present moment without care for the morrow. I had yielded for some time to the pleasure of dreaming with my eyes open, when two horsemen drew up by my side. I raised my head; to my great surprise, I recognized the sombre Brown and the amiable Truth.

"What are you doing here?" asked I. "What means this great hat, this heavy overcoat, this sword by your side? it is neither the costume of a soldier nor a pastor."

"Doctor," said the Puritan, "war is a cruel malady; it endangers the soul no less than the body; you care for the one, we for the other; we are physicians like you."

"I am delighted to have you as comrades," said I; "but it is a rude vocation. A surgeon is inured to it; tenderness is to him an unknown evil; that the hand may not tremble, the heart must be silent. But you, Truth, how will you resist the cry of the wounded, the despair of the dying?"

"It is my duty," said he. "God will give me the strength, as long as he deems my service useful or necessary. I belong to the Lord."

The stage was not a long one; at eight o'clock we halted. The colonel had wished to teach us to march;

the lesson was not useless, the regiment had the appearance of a flock of sheep in flight. Nevertheless, the brave Colonel St. John complimented all the novices, accustoming them by degrees to look on him as a father and have confidence in him.

"Major," said he, "do not laugh. Before a month, we shall equal the Prussians. When a man believes himself a soldier, he is half one already; you will see what an army of citizens is."

The bivouac was pitched in the midst of the fields. The fires lighted and horses picketed, we supped heartily on the provisions which each one had brought. To conscripts, this first repast in the open air was a festival; war had not yet inspired them with regret of comfort and love of the fireside.

The supper ended, and it did not last long, the soldiers, instead of laughing and shouting, seated themselves in silence on their cloaks to listen to the minister. Our staff formed a circle; Truth advanced in the midst of us, and, opening the Bible, read in an inspired voice the psalm sung by David when the Lord had delivered him from his enemies.

"The Lord is my rock, and my fortress, and my deliverer; my God, my strength, in whom I will trust; my buckler, and the horn of my salvation, and my high tower.

"I will call upon the Lord, who is worthy to be praised: so shall I be saved from my enemies. . . .

"For who is God save the Lord? or who is a rock save our God? . . .

"He teacheth my hands to war, so that a bow of steel is broken by mine arms. . . .

"I have pursued mine enemies, and overtaken them: neither did I turn again till they were consumed.

"I have wounded them that they were not able to rise: they are fallen under my feet. . . .

"They cried, but there was none to save them: even unto the Lord, but he answered them not.

"Then did I beat them small as the dust before the wind: I did cast them out as the dirt in the streets. . . .

"The Lord liveth; and blessed be my Rock; and let the God of my salvation be exalted."

While Truth recited this beautiful poem, I looked about me. All the officers were listening prayerfully, their eyes sparkling with enthusiasm and faith. The last flames of our dying fires illumined these noble faces, and cast upon them an indescribable, mysterious lustre. I fancied myself transported back to the middle of the sixteenth century, into a camp of Roundheads. "And it is to these," thought I, "it is to these people that our journals of Paris deny all patriotism and religion! No, military tyranny will never be established over this generous land; this soil, opened and fructified by the Puritans, can bring forth naught but liberty."

The reading ended, I shook hands with Truth, then, profiting by my privilege, inspected all the companies, in search of my son and Alfred. I found them both, stretched on the ground, wrapped in their cloaks, and talking in a low voice. Of what were they talking? I knew well.

"Children," said I, "a soldier must husband all his strength; and the first condition of this is to sleep. Make room for me between you, and dream with your eyes shut."

Upon which I embraced both my sons tenderly, carefully wrapped my cloak about me, pulled my cap over my eyes, and fell asleep as tranquil and light-hearted as if in my own house. When one devotes himself for his country, when he is permitted to sacrifice himself for what he loves, fatigue is sweet, even danger has its attractions.

CHAPTER XXIX.

A PLEASURE VOYAGE.

In the midst of my peaceful slumber I had a vision. A man, or rather a phantom,. with mocking eye and wrinkled brow was stretched upon me, stifling me. I recognized Jonathan Dream; he alone had this terrible glance.

"Well, doctor," said he, in a piercing voice, "the thing is proved; you no longer doubt magnetism and its miracles. Here you are, become a Yankee in eight days."

"Yes," murmured I, "and I am proud of it. I have a wife and children according to my heart; I have a country to love, liberty to serve and defend; I am master of my life, I believe the Gospel, I am happy. If this be a dream, for pity's sake do not awaken me."

"Bravo!" cried the voice; "I am avenged. On the way now to France, to Paris!"

I felt a hand put aside my cloak and glide beneath my cap. I sprang to my feet, and sought to cry out. Vain effort! I was magnetised. An invisible hand seized me by the only lock of hair left on my bald forehead, and drew me into the air with frightful rapidity.

I had not yet recovered from a very natural emotion, when I found myself hovering in the sky like a bird, and fluttering above my house. The traitor who had deprived me of speech, and who still held me suspended, lowered me to the parlor window. In my cherished abode I perceived, gathered around a work-table, my Jenny, my Susan, and Martha. Poor Sambo was seated on the floor, sobbing in a corner. Susan, in a voice broken by sobs, was reading the Gospel. Jenny and Martha were tearing bandages and scraping lint.

My heart called to them and blessed them. Jenny directly raised her head.

"Susan," said she, trembling, "it seems to me that I hear your father. I am sure that he is thinking of us at this moment."

"Mamma," returned Susan, "what you say is strange: I have the same presentiment."

"The effect of magnetism," murmured Jonathan, laughing in a sinister manner. "What do you say to this experiment, learned doctor?"

"O God!" said Jenny rising, "thou who hast given me my husband, and commanded me to love him, protect him, I entreat thee. Put away danger and death from him and from my children. But, before all, O Lord, thy will be done, and thy name be praised!"

"Amen," said Susan; "Amen," said Martha. The three women burst into tears, while Sambo stuffed a handkerchief into his mouth to stifle his cries.

Oh, my beloved ones! I was opening my arms to you, when a second time I was hurled into space and borne away by an irresistible force. In the twinkling of an eye, the great city disappeared, with its flickering lights. After the city vanished the fields, the meadows, the woods, the earth. I heard nothing longer but the whistle of the wind and the moan of the waves. I perceived, as at the bottom of an abyss, the waters trembling beneath the pale beams of the moon: I was ten thousand feet above the ocean.

"Let us talk now," said the terrible sorcerer, who hovered above me like an eagle with a pigeon in his claws. "Dr. Lefebvre, I restore you your speech. I shall be delighted to enjoy your agreeable conversation."

"Monster!" exclaimed I, "how long shall I be thy victim?"

"My good friend," replied he, sneeringly, "you are not polite. To say *thou* to a man whom you have seen but twice is rude—it is more than awkward. I have only to open my hand to precipitate you into the waves; nor do I think that the French gendarmery, despite its vigilance, would be of much use to you here. Be courteous, therefore, and amuse me. I am tired; I have lost a great deal of fluid, it is difficult for me to make more than a hundred leagues an hour: we shall not be at Paris before to-morrow morning. There remains a whole night for us to travel together; the weather is fine, the route pleasant, let us be friends and talk."

Of what can one talk in the clouds, if not of metaphysics?

"Mr. Jonathan," said I, assuming my most respectful tone, "do you believe in God?"

"God!" exclaimed he, in the tone of a professor, as if repeating a lesson—"God is an old-fashioned word; it is the personalization of ideality."

"Speak French!" exclaimed I.

"So be it," said he. "God is the idealization of personality."

"If this is your French, Mr. Sorcerer, for pity's sake speak Greek to me."

"Very well," said he, in a courteous tone. "God is the category of the ideal; nothing more."

"I do not understand," said I.

"It is because you do not know German," replied he. "Philosophy is a peculiar language, which comes to us from beyond the Rhine. I have seen illustrious scholars who had spoken it for twenty years without understanding it, and had been none the less applauded for it."

"Explain your system to me," resumed I, with forced gentleness. "You are a great man, a genius; I shall be delighted to instruct myself in your school. Have the kindness also not to pull my hair quite so hard; my head is sensitive; and I am sure that Absalom had some trouble in philosophising, suspended to his tree."

"I am the pupil of Spinoza," said Jonathan, "but I have been further than my master. There is neither matter nor spirit in the world: there is nothing but a collection of organized forces, which are diversified to infinity. Plants, animals, men; so many forms of this universal life; so many bubbles of water, which rise to the surface of the ocean of beings, then break and return to the abyss to emerge from it anew. Life and death are simple phenomena, of no importance. The individual disappears, the species endures; this is the essential point. It matters little whom the wheel crushes, provided it revolves continually. This is my system; it accepts everything."

"And explains nothing," exclaimed I. "These forces —who created them?"

"What are you thinking of, doctor?" answered the magician. "To create would be to disturb the universal and fatal order of things: there never was a creation. To suppose a commencement is to suppose a will; this would derange the whole system."

"I thought," said I, "that systems were adapted to the facts observed?"

"That will do for natural philosophers," returned he. "We, on the contrary, adapt the facts to the system; we are philosophers."

"This is very ingenious," said I; "but solve me one doubt. I thought that man was not very ancient on the earth."

"So I think," said he; "it is twelve or fifteen thousand years since man appeared; but there was no creation. Nature"——

"What is Nature, Mr. Dream?"

"It is another name for the universal force."

"What is the universal force?"

"It is another name for Nature."

"I thank you for this philosophic explanation."

"Nature," resumed he, "experiences at certain periods a redoubling of energy, a sort of fever, and then she changes and, if necessary, transforms certain species. It was in this manner that man appeared on the earth; according to all appearances, he is an ape or a degenerated dog."

"And speech, consciousness?" exclaimed I.

"Are trifles," said he. "They pertain to a simple physiological modification. A little more fineness in the composition of the larynx, has made of a bestial cry an articulate language. There is no consciousness possible without a nervous apparatus, consequently consciousness is a matter of nerves. An accumulation of grey substance, a freak of nature, sufficed to give birth to this lord of creation."

"A poor lord, assuredly, if he is only the first and most wicked of animals."

"Not so," said Jonathan; "for thanks to his nervous apparatus, he has general ideas, and this it is that makes man a distinct species. He is the only animal that is amused and deceived by words. Man sees certain facts which are reproduced in regular series, and which he calls truths; he imagines a universal truth which comprises and supports all particular truths; he perceives beautiful things, and pictures to himself a beauty which is the model and type of all others. This is the ideal which allures and consoles him—it is what the good people call God."

"Very well," said I; "I begin to catch a glimpse of the category of the ideal. The soul is a mirror which reflects what does not exist; or, if you like better, man sees himself in this magnifying glass, and, a new Narcissus, falls upon his knees before his magnified image."

"Not bad for a novice," said the sorcerer.

"Thus there is nothing superior to man in the universe?"

"A logical conclusion," said Jonathan.

"If there never had been any men on the earth, there would have been no idea of God, and consequently God would not exist."

"Marvelous!" said he; "you are becoming a philosopher."

"No, indeed," exclaimed I; "I know not whether my manner of seeing pertains to my strange position, but it seems to me that all this system of metaphysics is like myself, suspended in the air by a hair. What is this Nature with its redoublings of energy? A word to replace the Supreme Being who, in his goodness, voluntarily created man and the world. What is this change of tissues, this metamorphosis of apparatus, if not a sonorous phrase which explains the unknown by the impossible? What is this inconscient and immoral force which produces a creature endowed with consciousness and morality? A chimera. At the height where I am, one judges things in quite a different manner, and is not satisfied with vain words; physical laws, that is, an intelligent order, a constant and continued creation, reveal and cry to me that a will always active and always present sustains the universe and prevents its dissolution. I see Nature nowhere, I feel God everywhere."

"Bravo! thrice bravo!" said the magician.

"It is not your system then that you are expounding?" returned I, greatly astonished.

"The system is mine," replied he, "since I stole it; but I have little belief in it. Yesterday, on my way to Tubingen, where I was going to visit one of my good friends, an honest theologian who dreams continually, I perceived a great metaphysician who, by dint of writing, had fallen asleep over Hegel. I rifled him at once of his pipe, spectacles, and system; when he awakes he will find no longer but his eyes to see with and his mind to reason with."

"Poor man!" exclaimed I, "what will he do with these instruments which he has never used?"

"Bah!" said the sorcerer; "you know little of German philosophers. They are silkworms who exist in books; they spin from the first old tome that comes a thread with which they envelope themselves in a fine system, which is proof against air and light. My man is only stripped to weave a new cocoon. Truth is nothing, logic everything. Hegel is dead, long live Schopenhauer! There is always a king in this dynasty of dreamers."

"Sir," said I, "your jests are cruel. You should not hold a man ten thousand feet in the air to deride him."

"Sir," said he, in a dry tone, "your questions are impertinent. How dare you ask a medium whether he believes in God? We alone know what the soul is, we alone have in our hands the proof of its immortality."

"What is the soul, then?" asked I impatiently.

"It is a magnetic force," answered Jonathan. "This monad, created by God and endowed with consciousness, makes itself an envelope, as the grain of wheat, cast in the earth, makes itself roots, a stalk, and blades. When the body has grown old, the soul, always young and active, throws off a decrepit covering, and takes flight to a better world, to seek a new form for its immortal energy. See yonder globes radiating in space—Jupiter, Saturn, Sirius—so many spheres inhabited by risen spirits. To ascend the infinite scale of creation, always to approach God without ever attaining him—such is our glorious destiny. Death is only a passage to a more intense life. Nothing is annihilated here on earth—no, not even an atom of dust; how, then, can the consciousness become extinct? Is God a capricious artist, who destroys the masterpiece of his greatness and goodness?"

"Sir," exclaimed I, "these words are beautiful, and go to my heart; but the proof—that proof which humanity has demanded for six thousand years—give it me."

"Nothing is easier," returned Jonathan. "Let us fly to Sirius, which is shining yonder above our heads; you will see one of the stations which you will some day inhabit. It is not long since I visited Washington there."

The offer was calculated to tempt a curious man, but the cursed sorcerer had already played with me; I distrusted his magic. Fearing the annoyances of a new voyage, I refused; I was wrong; it was an opportunity which perhaps I shall never find again.

"Are we almost at our journey's end?" asked I of Jonathan.

"That is an ungracious question," said he. "Look down; do you not see a speck of light on the sea? It is the signal-light of the Arabia, which sailed from Boston the day I carried you to America; it is half way to Europe; there still remain six hundred leagues for us to travel, or six hours' journey."

I sighed, and said no more.

"My good friend," said the odious magician, "you are sulky. If you do not like discussion, if metaphysics affect your nerves, choose some familiar subject on which it will be easy for us to agree. Let us talk politics."

"What do you think of slavery?" exclaimed I; "what do you think of the fratricidal war that is rending the United States? Upon this point there is but one opinion among honest men; I suppose that you detest despotism and that you hate servitude—you, Mr. Medium, who doubtless respect an immortal soul, whatever may be the skin that covers it."

"This is a wholly pacific question," said he, "but it is more delicate than you think. It is not the laws which make men command or obey."

"What is it, then?"

"It is the magnetic fluid," replied he, with insupportable phlegm. "What philosophers term will, energy, power, is nothing else than this fluid, which constitutes our soul. Each one possesses it in different and unequal quantity. Woman, for instance, is a more magnetic being than man; therefore, you see that, in the greater part of the households, whatever the code may say, it is the husband who obeys. Children, whom the law subjects also to their parents, are domestic tyrants, who impose their caprices on the whole house, and make their mother a slave. Why? Because they abound in magnetism. Old men, on the contrary, are cold blooded, and no longer exert an influence on those who approach them. Lovers"——

"I beg your pardon," said I, yawning, "we are not talking medicine, but politics."

"Patience," said Jonathan, in a satirical tone. "If it is proved that the negroes have less fluid than the whites, the question is decided; slavery is legitimate."

"Sir," said I, "your paradoxes weary me."

"Paradoxes!" exclaimed he. "You are behind your age, Doctor Rococo; read your great historians and your great politicians; study the question of races; you will see that to-day morality is no longer but physiology!"

I am of great natural gentleness, as all acknowledge, except my intimate friends, who, according to custom, see only my faults; but let any one put himself in my place, and he will understand that I could not but lose patience. Suspended by the hair for six hours, carried I knew not whither by I knew not whom, these were vexations enough, without having any one presume to differ with me in politics.

"Sir," said I drily to my enemy, "carry your wit elsewhere. I cannot entreat you to leave me, but I declare that henceforth I will no longer listen to you."

"And how are you to help it?" resumed he, in a mocking voice.

"Another word," exclaimed I, "is an insult, for which you shall give me satisfaction."

"A duel in these serene heights!" said the sorcerer, "that would be original; I will reflect on it; meanwhile, you shall listen to me, whether or no; I defy you to part company with me."

"You do not know," said I, gnashing my teeth, "you do not know of what a Frenchman is capable."

"I believe him capable of all follies," returned Jonathan, "except those which are impossible."

"Impossible!" exclaimed I, "that is not a French word."

Quicker than lightning, I drew a pair of scissors from my instrument case, and severed the lock of hair which held me in the power of this wretch.

Directly I fell, whirling right and left, like a broken kite. At the first moment, lost in the pleasure of my newly regained liberty, I was not troubled at this rapid descent. Reflection returned to me when I heard the roaring of the waves and the whistling of the gathering storm. It was too late. The sea opened to receive me into its depths, then, less fortunate than Jonah, flung me back upon the wave, breathless and chilled. I did not lose courage, but began to swim with desperate vigor. Five hundred leagues to make in this primitive fashion was a great deal, but might I not encounter some steamship on the great ocean highway? I was gazing in the distance, seeking some light, and seeing nothing but darkness, when the horrible phantom, ready to carry me away, hovered over me like a swallow over a fly on the surface of the water.

"Doctor," said he, sneeringly, "I hope that this bath has cooled your blood; let us resume the discussion where we left it."

"Rather die, than listen to your detestable sophisms," exclaimed I; and, clenching my fist, I struck my enemy so terrible a blow, that every bone in my hand cracked. I uttered a cry of pain, and——

CHAPTER XXX.

THE SHORTEST OF THE BOOK AND MOST INTERESTING TO THE READER.

I awakened in my bed——

CHAPTER XXXI.

SOME INCONVENIENCES OF A VOYAGE TO AMERICA.

On escaping from this danger, or rather nightmare, a little time was needed for me to recognize myself. Where was I? In what country had my executioner cast me? The curtains of the bed were closed; I drew them aside. The chamber was sombre and mute; it was the silence and twilight of a sick-room. When my eyes had become accustomed to the obscurity, I looked around me. A table, covered with papers, books and pamphlets, piled up at random; a bookcase, filled with books, stitched, bound and in boards, some standing, others lying; a heap of old tomes, rising from the floor and forming a tottering pyramid which threatened every instant to fall—everything in its place; it was really my study. I was at Paris, in France, and at last home from my travels. Shall I confess it? this return to the centre of civilization gave me indifferent pleasure; I had gained a taste for liberty.

I rang; Jenny entered on tiptoe, and asked in a low voice if I had called.

"Most certainly, my dear; give me some light, I beg of you; this room is like a tomb."

Jenny half opened the curtains and called Susan, who softly put her head in the door, then paused, and looked at me with an anxious eye.

"Well, miss," said I, gaily, "haven't you a kiss for your father to-day?"

Instead of throwing herself in my arms, she approached with a timid step, and took my hand, weeping.

"How do you feel, papa?" murmured she.

"Very well, my child, with the exception of the fatigue and excitement of the voyage."

"Ah!" said Susan. "Ah!" said Jenny.

There was in this cry so strange an accent that I gazed by turn at my wife and daughter; their countenances were full of consternation.

"What is the matter with you?" asked I. "What have I said to frighten you?"

"My dear," said Jenny, "I entreat you, keep silence; Dr. Olybrius recommends it."

"Who is Dr. Olybrius? Isn't he the coxcomb who wrote a thick volume on *Lent considered in the point of view of Hygiene and Navigation?* What is there in common between me and this sacristan pedant?"

"Daniel," returned Jenny, in a dry tone, "everybody consults Dr. Olybrius. For the last week, he has shown you all the care of a brother physician and friend."

"The last week!" exclaimed I, starting up in bed. "You are dreaming, my dear child. How could your doctor have attended on me in Paris when we were in America?"

"Listen to me, Daniel," said my wife, in an agitated voice, "listen, and do not interrupt me; your health and perhaps life depend on it. A week ago yesterday, Thursday, you returned home in a deplorable condition. You had consulted some quack who, if I am to believe the doctor, had administered to you a dose of opium or hasheesh, which might have killed you. The strength of your constitution, and perhaps our cares, have saved you. The whole week you have been in complete lethargy or frightful delirium. You have had terrible visions, which more than once have made us fear for your reason. To-day you have regained your senses, Dr. Olybrius predicted it; but he added, that the return to health demanded the greatest care; that, according to all appearances, you would need some time to shake off your reveries and accustom yourself again to real life, and that in such a crisis, repose and silence were of absolute necessity."

It was my turn to look at my wife with terror. What fable was this, uttered with so much assurance? I was certain of having been in America; never could French brain have imagined what I had seen; moreover, delirium is incoherent, and leaves no memories. But if Jenny had remained in France while I was in Massachusetts, who was that American Jenny whom I had clasped so tenderly to my heart? Had I been a bigamist without suspecting it? Were there two Susans and two Henrys, the one at Paris in France, the other at Paris in America? Was I double? Had I a single soul and two bodies? What confusion! what chaos!

"Accursed Jonathan!" murmured I; "the devil fly

away with you and spiritism likewise! Here I am, in a fine embarrassment!"

Suddenly, the truth struck me; I was vexed at myself for having listened to my wife, even for an instant. Had not Jonathan told me that I alone would preserve my memory, and that my family would become Yankee by birth? All was explained in the most natural manner: Jenny was the sport of an illusion. If any one was dreaming in my house, it was not I, but my wife.

This simple reflection restored me my courage and dignity.

"My dear," said I to Jenny, "do not trust to appearances. Your Olybrius is a fool; I have never been ill. The proof is that my pulse is not more than sixty-five, that I am dying of hunger, and that with your permission, I will rise and breakfast."

For her sole answer, my wife burst into tears, a fashion of reasoning which Aristotle did wrong to forget; it plays an important part in household rhetoric; a husband teased is half conquered.

Like a well-brought-up daughter, Susan did not fail to outdo her mother; she hung on my neck, sobbing.

"Papa!" cried she, "my darling papa, do not grieve us; wait for the doctor."

"I will wait for him on my feet, and not fasting," replied I; "nevertheless, my children, I do not wish to grieve you. I am a physician; I give you my word of honor that I am in excellent health; if my assertion is not enough for you, call in neighbor Rose; he is a doctor, and you will soon be reassured."

The offer was accepted. Rose entered as soon as called, with so awkward and solemn a mien that I laughed him in the face.

"Good morning, my old friend," said I, offering my hand.

"You do me honor, sir," answered he, seating himself in my large easy chair.

"Oblige me by feeling my pulse, and tell these ladies whether I am not in perfect health."

He took my wrist, gravely counted the pulsations of the artery, and turning to Jenny with an air of astonishment:

"If I might be permitted to have an opinion," said he, "I would venture to say that this pulse is not in the least capricious. It is regular, and even a little feeble, like that of a man who is fasting. The crisis is passed, admitting that there has been a crisis, which I would not dare affirm. I think," said he, unbending his brow, "that a cold chicken and a few glasses of Bordeaux are naturally indicated; it is a prescription which, sick or not, will do the doctor no harm."

The two women went out to order my repast; Rose, rising, approached me, his finger on his lips:

"Confess, doctor," said he in a whisper, "that henceforth you will play no more with opiates."

"You too," exclaimed I. "My dear sir, opium has had nothing to do with this matter; I have been magnetized."

"Good," said he; "you, doctor, a clear headed man, a free thinker, you believe in magnetism when the Academy of Medicine refuses it the civil state?"

"One must yield to proof," replied I, sighing. "You behold a victim of this deplorable discovery. I have been transported to America."

Rose drew back, pale and astounded.

"Yes," resumed I, "I have been transported to America, I, the house and the street. I saw you there, Mr.

Rose; you were a patriot, a brave soldier, a captain of Zouaves."

"Be silent, in Heaven's name, be silent;" said he, "what if any one else should hear you!"

"Do you doubt my word," said I; "must you have proofs?"

"God forbid that I should contradict you," exclaimed the apothecary; "we have served together in the ranks of the National Guard; I esteem you a worthy man, and I should be very sorry if anything unpleasant happened to you. Listen, therefore, to the counsel dictated to me by the respect I bear you. Be prudent; be discreet. You have been in America; so be it; you say so, and I believe you; but in your house, every one believes the contrary. You are alone in your opinion. Now, you know the proverb, '*Where everybody is wrong, everybody is right.*' If you persist in speaking of this magnetic voyage, I am afraid that the incredulous will avenge themselves in their own way, and make you pass for a man who"——

He stopped, tapped his forehead with his finger, shook his head, and looked at me with an air of pity.

"What," exclaimed I, "do you think perchance that my brain is deranged?"

"No, of course not; I know what to believe; but who can check too lively imaginations? Your adventure is so extraordinary that it would be wise to keep the secret of it to yourself alone."

"Mr. Rose," replied I, "sit down and let us converse; you will see that my head was never clearer. How are your nine sons?"

"Very well," said he, "I thank you; they are all in places, even to my Benjamin."

"Alfred, eh?"

"Yes," said he, smiling, "a handsome young man of twenty-four. It is a great happiness to a father to have at last established, and well established all his family."

"What are all your children doing? Tell me about them, neighbor; speak, incredulous; assure yourself that my heart and mind are younger than at twenty."

"The eldest," said he, "is the only one that has given me any trouble. He is the picture of his deceased mother. Headstrong, ambitious, always having ideas of his own, and unwilling to yield to any one, I could do nothing with him. I was forced, therefore to let him enter the Polytechnic School, which he left, as one of the first scholars. He might have had a fine place in the Tobaccos; but he is like a wild horse that no one can curb. The gentleman has been roving the world ever since, with inventions in his pocket; he is at present superintendent of a manufactory, and pretends that he is making a fortune; God grant that it may be so! but manufacturing is a perfidious vocation; one is never sure of having succeeded until after he is dead. I am in constant fear for this child.

"My other sons, all brought up by my care, have given me nothing but joy. They have received a literary education, and, thanks to patronage skillfully employed, I have pushed them all into the administration. I have two in the Customs, two in the General Taxes, two are already Collectors; the eighth is in the Waters and Forests; as to my Alfred, he is private secretary of a prefect, and on the road to greatness. In the course of a few years, if I obtain him some recommendations, he will be counsellor of prefecture with eighteen hundred francs' salary."

"What!" exclaimed I, "you, Rose, a patriot; you have made your children clerks, when you might open to them an independent career, and make them citizens?"

"Doctor," replied the apothecary, "I have followed the counsel and example of men of sense. If the service of the State is not brilliant, it is sure. One has no anxiety and little fatigue in it. If he has some small fortune, he jobs at the Bourse to better his possessions; he strives to marry a wife with a pretty dowry, and whose parents are not too young, lives tranquilly, and dies at his ease in a comfortable retreat in the suburbs of some provincial city."

"It is the life of an oyster."

"Oysters are happy," returned he: "that is the main point. Would you be a manufacturer, merchant, shipper? One day revolution ruins you; the next, a strong government makes war without apprising you. Then the taxes, which increase annually, and crises, and competition! Everything conspires against the man who labors. Our society is not made for him. He is mad indeed who runs such hazards, when nothing is easier than to live tranquil and honored, serving his country. The administration—it is France! Let republicans and fastidious spirits bark as they will, I had rather that my son should be among those who eat than those who are eaten."

"And to attain this you are forced to solicit—to hold out your hand like a mendicant."

"Yes," said he, laughing, "I have had to stoop a little. Right-handed and left-handed queens—I have implored all, flattered all; but I have succeeded, that is the essential point. Do not stare at me, doctor; I have done like every one else; you will do the same. I am none the less a patriot, and still of the opposition. I am left centre, with all France, and I pride myself on it, between ourselves; but when the future of my children is at stake, I put opinions which are of no service to me into my pocket."

"To take them out again on the day of revolution; do you not?" said I, ironically.

"Doubtless," said he, in a placid tone. "One serves a government, he does not destroy himself for it. It is one of the great advantages of the administration that it profits by every revolution; the head gone, the young men rise; there is a crisis every fifteen years; happy he who is in a position to seize the opportunity and draw the lucky number!"

"You are a wise man, Mr. Rose."

"Simply a man of sense," rejoined he, with proud modesty. "See my Alfred, for instance; he went through his studies admirably, and gained the prize for French oratory in the great competition. If I had listened to him, he would have become advocate—a glorious career, but long, difficult, laborious, and, at present, leading to nothing; while, with his wit, good mien, and a little tact, the boy needs only two or three good chances to be sub-prefect in ten years, prefect in fifteen, and, perhaps, senator."

"Heavens!" exclaimed I, "do you hear that noise in the street?"

Rose ran to the window.

"It is nothing," said he; "only a horse has stumbled, and a man has fallen over his head."

"I am lost! I shall be prosecuted again for five hundred dollars!"

"What ails you, my dear sir?" said the apothecary,

amazed at my dismay. " A stranger breaking his neck in the street is something that we see every day. How can it affect you? It is one of those misfortunes for which no one can be accused."

" It at least affects your administration," said I, returning to myself, and remembering that I was no longer in America.

"The administration is never responsible," replied Rose, in a bantering tone. "It takes care of us at our own risk and peril."

"There is an inspector."

"Doubtless," said he; " but the inspector is dependent on the prefect, who is dependent on the government, which is dependent on nothing but God and its sword. As my late father used to say, there are three accidents fortuitous and without remedy—shipwreck, fire, and the act of the prince. Against shipwreck and fire we now have insurance; against the act of the prince, there remains to us what our ancestors had—resignation."

"Things are not thus," said I, " in——"

Rose looked at me. I bit my lips, and was silent.

"Besides," resumed the apothecary, " you will soon be delivered from this detestable pavement, which for ten years has driven coachmen to despair. You will be expropriated next month."

" What! I expropriated?"

" Do you not know it? The inquiry has been opened within the last week."

"I object to it. I shall protest."

"Protest! to what purpose?" said he, with a paternal air. " My dear neighbor, you know the story of the earthen pot and the iron pot. Do not act wrong-headedly; it is useless, and sometimes injurious. Negotiate with the administration: it will give you a reasonable price for your house. What more do you need?"

"I will not be driven from the house of my father; the journals are at hand, I will write."

"The journals!" said the apothecary; "I wish they were all suppressed. Of what use have they been for the last ten years? Formerly, in the last reign, they said their say of the ministers, which was amusing; to-day, I know not what ails them; they are mute as fishes. They are no longer but placards. Do I want to pay fifty francs a year to have the prospectus of all the suspicious affairs sent to my dwelling, the praises of which are sung at a hundred sous a line? If I were the government, I would oblige the journals to tell the truth; since this is not the case, the *Moniteur* is enough for me, and more."

"And you are a liberal?"

"A liberal and free mason until death," said he, raising his hand with grotesque earnestness. "For forty years, my political creed has not varied an iota. Long live our immortal Revolution, and the emperor who carried to Moscow the glorious principles of '89! Down with the aristocrats and emigrants! Down with the Jesuits, who are the cause of all our calamities! I am not the enemy of religion; it is necessary for the people; but I wish patriotic curés and good men. I hate perfidious Albion, I execrate the Russian autocrat; I wish France to set free all the oppressed—Poles, Hungarians, Wallachians, Serbians, Greeks, Maronites, and Negroes. Furthermore, I love peace and the arts; we never can do enough for our first national scene, the French Drama, in which I applauded Talma in Sylla:

'I have governed without fear, and I abdicate without dread.

"I wish a strong and patriotic government, which listens to honest men, and silences advocates and praters. I wish an army that can cope with Europe, a navy that defies England; canals everywhere, railroads everywhere; I wish the government to give work and bread to every workingman. With these, I wish small expenses and few taxes. I do not mean that the state shall fatten on the sweat of the people. This is my symbol, and that of all good Frenchmen."

"And liberty?" asked I; "I do not see it on your programme."

"You are mistaken," rejoined he. "Have I not told you that I wish an energetic government—a government that will crush out all individual resistance? The day that the ruling power, enlightened on our true interests, shall force us to be free, we shall have liberty, and will enforce it on all the universe."

"What do you mean by liberty?" asked I.

"Neighbor," said he, "this question proves how clear your head is. There are a host of simpletons who cry liberty! liberty! without seeing the snare spread for them by fanaticism and aristocracy. I wish none of those false liberties which are only the privilege of wealth and superstition. A patriot, the friend of enlightenment, I do not wish a religious liberty, which would profit nothing but priestcraft. The priests must be muzzled, that the people may be free. I do not wish a liberty of association, which would serve the Capuchins; I do not wish that the poor should be corrupted, in the name of charity, by political alms, and fed on poisoned bread. I do not wish a liberty of education, which would deliver up our children to the Jesuits. I do not wish a departmental liberty, which would reconstruct provincial federalism. I do not wish a communal liberty, which would resuscitate the despotism of lord and curate, and make us serfs and villains. Better the hand of the state than these anarchical rights, abused by agitators, aristocrats, fanatics, and canters. I am for the people; long live equality!"

I gazed with terror at this honest Beotian. "To think," said I to myself, "that, before my voyage to America, I was also at this degree of imbecility! I, too, put my patriotism in the equality of servitude; I, too, made public liberty consist in the destruction of all private liberties, as if, after this annihilation, anything else remained than the brute mechanism of the administration. Jonathan! Jonathan! accursed sorcerer! why have you made me a stranger in my country, or why do you not transport all the Frenchmen to America for a week?"

"Well, neighbor," said the apothecary, surprised at my silence, "what do you think of my principles? Am I a man of the age? Am I a patriot and Frenchman of the old school? Are not these the doctrines which you have always defended?"

"You say truly, answered I; "but, after enumerating all the liberties of which we are afraid, I do not see that we have many left."

"Bah!" said he, "you are jesting. The liberty of baking—is that nothing? And universal suffrage—is not that everything? It is at the moment of balloting that we recognize the men who never flatter the ruling power. For forty years, I can render myself the justice that I have never voted except with the opposition. They may break me; I will not bend."

"Meanwhile, you suffer your property to be expropriated, without saying a word."

"Between ourselves, it annoys me," returned the

apothecary. "But how can it be helped? I am only an individual. A citizen, I brave tyrants; a simple licensed dealer, I do not intend to put myself on bad terms with the administration, of which I have need every day. Besides, this is a matter of principle; private interest should yield to public interest. Reflect that your house, if preserved, would over-run the line of the street at least two-thirds of an inch. Who would tolerate such a lack of symmetry? We Parisians are all born with the compass in our eye. There is not a passer who would not be shocked at this enormity, and lampoon our edileship."

"Yes," said I, "rights are nothing; the right line is everything."

"Sir," said the apothecary, "do not speak ill of the right line or you will give me a bad idea of your enlightenment and taste."

"You like the shortest way from one point to another so well then, that you would sacrifice your business to it without regret?"

"Do I like it? Listen to me, neighbor; I will confide a secret to you which, I am sure, will charm you as it has already charmed all my friends."

"I listen with all my ears, like a man who asks only to be converted."

"You see what is being made of Paris. Old houses, old memories, all these relics of a barbarous past are falling daily beneath the hammer of the demolisher, and being replaced by straight streets and palaces of yesterday. It is magnificent; a Parisian himself no longer finds his way among them. In ten years, Paris will be an entirely new city; the theatre, inn, and coffee-house of the whole world. Well, setting out from the same ideas, I have conceived a bolder and more glorious project; I will put all France in Paris. Provincialism will be dead; there will be no longer either Auvergnats, or Gascons, or Savoyards; there will be no longer even Frenchmen; we shall all be Parisians.

"The work is a great one," continued he; "the point in question is to strengthen and concentrate the national unity, which still leaves much to be desired; but the means is most simple. I prolong the boulevard de Sebastopol on the one hand, to Bayonne, on the other to Dunkirk; I carry the rue de Rivoli, at one extremity, to Brest, and at the other to Nice. On the way, I level everything, that nothing may impede the right line. What a perspective! what a horizon! And reflect that the expense is nothing! The expropriations will not cost dearly, and the plus value of lands will be enormous, since we shall be always in Paris. All the cities will be no longer but suburbs.

"In the middle of the way I place a railroad; on both sides are houses with arcades, that pedestrians may suffer neither from rain nor wind; I put theatres from place to place, and coffee-houses everywhere. Paris thus becomes the promenade of the human race. This is not all; I call the arts to my aid, to give style to my structures. At the Bayonne extremity of this boulevard, two hundred leagues in length, I erect a statue a hundred and twenty feet high—Glory; at the other extremity, at Dunkirk—Victory. At the end of the rue de Rivoli, at Brest—a group of warriors; at the bottom, at Nice, nymphs offering laurels. At the centre, lastly, that is at Bourges, I establish a Walhalla, a gigantic Pantheon. A column, or rather a vast pile, composed of cannon, laid one above another, will raise to the clouds a sort of

Minerva, with spear, casque, and buckler. This will be France, the queen of civilization, the arts, and peace. Around the column I arrange a vast portico, surmounted by explosive grenades and shells; in the interior I place the statues of all our national heroes—Duguesclin, Dunois, Condé, Turenne, Hoche, Kléber, Masséna, Murat, etc. Above, I place symbolic statues, each twenty-five feet in height; on one side, War, protecting Industry and the Arts; on the other, Conquest, bearing Liberty to foreign lands; in the midst, Fortune and Beauty crowning Valor. This will be noble, it will be imposing. Here will be one of those patriotic monuments which immortalize an age and enlarge the mind of twenty generations. Immensity, in uniformity—what an ideal!"

"The Greeks, I believe," replied I, "made beauty consist in proportion and variety."

"Frenchmen are not Greeks," exclaimed he; "we are Romans. Nothing pleases us but hugeness and symmetry; the gigantic is the beautiful."

I sighed, hung my head, and did not answer.

"Well, doctor, here you are, relapsed into your silence. What do you think of my project?"

"I think," said I, shrugging my shoulders, "that I come from a country which occupies itself in rearing men instead of moving stones and building monuments. Porticos, columns, triumphal arches and statues form beautiful perspectives on the horizon; but there is something nobler and greater, something more living which diffuses in the most narrow street an indescribably happy light, and which makes the most dingy habitation a palace—liberty."

"Good," replied he, in the tone of an irritated author;

"here are your black butterflies come again. I feel that my presence is indiscreet."

He rose; I let him go. What had I to do with the old fool? I heard him talking to my wife in the drawing room, and distinguished the name of Olybrius, and the words: "Make haste, it is time." What did these words signify? I did not trouble myself about them; I did very wrong. Fools are always to be mistrusted.

CHAPTER XXXII.

A PARISIAN FAMILY.

At length I rose and made my toilette, but not without more than once regretting my little American house. No bath in which to repose my wearied limbs, no fire in my room, no hot water; Frenchmen have not yet learned that the first of domestic liberties is to have everything at hand, and to stand in need of no one. I was forced to ring without ceasing, and every stroke of the bell brought a solemn, formal lackey, who stared at me from over his white cravat, and waited on me with majestic pity. Where were you, my poor Sambo? you were awkward and ridiculous, but you loved me.

Once shaved, I looked at myself in the glass, and experienced some pleasure in recognizing my former countenance. Not that it was handsome, but I was accustomed to it; nothing is so annoying as to seek one's self under a strange mask. I found my wife and daughter in the dining-room, awaiting me with ill-dissembled impatience. Jenny was embroidering tapestry, to keep herself in countenance; Susan was festooning, from time to time she fixed a sad and terrified gaze on me. I sat down to the table and breakfasted, nevertheless, with a good appetite. Eight days of excitement and cold water made me relish with delight a French breakfast and my old Bordeaux. I regained my country; my heart warmed; I had poetic ideas, which never happened to me in Massachusetts. Oh, my country! which I love as a lover his mistress, always quarrelling with her, yet wishing her every beauty and every virtue; oh, my beloved France! thou hast more than one defect of education, but nature has treated thee like a spoiled child. Nothing equals the softness of thy sky, the wealth of thy harvests, the warmth of thy wines. When the fever of revolutions does not seize thee, thy sons are polite, amiable and witty; thy daughters are more subtle than their husbands. What dost thou lack, then, to be the happiest and noblest nation on the globe? Naught but that liberty which thou deridest and dost not know.

"What are you thinking of, my daughter?" said I to Susan, whose silence astonished me. Usually she chattered like a bird.

"I am thinking of nothing, dear papa."

"Indeed? My little finger tells me that my pet is uneasy about her oldest friend."

"I will not say no, papa."

"Well, my child, we must drive away these bad thoughts. I am so well that I am anxious only about your happiness. My daughter, when are you going to be married?"

Jenny rose as if touched by a spring; Susan blushed to the whites of her eyes.

"No childishness!" exclaimed I. "You are almost twenty years old; you are not one of those little fools who begin to giggle at the word, husband. If your heart has spoken, tell me; I have full confidence in you, my dear; I adopt in advance the son-in-law whom you have chosen me."

"Susan," said my wife, in an agitated voice, "go to my room and bring me some worsted for my embroidery."

Saying this, she made my daughter a sign of intelligence, which, translated into good French, signified, "Leave us."

As soon as Susan had left the room, Jenny broke out.

"Daniel," said she, "you are cruel. What has this child done to you?"

"What! cannot I ask my daughter whether she is in love?"

"My daughter, sir," resumed Jenny, "is in love with no one. She is an honest woman, who will do like her mother, and wait till her wedding-day to love the husband whom her parents shall choose for her."

"Her wedding-day!" exclaimed I; "that is rather late. If love does not enter at night, he will find the door shut in the morning. To leave our happiness to the choice of our parents is dangerous. One marries for himself, not for his mother. Duty is a fine thing, but it does not replace the first holy tenderness of a heart that gives itself freely."

"I do not know where you get your doctrines," said Jenny, in an austere tone; "but you ought to respect your house enough not to bring such deplorable paradoxes here."

"But, my dear, in every country of the globe, young girls choose their husbands. Look at America?"

"Are we Iroquois?" interrupted my wife.

"Look at England, Germany, Spain even; people marry there for love, and I do not see that the households are any less happy than at Paris."

"You have not common sense, Daniel."

"That is to say, madam, one of us two is blinded by prejudice and reasons wrongly."

"Yes, sir, with the difference that you are alone in your opinion, and that everybody in France thinks as I do."

"Ah" murmured I, "behold my tyrant, Lord Everybody, again in my house. How much better my wife was in America!"

To discuss was useless, to dispute is odious to me; I had recourse to a remedy which Socrates lacked; I lighted my pipe and fell into a reverie.

The peace did not last long. Henry entered the room and came timidly to embrace me. I looked at my son; I had some difficulty to recognize him. He was no longer my bold volunteer, ready to set out for the East Indies or the battle-field; but a handsome, slight, young man, with the mien of a doll. His hair was parted in the middle, like that of a woman; he wore an embroidered shirt, standing collar, and Scotch ribbon, which served as a cravat; his whole person was indescribably graceful, delicate and indolent—one would have called him a young girl in a paletot.

"Where do you come from, my dear?" said his mother.

"From my hair-dresser's, mamma."

His hair-dresser! My son in need of a barber! I gazed at him as a curiosity.

"Have you been to the riding-school this morning?" continued Jenny.

"Yes, mamma, and to the fencing-school."

"That is right," said I, "I like these manly exercises. A boy must learn to ride on horseback, swim, box, use the sword and pistol; a civilized man should unceasingly combat the indolence of an enervating life; but, my dear

Henry, this is not all, it is necessary also to choose an occupation. You are sixteen; you are a man. What are you going to do?"

"Poor love!" exclaimed Jenny, "let him enjoy his happiest days; he is not yet even bachelor."

"Well, let him become bachelor."

"I have time enough, papa," said Henry, yawning. "Next year, you will give me a tutor."

"To what purpose?" said I.

"Everybody takes tutors," said Jenny, shrugging her shoulders. "See the son of Petit, the banker. He knew nothing, he was an idiot. In three months, a practised man crammed a whole encyclopedia into his head; he astonished even his examiners."

"And three months after, he was as ignorant as on the first day."

"What did it matter?" said Jenny; "he was bachelor; that title leads to everything."

"Be bachelor, then, my son, and do not wait till next year; at seventeen, I wish you to enter a profession."

"He has yet to go through his studies!" said my wife.

"Yes, spend three years in rambling in the Bois and elsewhere, except during a chronic malady styled the examination. Three years, the best of life, foolishly wasted in idleness or deplorable pleasures! I will not have this. Let Henry first enter a profession, then he will study in earnest. Speak, my son, what profession do you choose?"

"Whatever you like, papa," answered he, embracing his mother. Jenny smiled at him as if to say, "Have patience, my son, your father has not common sense."

"Have you no taste, no vocation?" asked I of Henry.

"No, papa, that is your business. Provided I stay in Paris, ride on horseback, and amuse myself with my friends, it is all the same to me."

"Dear child, how he loves us!" said Jenny, stroking his hair.

"Amuse yourself!" exclaimed I, "where did you get such principles? My son, we are not on earth to amuse ourselves. Labor is the command of God, the curb of our passions, the glory and happiness of life. In America, there is not a man of your age that does not already support himself, and has not the consciousness of duty and dignity."

"Daniel," said Jenny, with visible impatience, "why do you torment this poor child who is seeking only to please you. Wait a little, he will do like others."

"That is to say, he will do nothing."

"He will have a place."

"Just what I said," resumed I, indignant at this maternal weakness. "A place, that is the great word; my son will be a clerk."

"Everybody is now," said my wife. "Show me a young man of family that is anything else. Why should you make yourself singular?"

"What!" said I to Henry, "had you not rather be the artisan of your own fortunes, and owe your position only to your labor and talent? Is independence nothing? Would you not like to be an advocate, physician, manufacturer or merchant?"

"Why do you not propose to him to be a grocer?" said Jenny, with a contempt that wounded me.

"Very well, madam! To weigh sugar on one's own

account is disgraceful; but to seal letters and file receipts on account of the government is noble and glorious! And to attain this, it is necessary to entreat, to beg, to deny one's opinions, and to flatter men whose hand he would not take."

"Everybody does the same," said Jenny. "Do you believe yourself wiser or more virtuous than the whole world?"

"Oh prejudice! prejudice!" I exclaimed. "Paul-Louis, thou art right; we are a nation of valets."

I was furious, I strode up and down the room, and struck my clenched fist on the table; Henry hung his head and was silent; Jenny, pale and with compressed lips, followed me with her eyes.

"Daniel," said she, "put an end, I beg of you, to this ridiculous scene; you forget that I am not strong enough to endure such excitement. When you are cool, I hope that you will listen to reason. At this moment, you know no longer what you are saying."

"Madam," said I, "it seems to me that such language in the presence of my son is out of place; you are wanting in the respect you owe me."

"My dear," said she, "you are ill."

"Enough!" exclaimed I, "this pity is the heighth of indecorum. I will show you who is the head of the family. Despite your prejudices and despair, I will force my daughter to marry to her liking, I will force my son to choose a profession to his taste, and an independent one."

"Daniel, you are mad," said Jenny, clasping her hands.

"I have my reason, madam, and I will teach you that I am master of my own house."

"He is mad," cried my wife, bursting into tears; and she threw herself on the neck of Henry, who began to weep.

At this moment, the door was opened wide, and a voice announced, Dr. Olybrius.

CHAPTER XXXIII.

DOCTOR OLYBRIUS.

He entered; I see him yet. A bald forehead, with locks of red hair floating right and left, gold spectacles, a sanctimonious smile, a triple chin buried in the depths of a broad cravat, a green coat with a ribbon bedizened with the colors of the rainbow—all announced the successful fool. Behind him walked, like two bailiff's followers, the advocate Reynard, who with his weasel eyes, seemed constantly seeking a hole in which to burrow, and the fat Colonel Saint-Jean, leaning on his crutch, and dragging along his belly and gout. What did this grotesque cortége wish of me? Alas! I was about to learn at my cost.

"Good morning, fair lady," said Olybrius, taking my wife's hand and carrying it to his lips; "are you somewhat recovered from your fatigue and emotion? Spare yourself; the heart is the feeble organ among women; do not suffer your sensibility to kill you."

"Good morning, doctor," resumed he in a cavalier tone, extending me a hand which I dared not refuse; "I am delighted to see you on your feet again. I present myself as a friend and not a physician, as I told these gentlemen, who come as neighbors to learn of your health, and who dared not enter with me."

"Good morning, M. Lefebvre," said the colonel. "*Sacrebleu*, we have been sick then? But we have a good constitution. I am glad to see you, *sacrebleu!*"

"How are you?" said Olybrius.

"Very well," answered I.

"So much the worse," said he, "it is unnatural; it is a proof that the poison is not yet exhausted. After eight days' ravages caused by opium, you ought to be half dead, without pulse or voice."

"He is made of iron," said the colonel. "*Sacrebleu!* what a carabineer he would have made!"

"My dear brother," said I to Olybrius, "you have been mistaken in your diagnosis. My case is so extraordinary that any other scholar in your place would have equally wasted his Latin. I have not been poisoned by opium; I have been magnetised and transported to America, whence I have returned this very night."

"*Bigre!*" cried the colonel, "this is strong! I commanded a regiment of Gascons once, that had not their equals for drawing the long bow and fighting, but you carry off the palm!"

"My dear brother," said Olybrius, in a harshly gentle voice, "I always know what I say. The facts are at hand, and nothing is so rude as facts. That you imagine that you have been in America astonishes me little; it is the effect of the opium; but I who have attended on you eight days and nights, I affirm to you that you have remained in flesh and blood in your bed, and that you have not quitted Paris."

"Sir," answered I, "I come from a country where truth reigns without alloy. I have acquired an abhorrence of falsehoods, whether officious or official; believe what you please, I can say but one thing; in flesh or spirit, I know not which, I have passed eight days in America."

"The effect of the opium," said Olybrius, taking out his snuff-box, and inhaling a pinch of snuff. "The brain is not clear, the illusion persists. My dear sir, it is necessary to react with your reason, otherwise the cerebral lobes will become the seat of a grave and persistent disorder. In such a case, as you know, the first thing is to expel a fixed idea, and to believe things on the word of your physician. You have not been in America," added he, scanning each of his words with an imperious tone.

"Sir," said I, "permit me to keep my opinion."

"Daniel," cried my wife, in tears, "for heaven's sake, do not insist, you are destroying yourself."

"Good God! my dear," resumed I, smiling, "with what an air you say this. I seem to hear poor Rachel, as Roxana:

"'Listen, Bajazet! I feel that I love you,
You are destroying yourself; beware how you let me go.'"

For her only answer, Jenny raised her hands to heaven and, taking Henry by the hand, fled from the chamber, hiding her face in her handkerchief.

"*Sacrebleu!*" said the colonel, "you grieve your wife. The devil! one may lie to please the ladies. You are not a Frenchman! *Sacrebleu!*"

"My dear neighbor," said the advocate, speaking in an undertone, as if beginning a plea, "let us reason on the matter. If you have been in America, you have seen the country in detail, you are thoroughly acquainted with it; if you have been dreaming, your ideas on this point are only incomplete, confused, and in short, chimerical. Permit me to put to you a few questions which will bring you back into real life, and enable you to convince us yourself of the falsity or truth of your impressions."

"Speak, sir, I am listening."

"During your stay in America, did you see men shooting each other in the street? Were two or three persons hung a day by virtue of that lamp-post justice—that Lynch law, the name of which the Americans borrowed from us, and perhaps the idea?"

"Sir," said I, "leave this stuff to the journals. The Americans are a hundred times more civilized and peaceable than we. Duelling even is unknown among them."

"*Sacrebleu!*" cried the colonel, "this is too much. To say that a country exists where men do not fight! Are they all nuns of the Sacred Heart in the convent over yonder?"

"The effect of the opium," said Olybrius. "One sees everything on the bright side."

"Say rather the dark side," rejoined the colonel. "*Sacrebleu!* if I were in their barracks, I would slap them all in the face to see if they had any courage."

"Is there a government in America?" said the advocate; "or, at least, did you find any trace of one by chance?"

"Sir," said I, "there is the finest of governments—that which administers the least; that which leaves to the citizens the liberty of governing themselves."

"The effect of the opium," returned Olybrius. "Every one knows that America is pure anarchy."

"Sir," said I, impatiently, "take the trouble to go to the United States; you will find there a central government; thirty-four individual States, thirty-five senates, and thirty-five houses of representatives. I do not suppose that savages would have ever invented such combinations."

"*Sacrebleu!*" said the colonel, "thirty-five nests of lawyers and praters! If such follies were possible, I would make the voyage expressly to fling the brood out of the window! Shoulder arms, cross *ette!* the birds take flight; and then, *sacrebleu!* we have a government that does not sulk."

"Are there ministries?" resumed the advocate, in his least shrill tone.

"Of course."

"A Ministry of Public Worship, for instance?"

"No; the churches are independent societies. Any one can open a church without having anything to fear, except the law."

"It is impossible," said the advocate. "This would be to abandon society to the intrigues of the priests and sectarian hatreds. There would be a St. Bartholomew every day."

"Sir," answered I, "the thing is, perhaps, impossible, but it exists; and I add that in no country is there more tolerance and charity."

"The effect of the opium," said Olybrius.

"And not only is the church free," continued I, becoming animated, "but the school and the hospital are so likewise. Any one can teach; any one can relieve wretchedness, without needing to solicit the government and apply to the police, as if it were in question to open a house of ill-fame."

"It is a dream," said the advocate. "It is materially impossible."

"The effect of the opium," said Olybrius.

"Dr. Olybrius," exclaimed I, "if any one has a fixed idea at this moment, it seems to me that I am not the one."

"I have no idea, Dr. Daniel," returned he; "I call these honorable gentlemen to witness it. It suffices for me to state that until now you have not said a word of common sense to us."

"Is there a Council of State in America?" resumed the advocate, who had all the tenacity of an examining magistrate.

"No, sir; the courts suffice for everything. The administration is amenable to them."

"What a chimera!" said Reynard. "A people would not live six months without that admirable separation of powers, which makes the glory of our immortal Constituent Assembly. Suppose that the safety of the State required your arrest, what would be done in your country of Hurons?"

"What would be done?" replied I. "The course of proceedings is all arranged. The audacious man who placed himself above the laws would be indicted and sentenced to pay several hundred thousand francs' damages."

"Think of it; what would become of the prefects? Their occupation would be gone."

"The prefects!" returned I. "There are none."

"No prefects!" exclaimed he, laughing, "no prefects! What can the citizens do with no one to act for them?"

"Heavens!" exclaimed I, "they transact their own business themselves. Did you never think of that, Mr. Statesman?"

"No," said he drily, "I do not think such things possible. Who guides the public mind yonder, and teaches the citizens to think?"

"No one, assuredly."

"What!" there is no superintendent of the press?"

"No, sir. In this country of Hurons, as you style it, every one says and prints what he pleases, under the sole guarantee of the courts and the laws. Newspapers are considered there as a blessing: they are encouraged and multiplied on every side. There is no security, no stamp, nothing to hinder the diffusion of light, nothing to fetter liberty."

"*Bigre!*" said the colonel. "This is a country where the gendarmes must be busy."

"There are no gendarmes, Mr. Colonel."

"No gendarmes!" exclaimed he. *Sacrebleu!* I am in love with it: I ask nothing more. If you are not crazy enough to be chained, neighbor, then tear down Charenton! I never saw anybody of your calibre. No gendarmes! Why not say immediately after—no army, no infantry, no cavalry, no artillery, no generals, no colonels, no captains; a society of lambs or Iroquois, such as the world has never seen."

"Colonel," said I, "for seventy years America had no army; let peace come, and the Union be reëstablished, and it will dispense with it anew. As you say, it is a society of lambs."

"Enough, young man," said he, bending his brows; "respect my white moustache. I am a good fellow, *sacrebleu!* but I have spitted those who had not tried to humbug me half as much as you have done within a quarter of an hour."

"The effect of the opium," said Olybrius. "How could men live without gendarmes or army? They might assemble every hour in the day, in the street or elsewhere, to talk politics, find fault with the government, go armed, and I know not what besides."

"Indeed, sir," resumed I, "all this is done, and the peace is not disturbed by it. Free citizens, accustomed to liberty, know how to conduct themselves. In case of need, the law is at hand; a police officer and a judge suffice to maintain order or avenge it."

"Enough of this," said Reynard, casting a glance at Olybrius. "Doctor, I am convinced."

"And medicine," said the solemn imbecile, twirling his snuff-box in his fingers, "how is it practised in your land of Cocagne?"

"That is one of the things which struck me most," answered I; "women practice there, and with success."

"*Bigre!*" said the colonel. "Why had not I a major in petticoats when I was three months on my back at Constantine, with a ball in my calf? I would have given all the doctors in the world for one doctress! It is a fine yarn, but it is good, *sacrebleu!*"

"And," added I, "this is not the only profession practised by women; they have taken possession of teaching; it is they who educate Young America."

"This must make fine troopers!" said the colonel. "A nice school to teach the art of fisticuffs, the true apprenticeship of war and civilization! What come out of such shops? Day-books and calicoes?"

"There have come out of them seven hundred thousand volunteers, who fight like heroes."

"*Sacrebleu!*" said the colonel, "don't recite the newspapers to me. For two years, my gazette has told me every morning of these famous conscripts, who chase without ever overtaking each other. Ah! if I were there, with nothing but my Light Fourteenth, how I would strike, no matter whom, according to the wish of the government! I am over head and ears in America; I wish the revolution would shift to some other country, to give me a little change and amuse me."

"Colonel, I do not suppose that you would defend slavery."

"What do I care for those half-whitewashed wretches? But as for your Americans, I execrate them. They are a heap of beggarly democrats who set the worst examples to Europe, and are a blot on civilization. I hope that the North will swallow the South, and be choked with the morsel! These are my politics, and I am not the only one of my opinion, *sacrebleu!*"

"Sir," said Olybrius, rising with majesty, "permit me to sum up our conversation in a few words. The answers of these gentlemen, your friends and neighbors—these answers, full of good sense and truth, ought to have convinced you that your brain is not in a normal state. A society without administration, without army, without gendarmes, with the savage liberty of praying, thinking, speaking, and acting, each in his own way, is, you must grant, one of those abominable nightmares which opium alone can bring forth. Your system would not last a quarter of an hour; it is the negation of all the principles and conditions of that civilization which makes the unity of our great nation. By constituting a hierarchical and centralized administration, the wisdom of our fathers long since raised France to the first rank, and taught Frenchmen that liberty is obedience. In this is our glory and strength; do not forget it, my dear brother, and return to yourself. These anarchical ideas which trouble your brain, and which have never before entered the head of a Frenchman, tell you plainly that you are ill,—and the more ill that you do not feel it. It is urgently necessary to watch over you; I add, even, that nothing but heroic treatment can restore to you the possession of yourself and the calmness which you have lost."

"Why do you not say at once that I am mad, and that it is necessary to shut me up?"

Olybrius sighed, took snuff with his thumb and forefinger, inhaled it slowly, and looked at me with a contrite air:

"My poor friend," said he, "you are seriously attacked; but I will cure you; I will save you despite yourself."

I felt my anger rising in my heart, and with difficulty restrained myself.

"Sir," said I, "let us end this farce; it has lasted too long; I am tired of it."

Olybrius blushed to the ears.

"Sir," said he, raising his voice, "you assume a singular tone!"

"Don't get angry, my dear doctor; you will give yourself a fit of apoplexy."

"Doctor Daniel," said he, gnashing his teeth, "I do not suffer impertinence. Do you know to whom you are speaking, my little gentleman?"

"Yes, my fat gentleman; to a fool!"

"Sir," said he, "do not forget that you have before you a man whom all the sovereigns of Europe have decorated."

"What does that amount to?" exclaimed I. "One has a book of nonsense bound in red morocco, and deposits it at the embassy, upon which he is made Commander or Chevalier of the Hippopotamus or Condor. Crosses! they are the alms which princes throw to the mendicants of literature."

"Do you know, sir," rejoined Olybrius, foaming with rage, "do you know that, at thirty-two, I was unanimously chosen member of the Academy of Medicine?"

"The deuce!" replied I; "I am nearer right than I thought. If you had had talent you would have had enemies; you would have been kept waiting at the door until fifty years old, and would have only been received then by a majority of one. Fools stand in nobody's light, therefore they enter the Academy like a mill."

I had gone a little too far; I felt it. The colonel laughed till he cried, but Reynard looked at me strangely, and Olybrius was suffocating with rage. I saw the moment approaching when the tables would be turned, and the patient would have to bleed the physician. The advocate, doubtless, had the elixir of gold in his throat; two words dropped into the ear of Olybrius restored to my imbecile all his serenity. A diabolical smile lighted up the wrinkles of his face. He approached the colonel, tapped him on the shoulder, and took him into a corner, followed by Reynard, his faithful counsellor.

This style of acting, this cabal held in my house without me, appeared strange to me. I was striding up and down, ready to make a scene when Olybrius went out without saluting me; Reynard, on the contrary, made me a low bow. The colonel approached me with a joyful air. His eyes sparkled.

"Do you know," said he, rubbing his hands, "that you dressed out that parishioner finely?"

"I was wrong." answered I.

"I do not say that," resumed Saint-Jean; "you gave me real pleasure, *sacrebleu!* I detest these sneaks who get themselves covered with decorations without ever having risked anything but other people's skin; but between ourselves, our man is not satisfied. It is natural, is it not? He says that you have insulted him, and demands that you shall apologize."

"I," I exclaimed

"Be tranquil," said the colonel; "I have given him his answer; he is reasonable. I have arranged the matter."

"Very well."

"You are to fight."

"We are to fight?" said I, greatly astonished. "And when?"

"At once. *En chaude colle*, as they used to say in the regiment. Nothing is so dangerous as to let these things get cold. By waiting twenty-four hours, I have lost ten opportunities. My carriage is below; we can set out immediately. I have excellent pistols; you will be delighted with them. At thirty paces I carried away the ear of a jackanapes with them who looked at me askance under the pretext that he squinted. Come, my brave fellow, the moments are numbered. On our way, *sacrebleu!*"

"In a moment I am yours," replied I.

"You are going to embrace your wife and children. A bad plan; it excites you and makes your hand tremble. No tragic adieus; drink a glass of Madeira and smoke a couple of cigars; that will raise your courage and steady your wrist."

I had no occasion to raise my courage, I was beside myself with anger. I entered the drawing room; Jenny was there, pale and speechless, with her children clasped to her breast; they had heard all.

"Are you going with the doctor?" said Jenny, in a despairing tone.

"Yes, my dear; I shall probably be absent a few days."

"You will soon return," said she; then paused, as if affrighted.

"Yes," answered I, "I shall soon return if it please God. Let me embrace you all before I go.

"Adieu, my dear Henry, remember my counsels. Nothing has been done to cultivate your will; it is a great pity, for the passions take the place in the soul which the will does not occupy. Form for yourself studied convictions and an energetic character—these make the man. Choose an independent avocation; expect nothing but from yourself. Bow your head before no one, never have to blush before God, and never trouble yourself about the future. Happiness is not in the things of earth, but in the joy of a good conscience; true greatness is that of an honest man who has elevated himself by labor and virtue. Adieu, be a Christian and citizen. Remember that, to surmount the selfishness which devours us, there are two invincible forces—the love of God and the love of liberty.

"Adieu, my Susan; choose your husband yourself. Look neither at position nor money, but at the heart; therein is the only wealth that has nothing to fear from time or chance. Choose above all a man who esteems you and who shares your opinions; be proud of the father of your children. Love takes flight, confidence and respect remain by the fireside, and become sweeter and more holy than love as old age draws nigh. If you have children, let their souls expand freely; do not teach them the cruel wisdom of that society which reduces everything to interest; let them dream like their grandfather, should they suffer like him. The most unhappy here on earth are not those who weep.

"Adieu, my dear Jenny, forgive me if I have wounded you, and permit me a last counsel. You Frenchwomen have too much wit and finesse; it needs more simplicity to be happy. Why always go out? the world can offer you nothing but agitation and ennui. Remember what St. Paul says—'The man was not created for the woman, but the woman for the man.' Espouse your fireside, make it your pleasure to do the will of a husband; be the queen of the hive where God has placed you—there is the happiness which you seek abroad, and which awaits you in vain in a deserted house. Ah! my Jenny, would that we were in America; there were love and felicity!"

My wife was greatly agitated; she wept, but at the last words she withdrew from my arms, and shrunk from me when I embraced her. Henry received my caresses with a cold and constrained air; Susan alone hung on my neck, and inundated me with her tears.

Once more I clasped them all to my breast, and departed never more to return. To descend the staircase and enter the carriage, where the colonel was awaiting me with his pistols, was the work of an instant. I asked Saint-Jean where we were going.

"I know nothing about it," said he. "We are following Olybrius' carriage. I think that he is taking us to Saint-Mandé, to some private garden. Since Vincennes and the Bois-de-Boulogne have been disfigured to make English parks of them, there is no more pleasure to be had. Fight in a winding path, and foil the people who track you to rake the mark of your footsteps, if you can. We have no duelling-ground at Paris; it is a shame on old French honor, *sacrebleu!*"

The colonel was monotonous and repeated the same things over and over again; I hastened to offer him a cigar to shut his mouth and, sinking into the corner of the carriage, I followed the French fashion of reflecting when it is too late. At my age, and for such a cause, this duel was a piece of folly into which I had let myself be drawn by a brute and a fool. I was determined not to answer Olybrius' fire; but this did not justify me. What! I had not had strength to resist a stupid prejudice! My thoughts and remorse carried me to America; I saw again those mild and honest faces, those good and sincere friends who had raised me to their level. Truth, Humbug, Naaman, Green, Brown himself smiled on me, and with them all that American family which had made the joy of my heart, without forgetting either Martha or Sambo. What a difference between the two countries! The Paris where I was appeared to me a stranger city; the streets of my childhood had disappeared, and my memories with them; my neighbors seemed to me ignorant, vain and egotistical; their actions, their language, all was conventional; no truth, no simplicity. In eight days, in Massachusetts, in the pure air of liberty, I had lived more than at Paris in fifty years. My eyes were opened, I had put off the old man; my country was yonder, where I was beloved; my soul took flight beyond the ocean.

Buried in these reveries, I did not return to myself until alighting from the carriage. We were in the courtyard of a large house with grated windows, something like a college, convent or prison. At the back was a garden, which Reynard pointed out to me as the place of combat, and invited me to repair thither while he arranged the conditions of the duel with the colonel and a couple of friends.

I advanced without suspicion; all at once a grating was shut behind me; I turned round, four strong men seized me by the arms and legs; I resisted like a madman; I shrieked, my voice was stifled. In the twinkling of an eye, I was carried into a low hall, thrown down, secured, and fastened in an easy-chair. Everything began to whirl before my eyes with incredible velocity; a sheet of icy water fell on my head, and I fainted.

CHAPTER XXXIV.

A MADMAN.

Saint-Mandé, house of Dr. Olybrius.

APRIL 20, 1862.

THERE are three sorts of persons whom the law disdains and abandons to the administration—unmarried women, lunatics and journalists. But, whatever may be their profligacy (I speak of the journalists), or whatever may be their fault, I esteem these wretched beings unworthy neither of justice nor pity. If they are criminals, why not try them? If they are unfortunate, why treat them as criminals? I recommend the question to philanthropists out of employment. It is noble to ransom young Chinese, it is noble to save from the fire Malabar widows who follow their husbands even unto death (the example might be contagious); but it would not perhaps be wrong to defend humanity in France, and to give the guaranties of the common law to poor creatures, victims of education, birth and society. Another dream which I must keep to myself, or beware of shower-baths and bleeding!

My fate is fixed; I have played a dangerous game, and lost. A fool, who entitles himself a physician, has declared me mad; my good friends joyfully confirm the decree of ignorance. Here I am shut up, and forever. Can I extinguish the flame which illumines my brain? Can I deny the truth? No; I have known liberty; I have tasted on my lips this intoxicating honey, I have caught a glimpse of the eternal ideal, I am mad! I will not be cured!

Frenchmen have even more wit than they attribute to themselves. To imprison those who think, speak and reason is a master-stroke, the success of which is infallible. Where force is, there is public opinion. Go, happy sheep, browse in silence; bleat to yourselves that you are the kings of the world, your shepherds will not be the ones to refuse you this innocent pleasure. Amuse yourselves, enjoy life, you have nothing to fear; the mad men are under bolts, they would disturb your quietness; the wiser one is, the more he laughs.

My wife does not come to see me, she is so sensitive! She would die of pity. I do not want my children. Poor Henry, if he should get my disease, how would he make a fortune? And you, my Susan, I love you too well to make you weep. A daughter's tears are the only trial that could shake a martyr.

My neighbors have not forgotten me. Rose writes me that he is not surprised at my misadventure. He recognizes in it the hand of the Jesuits; my wife went too often to mass! He is on the track of a vast plot framed by the reverend fathers; it is they, says he, who set the North on the South, who stir up Europe, who pave the way for the downfall of the Sultan. Every revolution is their work; they are the cause of every calamity; his journal has revealed to him this mystery of horror and iniquity. Rose is a sane man, since he walks the streets; I am mad, since I am confined.

Here is a letter from the colonel. The brave Saint-Jean apologizes for having aided in my arrest without knowing it.

He wished, he says, to cut off Olybrius's ears, but the puppy refused to submit to the operation. The colonel adds, that if he has wronged me he is ready to make reparation. To deprive me of the right of complaint, he proposes that we shall mutually blow out each others' brains. The stakes are unequal; I cannot accept this amiable proposition. Saint Jean talks politics to me; he foresees war breaking out on all sides this spring, and his joy is prodigious. He is a soldier; he is convinced that men are on earth to slaughter each other. If mothers, through infinite pangs, rear their sons to twenty, it is to send them to the shambles. The colonel is free, he is a reasonable man; I am mad!

Let us read the journal. I am no longer but a spectator who, from his grated cell, watches the comedy and actors. I will use the only right that is left me: I will hiss!

"A new work has just appeared by Mr. Reynard, our great orator and celebrated publicist. This book, which cannot fail to open to the author the doors of the Academy of Political and Moral Sciences, is entitled *Unity*. M. Reynard demonstrates irrefutably that all the sufferings and revolutions of France proceed from a single cause—the weakness of centralization. Now that railroads and telegraphs have suppressed distance, France, the model nation, can at last find a constitution which will permit her to fulfill her great destinies. The author unites the spiritual power and temporal power in the same hands; an admirable invention to put an end to the dissensions which have rent the world for fifteen centuries; he suppresses the municipal councils, the general councils, the Chambers, the press, and all those means of opposition, excusable, perhaps, at a critical epoch, in an age of struggle and transition, but which have no longer reason to exist in an organic century such as ours, and with the first centralistic race on the globe. A single man, a civilizing pope, placed at the nucleus of the state, having in his cabinet the key of the telegraphic network, will govern all France by his infallible and irresistible will. The organ of the popular sovereignty, he will be the democracy personified, the nation incarnated. Thenceforth, nothing can longer fetter progress; all divisions will cease; all the heads of anarchy will fall at one blow.

"On entering into details, it is impossible not to be fascinated by the simplicity of the system. This is the mark of all great inventions. Henceforth, there will be no longer in France but one soul and one thought. The whole country will be a great and ingenious piece of mechanism, conducted and regulated by a single motive power. What could disturb this great harmony, formed by the accord of a single note? One self-same dispatch, repeated in the forty thousand communes, will transform forty million citizens from night to morning. 'Work,' the telegraph will say; and directly there will be work for every one. 'Be instructed;' ignorance will cease. 'Be virtuous;' the Bourse will be closed. 'Be happy;' our happiness will be achieved.

"It is incredible that humanity should have lived so long without realizing this marvelous discovery, which will immortalize the name of M. Reynard. But what! steam is of yesterday, and the electric telegraph is of to-day! Our kings, moreover, have had the consciousness of this truth, which a man of genius places in full light. Without ever troubling themselves about right or justice, our great sovereigns have always thrown down all opposition which impeded their course; it is for this that history admires the Francis I., the Richelieus, the Louis XIV., and the Napoleons. Saint-Simon caught a glimpse of this glorious reform; but the honor of being its prophet belongs, without partition, to the illustrious and profound Reynard. There is not a Frenchman that does not envy him his discovery and success!"

"Alas!" thought I, "M. Reynard walks abroad, and goes where he will; he is admired and envied; he is more than a philosopher, he is a great man; and I am mad!"

What do I see? The name of my executioner! What can this intriguer be doing? Let us see:

"Yesterday the Academy of Medicine received a communication of the highest interest. One of our medical heads, the celebrated insane doctor, Olybrius, read a paper on wit, genius, and madness. He demonstrated that, through the effect of the sympathetic tie which unites the functions of the brain with those of the stomach, this last organ unmistakably produces and rules all those nervous forces popularly called faculties. Wit is a nervous affection, genius a chronic gastritis, and madness an acute gastritis. In support of his system, the doctor cites a very curious example. At this moment he has in his hands a most valuable subject for experiment. This is a certain Doctor L——, who, in his madness, imagines that he was suddenly transported to America, and remained there a whole week. There is in the delirium of this unfortunate man a mixture of hallucinations, memories, and original ideas, which Doctor Olybrius follows and observes with the greatest care. The malady is in the highest degree acute, but the learned Olybrius does not despair of reducing it to the chronic state, and transforming its character, by dint of bleeding, shower-baths, and a skillfully regulated diet. If he succeeds, the problem is solved. From a madman half cured, will be made a man of genius. As soon as the experiment is ended, the learned doctor will submit the subject to the inspection of the Academy. It is unnecessary to point out the consequences of this prodigious discovery. France is in need of great men, when nothing would be easier than to manufacture them and furnish them to the whole world. At Charenton alone there are three thousand patients, who, with judicious treatment, in less than six months might be transformed into poets, musicians, and artists of every kind. There are unknown Mozarts and Raphaels there by hundreds.

"The lecture, sprinkled with striking traits and ingenious sayings, was listened to in profound silence, frequently interrupted by flattering murmurs. No one has more wit than Doctor Olybrius; to hear him, we might fear for his health; but to see him, we are reassured by the solidity of his muscles and the vigor of his lungs."

Triple fool! less silly nevertheless than those who listen to thee! thou art a scholar, an academician, a philosopher; and I, who hiss thee, am mad!

No, I will not return into this society, full of vanity, which is afraid of the truth, and which is caught like larks, by the dazzle of a mirror. If the crowd rejects me, I for my part exile it from my peaceful abode; solitude restores me liberty. Here I wish to live and die, consoled by the Gospel, surrounded by those old friends who are always faithful and never lie to me—Socrates, Demosthenes, Cicero, Dante, Cervantes, Louis de Leon, Milton. You, too, poets, orators and citizens, men disdained, execrated, exiled, imprisoned, assassinated. Madmen and seditious spirits during your life, you became sages and patriots after your death. The world erects altars to the victims whom it has slain. The history of humanity is the history of martyrs.

Why should I not have my home? If I am not a great man, have I not supported a great cause? Who knows whether my country, disgusted with the insipidities that enervate it, will not forgive me my reserve and harshness? "What is bitter in the mouth is sweet in the belly," says a proverb; so it is with truth. It is healthy as the scent of the grass and trees, as the wind which passes over the glaciers and ocean; he who has lived in this bracing air suffocates in the low grounds and marshes.

I hope against all hope, I am mad. If I were wise, I

should do like the shrewd; I should resign myself and shout with the crowd. I will have none of these saddening joys, I like better my prison and my dream.

Every morning, in the silence of my wretched cell, a vision consoles me. I behold in the distance the whitening summits—it is the breaking of the dawn, the dawn of a day which I shall never see, but what matter? What is that luminous point which pierces the horizon and seems to drive away the fleeing shadows? It is the New Jerusalem, the city of the future. There, all is changed; the last vestiges of paganism have disappeared; the individual commands, he is king. Respected by all as he respects others, he is the sole master of his actions, alone responsible for his life, he has nothing to fear from the laws. The Church has reconquered evangelical independence, she has broken that adulterous chain which Constantine imposed on her to the misfortune of the world. Returned to her divine spouse, she is the curb, consolation and hope of souls; the Gospel is the charter of liberty. Scattered broadcast, education opens hearts to the truth; charity, the work of all, gives scope to that instinct of union, that need of common action which makes the greatness of societies. The province has resumed its ancient vigor; the love of the village doubles, while strengthening the love of the whole country. The commune has broken the bonds which hold it; it lives, it acts; it calls and retains its children within its limits. The *Times* is no longer the organ of France; the press is free; every one says what he thinks and thinks what he says. Confined within its bounds, the State is no longer but a blessing. Outside, it is the sword of the country, within it is the law, nothing less, nothing more. Truth, justice, liberty, ye shine in this new sky like pacific stars; before you are eclipsed the scourges of old Europe—despotism, intrigue, and falsehood. France, happy and proud, blossoms out in abundance and peace, it is the example and envy of nations; there it is glorious to live, there it is sweet to die.

Such is my dream; it casts into my prison an indescribable, serene light which warms my heart. How glorious will it be on the day when the masks shall fall and the madmen be the sages, the sages the madmen! Then, about the year 2000, pious pilgrims as numerous as the sands on the seashore will visit the cell where, a new Daniel, I foretold the future. Then, too, some curious men, some antiquarians, laboring continually to do nothing, will seek beneath the rubbish of the past, what certain varieties of Frenchmen of the nineteenth century could have been—varieties disappeared forever, like the carlin, the everlasting regret of porters. It will be asked what was the devourer of Jesuits, the leather breeches, the inventor of centralistic races, the adorer of the God-State. And the father, passing through the halls of the Museum of Natural History, will point out to his astonished children a gigantic bottle where, embalmed in spirits, with his crosses and diplomas, will repose the last of the Olybriuses.

Amen, *amen*, AMEN, **AMEN**!

CHAPTER XXXV.

A SAGE.

Doctor Olybrius, etc., etc., to Madame Daniel Lefebvre.

"April 22, 1862.

"Dear Madame:

"Our poor friend has suffered greatly. He is a little better: he eats, drinks, and sleeps, and no longer has a will of his own.

"The crisis was terrible. As soon as we attempted to treat him, he became furious. It is one of the most characteristic symptoms of this fatal malady. The Frenchman is naturally gentle, amiable, polite; always ready to do what his masters, friends, or wife prescribes. See the history of our glorious Revolution! To save France, and inoculate it with the love of equality, justice, and fraternity, the Convention placed all Frenchmen outside the protection of the law. It ruined, exiled, deported, cannonaded, shot, and guillotined them. Did a single one resist? Is there anything to-day more justly popular than this immortal Assembly? But, alas! As soon as madness seizes him, the Frenchman becomes willful and wicked. If he is arrested, he resists; if he is shut up, he rebels: he thinks and speaks only of liberty. Such is the intellectual and moral degradation which a violent nervous affection produces among our enfeebled subjects.

"This is what happened to our poor friend. Happily for him, I was on the watch. Two profuse bleedings, three violent purgations, and icy shower-baths have restored to him the calmness of which he was in need. The disease, I hope, is passing the acute stage. In becoming chronic, it will give surprising results, on which I found the hope of my reputation.

"At this moment he is tranquil. He busies himself in scribbling, too certain a proof, alas! that he is still far from a cure. I send you this trash, which he entitles *Paris in America.* I have refrained from retrenching anything in it, even the abuse which he addresses to me, and which falls at my feet. The chevalier of twenty-seven orders, and member of thirty-three foreign academies and eighty-two provincial societies—my name has nothing to fear from time or envy. France has always venerated the Olybriuses. Beware, however, of speaking or printing such follies. Nothing is more contagious than chimera. The brain of man is weak, and nervousness is a malady always to be distrusted. Lock up these papers; they will be of use to you in procuring a too necessary interdiction. I do not suppose that any reasonable Frenchman, acquainted with his age and country, could read two pages of these dreams without declaring that their author is mad, and that it is necessary to keep him confined.

"Let us come to yourself, dear madame. Permit me to touch on a delicate point. Sensitive as you are, you need the greatest care: see the world; surround yourself with society; seek to distract yourself, ennui would be fatal to you. I prescribe for you distractions and pleasure. Return to life; accustom yourself to an independence and solitude, which all your friends will strive to alleviate. Do not cherish vain hopes; these emotions would weaken your health, already too much shaken.

The poor doctor will never return home. Whatever form his disease may assume—even though it should become a literary madness resembling genius—it will always be necessary to keep under restraint a man as dangerous to his family as to society. You may believe me, dear madame; science is infallible, and an Olybrius is never mistaken. The madness of love is cured when one is young; if old, he dies of it; the madness of ambition yields sometimes to age and the contempt of mankind; the madness of liberty is never cured.

"I place myself at you feet, dear madame, etc."

FINIS.

III.

LIFE OF OUR LORD UPON THE EARTH:

Considered in the Historical, Chronological, and Geographical Relations. By REV. S. J. ANDREWS. 1 vol., post 8vo. $2 25.

"The most sober, scholarly, reverential, and trustworthy work of the sort which has lately been laid before the public. It is, indeed, a treasure house of explanations on all disputed points, and from its clear and methodical arrangement, it is easy of reference, and will be a permanent and valuable assistant to every devout student of the Holy Gospels."—*Church Journal.*

"It exhibits an extent of information, a patience in the investigation of the most perplexed and difficult questions, and a calmness and candor of judgment, with an individuality of view, that are very rare. Ministers, theological students, Sabbath-school teachers, and private Christians will study it with profit."—*Hartford Courant.*

IV.

"ONE OF THE VERY BEST BOOKS ON THE REBELLION."—*Boston Traveller.*

POLITICAL FALLACIES.

An examination of the false assumptions, and refutations of the sophistical reasonings, which have brought on this civil war. By REV. GEORGE JUNKIN, D.D. 1 vol. 12mo. Portrait of Author. $1 25.

"It contains many things that are not to be found in any other work, and the author's long residence at the South enables him to deal with the fallacies and assumptions of the rebels in a very satisfactory manner, because he knows well the men who head the rebellion, and he understands their purposes better than they are understood by persons living far from the Confederacy."—*Boston Evening Traveller.*

V.

WILD SCENES IN SOUTH AMERICA;

Or, Life in the Llanos of Venezuela. By DON RAMON PAEZ. 1 vol., post 8vo., with 38 illustrations. Price, $1 75.

"The author is a genuine lover of nature; has the ardor and enthusiasm which prompt a traveller to explore her untrodden ways and secret recesses; and has, moreover, the courage and endurance which find in danger and fatigue only a new source of enjoyment—a new element to sport in. The work is, throughout, a narrative of personal adventure."—*Pittsburgh Gazette.*

"We regard the book as one of the very best about South America, both for its information and the admirable manner in which it is conveyed. The author has the scholarship, the artistic eye, and the love of a wild life, to make the narration of the journey very agreeable, while we feel that he is trustworthy."—*Hartford Evening Press.*

VI.

THE NEW TESTAMENT.

With Brief Explanatory Notes (or Scholia). By PROF. HOWARD CROSBY, D.D. 1 vol., 12mo., pp. 540. Price, $1 50.

This book is intended to meet the wants of the Bible reader, by solving in a brief and suggestive manner the difficulties of the English text. There is no commentary or discussion of doctrine, but simply an explanation of text and context. It gives the result of Biblical scholarship. Its brevity and point will commend it in these days of prolix commentaries.

VII.

THE TRIUMPHS OF THE BIBLE:

With the Testimony of Science to its Truth. By REV. HENRY TULLIDGE. 1 vol., 12mo. $1 50.

"A work of Christian Evidences suited to the wants of the present time. In the conflict now joined between belief and unbelief, the old standard works of Christian apology are to a considerable extent deficient and unavailable. They were written with reference to phases of skepticism prevalent in their day, and do not meet the peculiar scientific difficulties and objections with which Christianity has now to contend. The object of this work is to meet these difficulties, to vindicate the truth and authority of the Divine Word. The writer first undertakes to show that the Triumphs of the Bible—the wonderful achievements it has wrought in the world—demonstrate it to be from God. In the following part two special objects are proposed. *First*, from a careful examination of the relations of Science and Scripture, to show that there is no collision, but entire harmony as soon as the latter are properly understood. *Second*, to bring forward a new class of evidences which have been preserved for discovery until the present age as material for vindicating *The Historic Reality of the Bible*."

VIII.

A NEW BOOK ON HUMAN RACES.

THE RACES OF THE OLD WORLD: A Manual of Ethnology. By C. L. BRACE, Author of "Hungary in 1857;" and "Home Life in Germany." In 1 vol., post 8vo. Printed on tinted paper.

This should be in the hands of every student of history, and of all teachers in schools and colleges. It is the only general work in so brief a form on this subject. It treats of "The Earliest Historical Races;" then of "The Races of Asia in the Middle Ages;" of the "Modern Races of Asia, Africa, Oceanica, and Europe," including the latest information in regard to the tribes of the Pacific, the interior peoples of Africa, and such races as the *Basques* and the *Gipseys*. The subject of Acclimation, Hybridity, Degeneracy, and the formation of Varieties, as bearing on the question of Unity or Diversity of Origin, are discussed at length. The final chapter is devoted to the recent discoveries bearing on the "Antiquity of Man." This work is designed to fill a much needed place in the studies of our higher schools and colleges.

IX.

LABOULAY'ES GREAT WORK,

PARIS IN AMERICA. Translation by MISS MARY L. BOOTH. 1 vol. 12mo.

"A very ingenious, humorous, pungent satire on the faults and defects of French manners and customs, under the restrictive influences of French administrative custom, as compared with the free and easy self-developing independence of American manners and customs. There is a grave, thoughtful censor's visage under the extravagant laughing mask. Nay, looked at closely, here is satire, not only of French national defects, but of American foibles. It is a singularly clever book."—*Paris Correspondent of New York Tribune.*

"It is a sarcastic, witty, and philosophic criticism on French political and social life as compared to that of the United States, and deals such hard blows at certain high dignitaries in France, that one is astonished at not seeing the book seized by the police. It is an important and most entertaining book."—"*Malakoff*," *Paris Correspondent of New York Times.*

X.

THE SECTIONAL CONTROVERSY;

Or, Passages in the Political History of the United States, including the Causes of the War. By WM. C. FOWLER, LL. D. 1 vol., octavo. Price, $1 50.

"A well-stored repository of historical facts and documentary papers, relating to the sectional controversies which, at different periods, have arisen between the States. The reader here has in a condensed form a statement of the causes and occasions which have contributed to bring about an unhappy alienation between the North and the South. The compiler has performed his task in a candid and dispassionate manner." —*Washington National Intelligencer.*

XI.

MULLER ON LANGUAGE.

LECTURES ON THE SCIENCE OF LANGUAGE. By MAX MULLER, M. A. From the 2d Revised London Edition. 1 vol., large 12mo. Printed at the *Riverside Press*, on laid tinted paper. Price, $1 88.

"Easily comprehensible, and yet always pointing out the sources of fuller investigation; it is ample, both to satisfy the desire of those who wish to get the latest results of philosophy and to stimulate the curiosity of whoever wishes to go further and deeper. It is by far the best and clearest summing up of the present condition of the Science of Language that we have ever seen, while the liveliness of the style and the variety and freshness of illustration make it exceedingly interesting."—*Atlantic Monthly.*

XII.

TRENCH'S NEW WORK.

A COMMENTARY ON THE EPISTLE TO THE SEVEN CHURCHES IN ASIA. By R. C. TRENCH, D.D., Author of "Study of Words," etc. 1 vol., 12mo. Price, $1 25.

"The Commentary is a model of its kind, and expounds one of the most instructive and attractive portions of the New Testament."—*Christian Review, Jan.*, 1862.

"As investing the second and third chapters of the Apocalypse with a new and profounder interest, worth, and deeper significance, and this especially to the scholar and thinker on the same intellectual plane with the author, it can hardly be praised to excess."—*North American Review, Jan.*, 1862.

XIII.

GASPARIN'S WORKS.

AMERICA BEFORE EUROPE—PRINCIPLES AND INTERESTS. 1 vol., 12mo., 420 pages. Price, $1 50.

"The most complete and satisfactory vindication of this Government in its measures to subdue rebellion. The task has been accomplished, not only with great ability and eloquence, but with the constant recognition of the paramount claims of Christian truth and duty. Such a book will do immense good both in Europe and America. Spread broadcast in our own country, it could not fail to obviate the objections urged by ignorance and prejudice."—*New York Evangelist.*

BY THE SAME AUTHOR.

UPRISING OF A GREAT PEOPLE.

1 vol., 12mo. Price, $1 00.

www.ingramcontent.com/pod-product-compliance
Lightning Source LLC
LaVergne TN
LVHW020127110826
845151LV00001B/299